WORDS OF DEFIANCE

WARTIME SPEECHES BY UKRAINE'S FOREIGN MINISTER DMYTRO KULEBA

BJORN BERGE

Biteback Publishing

First published in Great Britain in 2026 by
Biteback Publishing Ltd, London

ISBN 978-1-83736-052-9

10 9 8 7 6 5 4 3 2 1

A CIP catalogue record for this book is available from the British Library.

Set in Minion 3 and Anton

Printed and bound in Great Britain by
CPI Group (UK) Ltd, Croydon CR0 4YY

FSC
www.fsc.org
MIX
Paper | Supporting responsible forestry
FSC® C013604

CONTENTS

FOREWORD
BY ANTONY J. BLINKEN

In January of 2022, as Russian tanks and troops were massing along the Ukrainian border, I sat down with Foreign Minister Dmytro Kuleba in Kyiv. The shadow of war was looming, yet my friend Dmytro was unbowed. 'Tony, I know we may face some dreadful challenges soon,' he told me. 'But one thing I am confident about is that I don't want to be writing my memoirs in exile. I will be writing my memoirs in Kyiv.'

A month later, Vladimir Putin unleashed his full-scale invasion of Ukraine. In the years since, Russia's war of aggression has been devastating, killing tens of thousands of Ukrainians, displacing millions, upending Ukraine's economy, exacerbating global food and energy crises and trampling the principles at the heart of the United Nations Charter.

As I write this, however, the people of Ukraine have endured. In the early days of the war, they beat back Moscow's assault on Kyiv, then reclaimed Kharkiv and Kherson. They regained more than half the territory Russia seized in the opening weeks of its 2022 invasion. Ukraine even pushed Russian ships out of the Black Sea

– without a fleet of its own. Through victories big and small – on land, by sea, in the skies – through sheer courage and grit, Ukrainians have denied Putin his goal of erasing their nation from the map. I am proud that the United States rallied the world to support them.

The world has been inspired by the bravery and sacrifice of Ukraine's defenders as they fight for their country's security, sovereignty and ability to choose its own path. And few figures were as critical to Ukraine's success as its skilled and tireless Foreign Minister, Dmytro Kuleba.

Dmytro was President Volodymir Zelenskyy's leading emissary in rallying dozens of nations from every part of the world in support of Ukraine. He and I spent countless hours together working to galvanise this global coalition, from Washington to Brussels to Kyiv. Leaders and people around the world understood that while Russia's unprovoked invasion was directed at Ukraine, it was much bigger than Ukraine. Had we allowed Putin to proceed with impunity, it would have signalled to would-be aggressors everywhere that they could get away with it, too.

In these pages, you'll glimpse the Dmytro I've had the privilege to see up close – through countless phone calls, in meetings on the margins of major diplomatic summits and even over French fries and cherry pie at a McDonald's in Kyiv.

A man of great foresight, speaking before the United Nations Security Council hours before the first Russian air strikes, calling on the world 'to put out the fire in the center of Europe, which is about to flare up'.

A leader of profound patriotism, defiantly declaring that 'every Ukrainian is a weapon ready to defend Ukraine and the principles enshrined in the UN Charter'.

A skillful and relentless diplomat, constantly pushing for more battlefield support, telling his foreign counterparts, 'we have to provide enough shells for the tired and oily hands of our artillerymen.'

A passionate advocate for his people, condemning Putin's atrocities – missiles raining down on shopping malls and power grids, Ukrainian children abducted and taken to Russia, mass graves in every city liberated – and demanding 'no more impunity for Russia'.

Above all, you will see a citizen with great faith in his country's future. As Dmytro tells a group of students at Harvard University, 'Modern Ukraine is not only a state; it's a project in the making. The Ukraine we want to be is always ahead.'

Ukraine's friends around the world – all those who value freedom – remain determined to ensure that Ukraine can stand strongly on its own feet – militarily, economically, democratically – and continue to realise that 'Ukraine is always ahead'.

Dmytro has many more chapters of public service ahead of him. But because of the efforts captured in the following pages, we can be sure the memoirs he mused to me about that day in January will be written from a free, prosperous, secure and democratic Kyiv.

Slava Ukraini!
Antony J. Blinken

PREFACE
BY PHILIPPE SANDS KC

On 24 February 2022, Russian President Vladimir Putin announced his decision to launch a 'special military operation' against Ukraine. Two days later, the *Financial Times* approached me to write an opinion piece on Ukraine and international law. They did so because of my work on the rule of law in the global context, and because I had written *East West Street*, a book on the origins of the legal concepts of genocide and crimes against humanity, tracing their origins to the city of Lviv, in the Ukraine.

'Putin's use of military force is a crime of aggression' was published on 28 February. I wrote,

> President Vladimir Putin's decision to launch attacks on Ukraine poses the gravest challenge to the post-1945 international order, one premised on the idea of a rule of law and principles of self-determination for all peoples and the prohibition of the use of force. It is not the first time that Russia has taken a military interest in the territories it now seeks to occupy: in September 1914, Russia occupied the city of Lviv, causing tens of thousands to flee

> westward, including my ten-year-old grandfather. The Soviet Union returned in September 1939 for a second bite, and then again in the summer of 1944, remaining in control until Ukraine achieved independence in 1991.

I expressed the view that President Putin had taken a gamble, hoping that the West would blink, that it would not have the stomach to stand up to his actions and that his bet posed a grave challenge to the existing international order, one that sanctions and financial measures alone would not be able to address. 'In the face of so flagrant a violation of the rules,' I wrote, it was 'lawful to act jointly to protect Ukraine and the fundamental rights of its people, by offering military hardware, taking steps to prevent Russia from using air power and, ultimately, putting boots on the grounds to enforce safe areas and draw lines that Russia must not be allowed to cross'.

I also addressed the matter of criminality, including the crime of aggression, even if I was 'not starry eyed about such labels'. I noted that the International Criminal Court (ICC) – which was established in 1998 as a child of the Nuremberg trials – had jurisdiction over certain of the crimes that may be committed on the territory of Ukraine (including war crimes and crimes against humanity) but not the crime of aggression. On these matters, the ICC had the power to open a formal investigation and, if the evidence supports and the judges authorise, to proceed to an indictment and prosecution.

I wrote,

> The ICC has a gap, however, as its jurisdiction does not yet extend to the crime of aggression perpetrated on the territory of

> Ukraine. Why not create a dedicated international criminal tribunal to investigate Putin and his acolytes for this crime? After all, it was a Soviet jurist, Aron Trainin, who did much of the legwork to bring 'crimes against peace' into international law. As Francine Hirsch has noted in her book *Soviet Judgment at Nuremberg*, it was largely Trainin's ideas that persuaded the Americans and the British to put 'crimes against peace' into the Nuremberg Statute and the indictments against the German defendants. [...] There can be no appeasing of Putin. Chechnya, Georgia, Crimea and now all of Ukraine. On it goes. Let him reap what he has sowed, including the legacy of Nuremberg. Investigate him personally for this most terrible of crimes.

The *Financial Times* article seemed to touch a chord. Within days I had received hundreds of communications, among which two stood out. 'This should happen,' said Dmytro Kuleba, Ukraine's Foreign Minister. 'How can I help?' asked Gordon Brown, the former British Prime Minister.

One thing led to another. Chatham House – the foreign policy think tank in London – convened a meeting on the idea of creating a special tribunal, which drew over a thousand attendees from around the world, on Zoom, apparently its largest meeting ever.

Dmytro Kuleba became active, engaging with colleagues and garnering the support of President Zelenskyy and the Ukrainian government. Over the course of a month, Gordon Brown set up a series of Zoom meetings with former heads of state and government of dozens of countries across Europe and beyond, who in turn persuaded prime ministers and presidents of numerous countries to support the idea.

An informal core group emerged, including legal advisers from the Baltic states, Poland and the Netherlands. Ukraine established its own informal advisory group, on which I was privileged to serve, along with academics and other lawyers from Australia, Britain, Germany and the United States, who worked on draft legal texts.

Over time, a more formal core group emerged, some forty countries and the European Union, which led to over eighteen months of negotiations, under the auspices of the Council of Europe.

In March 2025, as the war continued to rage, the Council of Europe and Ukraine reached an agreement. Article 1 provides: 'There is hereby established a Special Tribunal to investigate, prosecute and try persons who bear the greatest responsibility for the crime of aggression against Ukraine.'

On 9 May 2025, delegations of thirty-five European countries gathered in the Ukrainian city of Lviv to announce publicly the creation of the special tribunal. Ministers adopted the Lviv Declaration, noting the significant role of the city 'in the formation of international legal scholars who laid the foundations of modern international criminal law'. They reaffirmed the critical importance of the Special Tribunal in 'delivering justice by holding accountable those who bear the greatest responsibility for this most serious international crime committed against Ukraine'.

The ministers further underlined that the Special Tribunal would 'conduct its proceedings in full respect of international law and human rights, with the aim of securing accountability for the crime of aggression and strengthening the international legal order'. In this way, they honoured the ideas and work of Hersch Lauterpacht and Rafael Lemkin, two former students of what is now the law faculty at the University of Lviv who, in 1945, gave the world the legal concepts of crimes against humanity and genocide.

The Special Tribunal is an act of continuity and an expression of hope and commitment. It is the first international tribunal established specifically for the purpose of addressing the crime of aggression since the Nuremberg and Tokyo tribunals, eighty years ago. That is not without significance, a development that is in large part due to the commitment, persistence and ingenuity of Dmytro Kuleba.

It is increasingly said that we live in a post-rules world, one in which the very idea of an international legal order has been cast asunder. It is certainly the case that there are forces and even significant and powerful individuals that would support such a situation. It also remains to be seen what the special tribunal may yet achieve, in hard and practical terms. Yet I have come to understand that international law is a long game, and that symbols are important, as they were in the construction of domestic legal orders that have been established over many centuries.

I have also come to recognise that in the most difficult of times the ideas and actions, and courage and foresight, of particular individuals can make a difference. Dmytro Kuleba is one such individual, as the pages of this book make clear. It has been a privilege to work with him, in support of the ideal of an international rule of law, and in its practical elaboration.

Philippe Sands KC
London, 15 September 2025

INTRODUCTION

GALVANISED BY WAR

On a Monday afternoon in July 2025, I sat down with Dmytro Kuleba. For over two and a half years we had worked together on finalising this unique book. I believe we both want this project to make a difference, at the very least to bring accurate and reliable information to a public throughout Europe and elsewhere that have been misled and manipulated over the years by Russian propaganda.

Serving as Ukraine's Deputy Prime Minister and Foreign Minister for over four and a half years during the crucial period from March 2020 until September 2024, Kuleba was one of the most well-known faces of Ukraine at war. Travelling the world, from Brussels to New York, Rabat to Lusaka, Beijing to New Delhi, rallying political, military and financial support to Ukraine, the young and popular Ukrainian Foreign Minister had a huge impact. In many ways, the war truly galvanised him.

On this hot summer day in Kyiv, he was elegantly dressed in a pink polo shirt. On the wall behind him was a painting one could not help but observe. It was by Yurii Solomko, a well-known Ukrainian painter renowned for his unique use of geographical maps as a canvas. At the heart of this unique piece, he overlays the iconic image of Cossack Mamay – a legendary figure in Ukrainian history – onto the central outline of Ukraine. Surrounding him are the dancing figures from Henri Matisse's celebrated composition. It's a striking fusion of national identity and global artistic dialogue.

'Is there a little of the great Cossack Mamay in you, Dmytro?' I asked. 'And do you have a *kobza* [the legendary musical instrument associated with Cossack Mamay that is the symbol of the Ukrainian soul] hidden somewhere in your apartment?'

Kuleba laughed. 'No, I don't have a kobza, but like every Ukrainian I admire Cossack Mamay and the Cossacks. Their impact on our Ukrainian identity and culture has been monumental. Actually, Mamay reminds me more of my father,' he said with a smile.

'My father, Ivan, comes from a tiny village in the famous Poltava region in central Ukraine,' Kuleba explained. The region has been a source of inspiration for numerous artists, writers, mystics and religious figures for centuries – and now also prominent politicians, it seems. Kuleba continued,

> Life in the village was far from easy, and my grandfather's job was to drive a tractor, while my grandmother worked on a dairy farm. They were very poor. Eventually they had four children, and they all lived in a tiny little house in a forgotten village. Three of their children stayed in the village, but my father was different. He always had this passion for escaping the reality that was destined to him. He did something unusual and very adventurous as a young teenager. One day he left the village and fled to Leningrad, now Saint Petersburg. Why? Because he wanted to enter the Soviet Naval Academy. I don't know where he got this idea from, living in landlocked central Ukraine, but off he went.

For various reasons, the plan didn't work out, so Ivan Kuleba had to return to his village. Evidently, he now had to reconsider his plans, so he decided to embark on a completely different kind of career. He began studying at a regional college.

'My father was a very bright young man, so wisely enough he decided to become a student,' Kuleba said. Astonishingly, his father was able to join one of the main Soviet academic institutions at that time, becoming one of a very small, privileged group who were invited to study at the Soviet Academy of Foreign Trade in Moscow.[1] Together with the Soviet Diplomatic Academy, it was one of the top academic institutions in foreign affairs in the then Soviet Union.[2]

'It was definitely quite an achievement for him, as usually the students at the academy were children of the Soviet elite, and typically you also needed a strong lobby and even a special recommendation from Politburo in the Kremlin to be enlisted as a student,' explained Kuleba.

> But of course my father didn't have any such lobby, but through hard work he became part of a group of highly promising students from the poor and lower classes in the country. They were added to the list of elite offsprings for communist balance. His journey from a poor village to the most prestigious academic institution in the USSR, became in many ways a perfect example of a model Soviet career seen from an ideological point of view.

During Soviet times, about 80 per cent of the enlisted students were somehow connected to Soviet elites, while only 20 per cent could be described as 'living the Soviet dream'. One could, of course, question to what extent this dream ever existed; it might more accurately be described as a fictional part of the Soviet propaganda machine. But Kuleba's father must have been a unique case, being the son of a poor, rural tractor driver who ultimately became a student at the most prestigious academy in the country. 'Yes, this is how he made it,' underlines Dmytro.

In 1991, when Kuleba was ten years old, the collapse of the Soviet Union took the family by surprise. 'My father was encouraged to stay in Moscow, but he was very determined to go back to Ukraine,' said Kuleba. In Kyiv, Kuleba's father joined the Ukrainian Ministry of Foreign Affairs, first as counsellor. He rose through the ranks to the top position as Deputy Minister, and he also served as Ukraine's Ambassador to four countries (Egypt, the Czech Republic, Kazakhstan and Armenia).

'I could have been the son of a Gazprom oligarch, but I am the son of a Ukrainian diplomat. Which is obviously very different,' Kuleba once explained in an interview with *Le Monde*. 'He truly had a distinguished career, which has been a great inspiration to me,' Kuleba points out. 'If you look at his life, it's literally the story of a man that went from "zero to hero" and it became a truly great example to me in the sense that everything is possible if you work hard.' He quickly added, 'Yes, you definitely need to work hard, but at the same time you need a bit of luck, of course. But the fundamental premise is that everything is possible if you work hard.'

With hard work, Dmytro Kuleba graduated with merit from the Institute of International Relations at the prestigious Taras Shevchenko National University in Kyiv. Later on, at thirty-eight, he became the youngest Foreign Minister in the country's history. I like to think this is due largely to his successful work as Ukraine's Ambassador to the Council of Europe in Strasbourg, where in 2017 he was ranked number one among Ukraine's ambassadors abroad by seventy experts from the Institute of World Politics.

Kuleba told me that he spent last week together with his parents and his extended family.

> It was my father's seventy-second birthday last Friday. I offered a toast at the dinner and I said to my father a few words that I really mean and that I feel strongly about. I told him, 'You started from the bottom of the sea and you spent your life swimming up to the surface, so that I could start my life from the surface. I will always be grateful to you for that, because you gave me a completely different start in my life. At the same time, I know what it took for you to get there, and I will always acknowledge and appreciate that. I do not take this for granted in any way, but I take it first and foremost as a duty and responsibility for me to take it further, so that my son can start from the sky.

'Today, do you see some of your father in yourself?' I asked.

'I believe we all see something we know in ourselves that comes from our parents,' he replied. 'But the interesting part is that my father never tried to teach me, nor did he ever ask me to sit down so he could share his wisdom with me. No, it was more like I watched him and observed him, just by being next to him. And the most important lesson that I learned from him is definitely the one that I already explained: that everything is possible if you work hard.'

I asked him if there is anything that has made a profound impact on him as a person, or that has helped change him. His considered reply came surprisingly quickly.

> I would say there are three key moments in my life that changed

me and shaped me as a human being. The first one occurred in 2010, when I was returning from my posting in Vienna and I was appointed as assistant to then Foreign Minister of Ukraine Kostyantyn Gryshchenko. I was very close to him, and I was spending days and nights in the office continuously working. Sometimes I would pack my suitcase, go to the office and then spend the whole day and night working on documents, and then at five o'clock in the morning leave to the airport to accompany the minister on his trip. There was so much work that I just couldn't go home, and there was generally very little sleep. Well, my son Yegor was five years old then and I was absent in his life, because I was always choosing work over family life. Work was more important than my children. Once I promised Yegor that I would attend a concert at the kindergarten where he was singing with other children. But I did not come, because I was too busy at work. When I came home that evening, I saw how sad he was, how depressed he was, and I promised myself that from now on, it doesn't matter how busy I am, I have to be present in my children's lives, at least during the moments which are important to them.

This was a bitter lesson, and I started balancing my life in a way that would always allow me to reconcile my working duties with my family commitments. These efforts of mine culminated in one of the most extraordinary situations that I have ever experienced. It was while I was Foreign Minister, in the summer of 2024, and I was attending the Foreign Affairs Council of the EU in Brussels. I was sitting next to Josep Borrell, the High Representative of the Union for Foreign Affairs and Security Policy, who also chaired the meeting. Sitting around the table were the Foreign Ministers from all the EU countries. My mobile phone was on the table in front of me, and I saw it was ringing. It was my son calling me. I told Borell, and he said to me that if I need to pick it up, I should do it. Other EU ministers started noticing it and a few of them even said, 'Dmytro, you know we can wait. Our children are important, so you may answer the phone.' I replied, 'Well, thank you very much. Many years ago, I made a promise to my two children that I will always answer their calls.' The consequence was that a formal EU Foreign Ministers conference was abruptly interrupted because of a telephone call from my son. I must say that this was a very special moment for me, as again I realised that you have to work hard, but work is certainly not everything!

The second moment that had a profound impact on my life happened in 2011. My daughter had just been born, but she became seriously ill with a very dangerous disease. My ex-wife and I spent a year fighting for her life; it became a very painful experience for both of us, and it made me think that this was the moment that made me an adult. You see, I was a young and very ambitious person, but through that painful experience I became a grownup. I was thirty years old when I actually had to assume the responsibility for the life and health of my daughter. I had to make very difficult decisions about whether we do the surgery, or we find another way of treatment, and that was really the moment when I became a mature man – an adult.

The third episode occurred in 2014 during the Revolution of Dignity. I was on Maidan Square on the night when [President Viktor] Yanukovych ordered the violent crackdown of the protests. I was together with the fighters, trying to help them, though I wasn't a fighter myself. But then around three or four o'clock in the morning, I realised that we were losing. I mean everything was burning down and thousands of people left Maidan. The guys who were fighting and I had to make a choice, and, as a rational person with a certain experience in government and with a PhD degree, I confidently concluded that this battle was lost. I believed we must retreat but continue fighting against Yanukovych in different ways. I went home, absolutely convinced about this. But when I woke up in the morning and opened the news, I saw a big headline that read, 'Maidan stands!' I realised that the police had failed and that I had completely misjudged the situation. I immediately rushed back to Maidan Square and I saw these guys who had stayed and fought against the police until the very early hours of the morning. This moment is when I realised that these guys, these great ordinary people – many without college education, not to mention PhDs, and certainly not with any experience from government – knew much more about life than I did. Because they were guided by their honesty, instincts and their will. And that very same morning, standing there among the fighters, I promised to myself that whatever kind of hardship I encounter in my future life, I will never walk away until the situation is resolved. How it will be resolved, in a good or a bad way, that's a different story. But I promised to myself that I will never walk away.

I continued our conversation by asking him about today's Ukraine. 'You have repeatedly said that Ukraine has never been stronger than it is today. In what way?'

His eyes lit up as he responded.

Throughout our history, Ukraine has been fighting for itself and for the right to be itself. Yes, we have won many battles, but we always lost wars. And we lost those wars for one of the following four reasons. Firstly, the absence of a state that was able to run

> the war machine and effectively defend the nation; the second reason was disunity among elites and society; the third was the lack of a proper army; and the fourth was the absence of friends we could rely on.

Kubela made a quick sweep through recent Ukrainian history to offer some telling examples.

> In 1918–1920, those who lost Ukraine to Moscow wrote in their memoirs that we were always arguing with each other. The society was divided. Our people were divided. At the same time, we failed to build a strong army, and no one in the world cared about Ukraine.
>
> Let's go back in our history to 1709, when our elites rebelled against Tsar Peter the Great during the war with Sweden. They again failed because the Tsar was more effective in communicating with public opinion in Ukraine; he reminded the public that he was the Orthodox Tsar and that their elites betrayed them and sold them out by wanting to put them under the rule of a Catholic or Protestant, which for many Ukrainians was a very sensitive issue. So many turned their backs on their Ukrainian compatriots and important battles were lost. In the end, the war itself was lost.
>
> When we go even further back in our history to the seventeenth century, it's more or less the same. Quarrelling among elites traumatised the country and the Russians – the Muscovites – could easily play us against each other. And again, of course, we didn't have any friends. Because if you start fighting against Moscow, you need an ally. But Poland could not be an ally to us because it had just finished its own war with Russia. The Ottoman Empire could not be an ally because they had their own interests, and

they did not want another strong player in the region. And no one else was really interested.

So, you see that throughout our history we did not fulfil the four requirements to be successful. But the most important thing today is that with the ongoing war against Putin's Russia, all the four requirements to succeed are very much present. We have a strong state. We are united. We have an efficient army. And we have very good allies. This is for the first time in our long history! This is why I say that our generation will have no excuses not to succeed.

Kuleba raised his glass and offered a toast to Cossack Mamay:

You see we can learn a lot from the Cossacks. In many ways they have come to symbolise our ethnic image, much like the medieval knights of Western Europe. Although over centuries only a minority of Ukrainians belonged to this legendary group, their influence on our history, culture and even the psychology of our country has been nothing less than deep and profound. And if you happen to know the history and mentality of the Cossacks, you won't be surprised to find that Ukrainians, who may seem rather quiet and humble at first sight, can go on to sacrifice their lives on the Maidan Square and become fearless warriors when called upon.[3]

CHAPTER 1

THE EVE OF DISASTER

The United Nations was not created to take mankind to heaven, but to save humanity from hell.

DAG HAMMARSKJÖLD, FORMER UN SECRETARY-GENERAL

It was like the beginning of a violent and devastating storm. Heavy, dark clouds had gathered on the European continent, a region that had survived a Cold War but had recently experienced years of renewed tension.

In February 2014, Russian soldiers dressed in 'unmarked green uniforms' had invaded and occupied Crimea, and soon afterwards the Russian Federation formally annexed the peninsula in a flagrant violation of Ukraine's sovereignty and territorial integrity. At the same time Russia started a war, led by proxies and so-called 'separatists' in eastern Ukraine. Then, in late 2021, a massive Russian military build-up started all along both the Russian and Belarusian borders with Ukraine. In October of that year, several months before the full-scale Russian invasion of Ukraine, US intelligence went public with what was taking place. It was an unprecedented move, an effort to warn President Zelenskyy and other leaders around the world. At the same time, President Joe Biden started to hammer out a new strategy to 'deter and dissuade' Russia, dispatching his CIA director William J. Burns to Moscow to warn President Putin that the consequences of a Russian invasion would be severe.[1] The steps that the administration of President Biden took well in advance of the invasion to publicly expose Russia's intentions created a unique opportunity 'to rally allies and partners, impose sanctions and ramp up military and financial support to Ukraine, steps that proved critical to Kyiv's initial success in repelling Russian forces and thwarting President Putin's grandest ambitions.'

To invent a pretext for the all-out Russian invasion of Ukraine, President Putin delivered the first of two major televised speeches to the Russian people on 21 February 2022, a little over two days before the invasion began. In his remarks he denied the right of Ukraine to exist as an independent state, while alleging that NATO and NATO allies 'completely ignore our concerns, protests and warnings.' He also announced that Russia would recognise Donetsk and Luhansk, the breakaway regions of eastern Ukraine, de facto controlled by Russia for eight years, as independent countries.

The world was now facing potentially the largest security crisis in Europe since the Second World War, though a sense of disbelief and denial were still palpable among many European and international leaders. They could not make themselves believe that a full-scale Russian invasion of Ukraine would take place. Rather, many saw the massive Russian military build-up along the border of Ukraine, the Black Sea and the Sea of Azov as yet another piece in a Russian intimidation plan designed to place maximum pressure on the leaders in Kyiv.

On the same day President Putin delivered the televised speech, Ukraine's Foreign Minister Dmytro Kuleba happened to be in

Washington DC to meet with, among others, President Biden in The White House. Kuleba and Biden had listened to parts of Putin's speech, which is as close as you get to a declaration of war. 'President Biden was comforting me,' Kuleba later told the American journalist Simon Shuster. 'It's like when you see someone who has cancer, the last stage of cancer, and you know the person is doomed, but you really sympathise with him, and try to help him, and you do your best while knowing that nothing is going to help. That was basically the atmosphere in the meeting.'

The Ukrainian Foreign Minister admitted that he was deeply moved but also terrified, as many international experts and observers had already predicted that Kyiv would fall within days of a Russian invasion. The Russian military was fast, so fast that the Ukrainian military stood little chance of resisting it in a conventional war, they claimed. And Moscow had spent billions of dollars in upgrading the Russian armed forces, both weapons and systems, as well as reorganising their structure and developing new and better ways of planning. Some also claimed that the Russians had proved themselves during the invasion of Georgia in 2008 and during its military intervention in Syria in 2015.

The prospects were therefore far from bright when Dmytro Kuleba left the White House on Tuesday 22 February 2022, setting out on his journey to New York City and the United Nations, where he would present what would become the most important speech ever delivered by a Ukrainian Foreign Minister.

'I was just back from Washington where I received a briefing saying that the invasion will begin in the next twenty-four to forty-eight hours. And I understood that this was the last speech in the international arena that would be delivered by a senior Ukrainian official before the invasion begins,' recalls Kuleba.

> I knew I had the right words in my mind. I knew that I would make all the right points. But the question that bewildered me the most, that almost tortured me, was what I should say that would prompt the UN member states to act. That would steer an anti-war sentiment, an anti-war campaign that could politically help put pressure on Russia, so that President Putin and the other Russian leaders in Moscow understand that this war is something that the nations of the world will stand against, and that Russia will not receive any kind of support. My main challenge in preparing for this speech was how to turn words into action.

Certainly not a minor task, as there is probably nothing more demanding and difficult in speechwriting and political rhetoric than to find the right words that will trigger not only empathy but determined and concrete action by others.

'I have to admit it didn't work', says Kuleba.

> The war began, but this was one of those moments in diplomacy when you know the stage, you know the play, but the reality is so grim that you still have to make an extraordinary effort and try to do something that is probably not going to work anyhow. That was how I was thinking the days before delivering the speech at the UN General Assembly on the eve of the Russian invasion of my country. I knew it was highly unlikely that I would achieve all that I wanted to do with the speech. I understood it was highly unlikely that it was going to work. And I must say this is something you intuitively know because you have some experience and you understand how the world functions. But still, you must try to do your absolute best. This was the main thing about this speech, as I see it.

'The UN General Assembly speech was very, very special,' recalls Heorhii 'Gosha' Tykhyi, Kuleba's eminent speechwriter.

> We realised that we couldn't expect any decisions from the General Assembly that would reverse the course of the events or stop the Russian invasion. But we also had some very practical goals with this speech, as we understood that the Russians had probably already made the decision to invade, but to justify it they would need to invent some kind of pretext. And one of the important goals with that speech was to deprive them of this opportunity. That is why you will find lines in the speech refuting Russian lies and underlining that Ukraine wants peace, that Ukraine does not intend to attack or to provoke Russia in any way. This was important.

Kuleba's speechwriter is correct, as in the speech there are several very clear and very strongly worded statements denying all such Russian allegations: 'Russia's accusations of Ukraine are absurd'; 'Ukraine has never threatened or attacked anyone. Ukraine has never planned and does not plan any such action. Ukraine has never planned and does not plan any military offensive in the Donbas. Neither any provocations nor acts of sabotage'; 'It is ultimately absurd to suggest that Ukraine could have prepared for anything like this and waited for months until Russia amassed an enormous military force along our borders to proceed with such alleged plans. This absurdity defies basic logic.' Later in his speech, Kuleba once again resolutely rejected 'all Russian insinuations about any alleged Ukrainian offensive military operations in the Donbas. We do not hold or plan any such actions.'

'I also remember how hard we worked on drafting the speech,' explains Gosha.

> It was very intense as we only had a limited period of time for the preparations of the speech. And it did not help that Dmytro was in New York, and I was back in Kyiv, so I was drafting it here in Ukraine. It was like table tennis, going back and forth, back and forth – but it worked out very well in the end. I also recollect that we were organising some of the broadcasts of the speech. And I recall the extraordinary moment when he was delivering this speech, you could literally switch on any TV channel in the world and you would see Dmytro speaking. I mean, I cannot imagine what he himself felt at that rostrum, because when you have the eyes of the entire world watching you and you are broadcasted live, this must be a very, very tough task. And I really admire how he handled it and delivered those key messages.

'I agree with everything Gosha has said, except one thing,' Kuleba says.

> When it comes to these historic speeches, it's not that you ask yourself, 'how do you feel now?' And then you start speaking. No, it just pours out of you. It's not manageable. You do not manage these emotions. It's just your mind and your heart that come together. And they tune themselves to the reality, and then it pours out. And when it happens, you also have this moment of exhaustion, because you gave it all. You gave it all for the sake of the result. So, the first feeling after delivering such a speech is complete exhaustion. As if, you know, as if you started with a 100 per cent battery charge and you ended up with zero. Usually, it takes you a day to kill your battery, but this time it only took a ten to fifteen minute-long speech to do it. But I want to stress that you become completely dissolved in this reality. But you still control

> it, in a way. Because if you feel that something goes wrong, that you do not have a connection with the audience, you begin to react to it. But it all happens intuitively. These are professionally the highlights of our work, the public part of the work. But again, you cannot prepare for that, because people will instantly feel if this emotion is pre-set or it's real.[2]

Facing this unprecedented and extremely alarming situation, Kuleba walked slowly towards the rostrum in the Grand Hall of the UN General Assembly in New York on the morning of Wednesday 23 February 2022. He wanted to make a final plea to President Putin and the world to avert an announced disaster. He sought to appeal for peace, to request help to halt the imminent Russian aggression and to find a way to resolve the crisis exclusively by diplomatic means.

'I remember the room was completely full, and this rarely happens in the UN General Assembly Hall. Everything was so tense, but at the same time quiet in a way, like before a big storm,' recalls Albana Dautllari, former Albanian Ambassador and Deputy Permanent Representative to the United Nations.[3]

The former Romanian Ambassador to the United Nations, Ion Jinga, explains,

> At the UN General Assembly session that morning, we did not expect the war to start the next day. In fact, we hoped that reason would prevail, not least because being a permanent member of the Security Council, the Russian Federation has a distinct responsibility to promote international peace and security. Unfortunately, it was not the case, and the subsequent developments turned into a nightmare. The atmosphere among ambassadors

> was tense, as the shadow of dark clouds over Europe was already floating on the horizon.[4]

In his speech, Kuleba warned the world community that Russian aggression would not be limited to Ukraine alone, and he underlined the absolute need for a severe and decisive response by the global community to Russia's belligerence, stressing that failure to do so would only undermine the entire international security system and a rules-based international order. He touched upon the current, dire situation in the Russian-occupied territories of Ukraine, including the unprecedented violations of human rights, as well as the need to release unlawfully detained individuals. Kuleba also voiced strong concern about the ongoing and wide-ranging Russian propaganda and disinformation campaigns. Finally, he ended the speech by stressing that Ukraine would 'not hesitate to exercise its right to self-defence under Article 51' of the UN Charter.

Overall, Kuleba delivered a truly exceptional speech, rooted in the founding values of the UN. As he finished, he made a strong appeal for action to the countries of the world: 'These days we have probably the last window of opportunity to do what Russia does not expect the United Nations and its member states to do. Demonstrate unprecedented ability and readiness to act in order to stop aggression. No matter what relations you develop among each other, it is your ultimate duty to defend the UN Charter.'

The UN Secretary-General, António Guterres, in his response to the Ukrainian Foreign Minister, stated in his speech that the Minsk agreements – a set of international accords that aimed to end the war in Ukraine's Donbas region – would be 'surviving in an intensive care unit thanks to a number of life-supporting devices' until the recognition by the Russian Federation of the 'so-called "independence"' of the Donetsk and Luhansk regions of Ukraine. He called for a return to dialogue and negotiations in pursuit of a peaceful resolution of the dispute, pledging that the UN would continue its humanitarian work to help all those residing within Ukraine's borders, 'independent of whoever might control the territory where people are living'.[5] Later that evening, upon learning that the Russian military invasion of Ukraine had commenced, Guterres delivered a powerful statement, concluding that the Russian military operations inside the sovereign territory of Ukraine were in direct conflict with the UN Charter and marked 'the repudiation of the principles that every country has committed to uphold'.

'Stop the military operation. Bring the troops back to Russia. We know the toll of war. With deaths rising, we are seeing the images of fear, anguish and terror in every corner of Ukraine,' the UN Secretary-General emphasised in his strong appeal to President Putin and the Russian authorities.[6]

Abdulla Shahid, then President of the General Assembly, recalled the pertinent and famed words of former UN Secretary-General Dag Hammarskjöld, reminding all delegates, 'The United Nations was not created to take mankind to heaven, but to save humanity from hell,' and that the organisation's mandate stipulates that disputes between member states must be settled by peaceful means and in accordance with international law.[7]

The US Ambassador to the United Nations, Linda Thomas-Greenfield, stressed that 'this is Putin's war of choice', and that if he chose to escalate further the Russian Federation would bear full responsibility. 'Former empires cannot lay claim to sovereign nations,' she stressed, urging the international community to show Moscow that it is isolated and alone in its aggressive actions.[8] The Canadian Ambassador, Robert Keith Rae, underlined in his response that

'Russia with all its acolytes can contort and spin all they like, but the pain and suffering caused are its responsibility'. 'It is never too late to stop and turn to diplomacy,' he pointed out, while emphasising that 'Ukraine is not a mistake. Ukraine is a sovereign nation.' He added that this was not about the North Atlantic Treaty Organization (NATO) nor the European Union, but the existence, and the right to existence, of a member state of the United Nations.[9]

The Chinese UN Ambassador, Zhang Jun, emphasised that his delegation's position remained unchanged with regard to safeguarding the sovereignty and territorial integrity of all states. The situation in Ukraine, however, is tangled in a historical web, and that in the current context all parties should exercise restraint, implement the principles of robust dialogue and seek responsible solutions through peaceful means. He welcomed all efforts aimed at facilitating a diplomatic solution.[10]

The Russian Federation's delegate, Vassily A. Nebenzia, alleged that since the 'failed Maidan coup' of 2014, Ukraine has conducted a 'hate-filled policy against its own citizens'. He claimed that despite Russian efforts for negotiations in Security Council meetings and other international arenas, Ukraine had avoided dialogue with the Donbas region and ignored the interests of broad swathes of the population, adding that Ukraine had also sabotaged calls by member states for an inclusive dialogue. He further stated that while the people of Crimea, Donetsk and Luhansk have declared their independence, Ukraine has no plans for dialogue on the matter; instead Ukraine had carried out bloody military adventures while waging war on the Russian language as part of a deliberate State policy of 'linguistic inquisition'. After eight years of economic, transport and food embargoes on the Donbas, the Russian Federation decided that the region's people could consider themselves independent, he declared, adding that his country, through its armed forces, would seek to ensure that the ceasefire there would be monitored.[11]

His statement was mostly a repetition of Russian lies, disinformation and propaganda, but it is worth noting that it made absolutely no reference to the imminent full-scale Russian invasion of Ukraine. On this point, it can be noted that President Putin delivered his second televised speech to the Russian people at six o'clock in the morning on the day of the invasion (24 February 2022), a mere two hours after it started, in which he announced that he had made a decision to carry out 'a special military operation'. Putin announced that 'the purpose of this operation is to protect people who, for eight years now, have been facing humiliation and genocide perpetrated by the Kyiv regime. To this end, we will seek to demilitarise and denazify Ukraine, as well as bring to trial those who perpetrated numerous bloody crimes against civilians, including against citizens of the Russian Federation.' Putin bizarrely claimed that 'it is not our plan to occupy the Ukrainian territory. We do not intend to impose anything on anyone by force.'[12]

In addition to the above mentioned national statements, the overall reactions to the speech can only be described as resoundingly supportive.

The former Finnish UN Ambassador, Jukka Salovaara, recalled: 'There was an unmistakable feeling that the indifference of earlier years had suddenly disappeared, and that there was support for Ukraine. Russia, on the other hand, had difficulty in mobilising even its closest henchmen and, in the end, after more than eighty speeches, only Syria supported Russia.'

Romanian Ambassador Jinga recollects,

> Foreign Minister Kuleba's speech was followed with great

> interest, as he was the most credible source to brief the UN about the reality on the ground and the grave consequences of the Russian Federation's recognition of the so-called 'independence' of Donetsk and Luhansk – and his intervention was impactful. He showed firmness and determination in defending the independence and territorial integrity of his country, while leaving the door open for diplomacy. Minister Kuleba was very clear on the point that Ukraine will not hesitate to exercise its right to self-defence, which really made a very strong impression on the audience and was received with admiration and respect. But probably the most important effect of his speech came the next day, after Russia started its invasion of Ukraine, because Kuleba's warning got a new significance: he anticipated the events to come and was visionary on their impact in Europe and around the world. His claims that 'there is no more important task today than not to repeat the mistakes of the past' and 'this is the largest security crisis in Europe since the Second World War' became so tragically confirmed by reality. And at the same time, his appeal to the international community to vigorously react against this aggression and the aggressor was heard. The heroic resistance of the Ukrainian people received unwavering international support, proving that the love for freedom is more powerful than the power of guns. And we should never forget that the security of Ukraine is an integral part of the security of Europe.[13]

Many of those who were present at the UN General Assembly meeting on that grim February morning, on the very eve of an announced disaster, would later recall the solemn words of Kuleba:

> I warn every nation in this distinguished chamber: no one will be

able to sit out this crisis if Putin decides that he can move forward with his aggression against Ukraine. Your governments and your people will face painful consequences together with our government and our people. This is why we need to use this last chance for action and stop Russia where it is. It is clear that President Putin will not stop by himself. [...] Every hour of inaction now is a threat to the lives of Ukrainians, not only the military but also civilians, including women and children. This is an escalating threat to our collective global security and to our freedom.

STATEMENT BY DMYTRO KULEBA

UN GENERAL ASSEMBLY, NEW YORK, 23 FEBRUARY 2022

Mr President,

I am grateful for your leadership in this main policymaking and representative organ of the United Nations.

You have chosen the word 'Hope' as a motto for your Presidency. The same feeling currently dominates the mindsets of Ukrainians and people around the globe. Hope for peace. Hope for common sense to prevail. Hope for diplomacy to ease tensions.

However, today we need much more than hope. We need swift, concrete and resolute actions. A new type of action by the UN and international community which is relevant to the level of threat we all, not just Ukraine, face today because of Russia's aggressive course.

The people of Ukraine need these actions by Ukraine's strategic partners and international community. We are at a critical juncture in world history and our actions today define it for decades to come. We all read history books. We all watched movies about the mistakes of politicians in the run-up to 1914 and 1939. About the feats of our grandparents and a catastrophic price at which a revanchist evil in Europe was defeated.

There is no more important task today than to not repeat the mistakes of the past. I do believe in the power of the free world and our joint ability to avert a new devastating catastrophe in Europe that no nation will be able to sit out. This is why today I address you on behalf of over 40 million Ukrainians who only wish to live in peace and prosperity. Not in fear, intimidation, not under Russian fire, bombs and shelling.

We are currently at the middle of the largest security crisis in Europe since the Second World War. This crisis was created and is being escalated by one side unilaterally, by the Russian Federation. Russia's accusations of Ukraine are absurd. Ukraine has never threatened or attacked anyone. Ukraine has never planned and does not plan any such action. Ukraine has never planned and does not plan any military offensive in the Donbas. Neither any provocations nor acts of sabotage. It is ultimately absurd to suggest that Ukraine could have prepared for anything like this and waited for months until Russia amassed an enormous military force along our borders to proceed with such alleged plans. This absurdity defies basic logic.

Not less absurd are accusations of Ukraine escalating by acquiring defensive weapons from its partners. The only – I want to stress it – the *only* reason for Ukraine to boost its defences is Russia's ongoing and planned military and political actions. Russia's actions and statements are outrageous, horrific and go far beyond threatening Ukraine.

In fact, in his address this week Russian president Vladmir Putin overtly denied Ukraine's right to exist. Anyone who might think I exaggerate as the Ukrainian Foreign Minister should just watch this horrifying speech. It is with a heavy heart that we all need to admit the grim reality of a new aggressive and revanchist rule rising over Europe.

This is the fourth time that the General Assembly debates the situation in the temporarily occupied territories of Ukraine. However, this is the first time we debate the situation in the new reality created by the illegal recognition of two territories of Ukraine by Russia. And the backdrop of our discussion today is much more dangerous as Russia attacked the very fundamental principles of international peace and security, the pillars of the United Nations and, as I mentioned, the very existence of the Ukrainian state, the founding member of the United Nations.

A Ukrainian state that signed the UN Charter in San Francisco in 1945 as a founding member and made the principle enshrined in Article 2 of the Charter a cornerstone of its foreign policy. A state that voluntarily gave up its nuclear arsenal under the security assurances of nuclear powers. A state that has endured years of assault by one of these powers, a permanent member of the United Nations Security Council.

Two days ago, on February 21st, the Russian President recognised 'independence' of the temporarily occupied parts of the Donetsk and Luhansk regions of Ukraine and ordered the deployment of the Russian Armed Forces in these areas. This is an affront attack on the United Nations and core principles of international law, an ultimate blow to years of peace process and Russia's unilateral withdrawal from the Minsk agreements.

What is happening right now in eastern Ukraine, where Russian tanks are rolling in, and along the Ukrainian borders, where Russian forces are amassed in enormous quantities, must be a concern for everyone, for all of you.

I warn every nation in this distinguished chamber: no one will be able to sit out this crisis if Putin decides that he can move forward with his aggression against Ukraine. Your governments and your people will face painful consequences together with our government and our people. This is why we need to use this last chance for action and stop Russia where it is. It is clear that President Putin will not stop by himself.

Distinguished representatives, the beginning of a large-scale war in Ukraine will be the end of the world order as we know it. If Russia does not get a severe, swift and decisive response now, this will mean a total bankruptcy of the international security system and international institutions which are tasked with maintaining the global security order. This is a grim scenario which will throw us back to the darkest times of the twentieth century. Russia will not stop at Ukraine. If a permanent member of the UN Security Council succeeds in breaking literally all rules, other actors will be inspired by him and follow his pattern. What he tries to do now is to prove that the United Nations are weak, indecisive and unable to defend their core principles – that rules do not apply to him, to Russia, to Putin.

What role for the UN does Russia see? A new League of Nations. We must deny Russia what it wants. I graduated from university with a degree in international law and a strong belief in multilateralism. After many years of practising diplomacy, I still do believe in both: rules containing aggression and the power of our collective and firm action. If the United Nations makes a pivot right now to become a strong and proactive player, which is not afraid of resolute actions and using all of its might and powers, I am confident that Russia will stop.

In this context, I welcome yesterday's statement by the United Nations Secretary-General which is truly different in tone. We need decisive actions of the same kind to follow these right words.

Russia shows signs of readiness to further escalate its aggression against Ukraine and we have limited time to stop, deter and contain it. Every hour of inaction now is a threat to the lives of Ukrainians, not only military but also civilians, including women and children. This is an escalating threat to our collective global security and to our freedom.

Ukraine expects decisive, immediate and proportional actions by the international community. The United Nations is the organisation that has to demonstrate leadership. Not just condemnations. Concrete actions to stop the Russian machine of war without stepping into a bloody conflict with many thousands of casualties, devastation and suffering. I do not want this. Ukraine does not want this. The world does not want this. We need your help right now to stop Russia from proceeding with aggressive plans.

Ukraine believes in diplomacy. We see no alternative to peaceful solutions by political and diplomatic means. There is still an opportunity for diplomacy to say its word. Even as Russia continues its escalation and provocations. For months, Russia pretended to pursue diplomacy while bringing more and more troops to our borders and in the temporarily occupied territories of Ukraine. Now this number stands at least at 150,000.

Under the OSCE [Organization for Security and Co-operation in Europe] Vienna Document on Confidence and Security-Building Measures, such actions fall under the qualification of 'unusual military activities' that would require explanation. However, Russia has persistently refused to provide it. Instead, it proceeded with threats.

Russia has literally stuffed the Black Sea and the Sea of Azov with at least forty-six military vessels. It routinely closes large parts of the seas under the pretext of holding naval exercises. In practice, it amounts almost to a blockade of Ukrainian seaports. This is already an attack on the global freedom of navigation, one of the sacred principles of international law.

Russia's propaganda machine is in full swing. It desperately tries to create a pretext for further aggression against Ukraine.

We resolutely reject all Russian insinuations about any alleged Ukrainian offensive military operations in the Donbas. We do not hold or plan any such actions. We remain committed to political and diplomatic settlement and together with our partners we maximise efforts to reduce tensions and keep the situation in line with diplomatic dialogue.

For now, we see that Russian occupation forces have already significantly increased shelling of Ukrainian territory and civilian infrastructure. Artillery fire at the contact line in the Donbas from the occupied territory hit a kindergarten in a town called Stanytsia Luhanska and a school in Vrubivka, among the latest terrible examples.

Recognition of the so-called 'republics' has no legal implications. It merely confirms Russia's own involvement as a party to the armed conflict in Donbas, which Russia vehemently denied all these years. The situation in the occupied Donbas has already been terrible for years, with residents living in the atmosphere of fear, lawlessness and insecurity.

The infamous secret prison called 'Izolyatsia' in the occupied Donetsk remains inaccessible for human rights and humanitarian missions. It continues to function as a literal concentration camp – in Europe, in the twenty-first century. Hundreds of people have passed through this camp and were subjected to heavy forced labour, humiliation, tortures. Cases of extrajudicial killings have been reported too.

Russia continues to block the release of the illegally detained persons. In September 2021 the President of Ukraine handed over to the Secretary-General the list of more than a hundred Ukrainians from Donbas and Crimea who had been unlawfully detained, sentenced or even transferred from the occupied territories to the Russian Federation. We reiterate our call on the Secretary-General to provide good offices and facilitate their immediate release. And I appreciate the readiness of the Secretary-General to do so.

Mr President,

Today, Ukraine defends not only global security, but also freedom, democracy and fundamental principles of international law. Peaceful life and the future of millions of people in Europe and around the globe rely on the rules that Russia tries to destroy. Diplomacy and international fora must prevail and stop Russian aggression.

Since 2014, the General Assembly has already adopted eleven resolutions reaffirming its commitment to Ukraine's territorial integrity and condemning the temporary occupation of Ukraine's territories by Russia.

The General Assembly has not and will not accept the Russian mantra that 'the case of Crimea is closed'. The occupying power persists in destroying the identity of Ukrainians and the indigenous people of the peninsula, the Crimean Tatars. Since 2014 more than 64,000 Ukrainian citizens have had to leave Crimea and move to mainland Ukraine due to fear, persecution for political and human rights activism or discrimination on ethnic and religious grounds. Political persecutions continue unabated.

Among many others, Mr Nariman Dzhelyalov, Deputy Head of the Mejlis of the Crimean Tatar people, participant of the International Crimea Platform Summit, remains behind bars. He is one of more than 100 political prisoners of the Kremlin.

On February 16th, a court in Simferopol sentenced journalist Vladyslav Yesypenko on trumped-up charges to six years in prison. He is one of fourteen Ukrainian journalists kept by Russians in prison. Russia may continue to pretend it doesn't violate any international norms and principles. Yet reports by the UN Secretary-General, OHCHR [Office of the United Nations High Commissioner for Human Rights], OSCE, their missions, as well as the report of the ICC [International Criminal Court] Prosecutor, all testify to the contrary.

If Russia doesn't agree with all the mentioned resolutions and reports, it should simply provide access to Crimea to the UN Human Rights Monitoring Mission in Ukraine and the OSCE Special Monitoring Mission. The access of international organisations to the occupied territories is critical. Ukraine guarantees such access throughout the government-controlled territory and continues to demand from the Russian side to do the same in the occupied territories.

Esteemed members of the General Assembly, the whole world witnesses today that Russia turns to threatening and blackmailing the global community to 'close the Crimea case'. It is in fact one of the points in the long list of its recent so-called 'security demands'.

Ukraine continues efforts to achieve de-occupation of Crimea by peaceful means.

The Crimea Platform is a tool designed exactly for that end. We are truly thankful to all the countries supporting the International Crimea Platform. Your active involvement in the Platform is a sound foundation for our future success. We are open to new members, and I call on you to join the Crimea Platform. Be it states or international organisations, you are welcome. We expect the UN will find proper modalities to engage with this initiative, established on the principles of the UN Charter.

Mr President, dear colleagues, Ukraine made a historic contribution to global security. In 1994 we denuclearised, giving up the world's third largest nuclear arsenal. We have no plans to regain nuclear weapons. Today, we expect the world to reciprocally ensure our security with relevant scale and resoluteness of actions in the face of a historic level of threat. This is the reason why Ukraine requested urgent consultations under Article 6 of the Budapest Memorandum.

The world owes Ukraine its security.

Ukrainian President Volodymyr Zelenskyy initiated a new format of negotiations to settle the security crisis created by Russia. Five permanent members of the UN Security Council plus Ukraine, Germany and Turkey. This is the format that we are trying to convene.

I reaffirm that Ukraine proposed some years ago to deploy a UN peacekeeping mission to Ukraine. Until now, the UNSC [United Nations Security Council] has failed to take necessary decisions.

Ukraine proposes to combine stark sanctions policy and strengthening of Ukraine together with keeping diplomatic channels open to persuade Russia to de-escalate and prioritise diplomacy.

We urge member states to use all available means to protect Ukraine and deter Russia. Whatever action you can take is appreciated. We are grateful for the actions already taken by many of you. We expect the international community to do its best to put out the fire in the centre of Europe, which is about to flare up.

The Russian security crisis must end with Russia returning to the path of diplomacy.

We call on all states and international organisations not to recognise any alteration of the status of certain areas of the Donetsk and Luhansk regions of Ukraine and to refrain from any action or dealing that might be interpreted as recognising any such altered status. The absence of proper reaction or a neutral stance will only contribute to further escalation and sufferings. And it will not be limited to Ukraine's border and territory.

On the contrary, active diplomacy, strong political messaging, tough economic sanctions and strengthening Ukraine can still force Moscow to abandon aggressive plans. Swift and resolute actions by the United Nations can reclaim the organisation's leading role at this historic and dark moment.

Russia must withdraw its forces from the sovereign territory of Ukraine. Russia must stop destabilising the international security situation. We, Ukrainians, want peace. And we want to resolve all issues through diplomacy. We stand ready for all possible scenarios and ready to protect our land and our people if Russia further attacks. Ukraine will not hesitate to exercise its inherent right of self-defence as outlined in Article 51 of the Charter of the United Nations in response to the armed attacks of the Russian Federation.

These days we have probably the last window of opportunity to do what Russia does not expect the United Nations and its member states to do: demonstrate unprecedented ability and readiness to act in order to stop aggression. No matter what relations you develop among each other, it is your ultimate duty to defend the UN Charter.

I thank you!

CHAPTER 2

THE NEXT THREE DAYS WILL BE DECISIVE

There's no time to waste. We have the resources, economic strength and expertise to help Ukraine win this war.

Kaja Kallas, EU High Representative for Foreign Affairs and Security Policy

Western intelligence had warned of the imminent danger of a full-scale Russian invasion and predicted Kyiv would fall in a matter of a few days. Especially unusual was the accuracy, detail and advance warning of Russia's plans and intentions provided by the US intelligence community.[1] The massive Russian onslaught seemed impossible to halt. As a last attempt to avoid a war, President Zelenskyy appealed directly to the Russian people.

His appeal was broadcast a little after midnight on the night of the invasion. He spoke in Russian.

> Between us there are more than 2,000 kilometres of common borders, where your troops are standing today, almost 200,000 of them, and thousands of military vehicles. Your leadership has

> ordered them to advance on the territory of another country. And that step could be the start of a Great War on the European Continent. You are told that these flames will bring freedom to the people of Ukraine. But the people of Ukraine are already free. You are told that we are Nazis. But how could there be support for Nazism among a people who gave more than eight million lives for the victory against Nazism? How could I be a Nazi? Put that question to my grandpa, who fought the whole war as an infantryman in the Soviet army and died a colonel in an independent Ukraine.[2] We know for sure, we don't want war. Not a cold war or a hot war or a hybrid war. But, if we are under attack, if someone tries to take our country, our freedom, our lives and the lives of our children, we will defend ourselves.

If the Russians invade, he warned, 'you will see our faces, not our backs'.

The Russian assault began a few hours later, on multiple fronts, shortly before 4am Kyiv time on 24 February 2022. The Russian armed forces quickly attacked Ukrainian command and control centres, air defences and critical infrastructure with short-range missiles. At the same time, columns of Russian tanks and armed personnel carriers began to cross the Ukrainian border from Belarus towards Kyiv, from Russia towards Kharkiv and from occupied Crimea towards Kherson and Nova Kakhovka in the south. Citizens in Kyiv, Kharkiv, Odesa, Zaporizhia, Zhytomyr, Mykolaiv and Kherson – to name only some of the main regional centres that were targeted – woke up to the sound of violence and explosions, as Russian missiles and bombs attacked airfields and military installations all over the country.

The entire military operation was underpinned by President

Putin's belief in the 'non-existence of the Ukrainian nation' and the 'desire of Ukrainians to live under Russian rule'. Russian soldiers only had rations for two or three days, as they were promised the whole operation in Ukraine would take no longer, and in burned-out Russian tanks and vehicles Ukrainians later found parade uniforms for Russian soldiers prepared for the imminent victory procession down Kyiv's main avenue, Khreshchatyk. Since the invasion is billed a 'mission of liberation', the Russian officers and soldiers were initially ordered not to show any hostility towards the local population.[3]

The Russians were in for a big surprise, having grossly underestimated Ukraine's resistance and the people's determination to fight for their freedom and their country. In addition, it would soon become evident that Russian plans for the military campaign were ill-conceived, and they would meet considerable logistical problems, as well as major issues related to the morale of their soldiers.[4] At one stage, Russian commanders achieved a twelve-to-one force ratio facing the northern approaches to Kyiv, but failed to turn that advantage into victory due to a lack of tactical competence. Another major problem the Russian forces faced was large Russian columns becoming easy targets for agile, small and mobile Ukrainian military units.[5]

On the eve of the invasion, the Americans kindly offered to bring President Zelenskyy, his family and advisers to safety, but the Ukrainian President flatly refused to evacuate Kyiv. The renowned historian Timothy Snyder interviewed President Zelenskyy on why he had remained in Kyiv.

> Explaining his choice, he began not from the specific predicament, dramatic though it was, and not even from himself. He

> spoke of his love for his parents, and what he learned from them. He had not chosen them, and yet in his love for them he was free. He compared that love to the decision to remain in the capital as the war began: something self-evident. Staying was not something he did alone: he was in the company of those who had taught him when he was younger, and those who elected him. He was in the company of others who were also taking risks. He understood the situation, he said, because of what it meant to represent others. A president, he said, was only the first grain of sand in a turning hourglass.[6]

Instead of leaving the Ukrainian capital, Zelenskyy began to mobilise his people to fight the invading army in what can be considered one of the most far-reaching and powerful strategic decisions of the entire conflict. He would play an extraordinary role in mobilising international support for Ukraine. *Time* correspondent Simon Shuster, who published an intimate account of the Russian invasion, praised 'the way he coaxed and inspired his peers in the West, convincing them that this war was their own.'

Zelenskyy's numerous short video messages of resistance, where he called upon the Ukrainians to do everything in their power to assist their armed forces and on those living abroad to help form an international anti-Putin coalition to save Ukraine, greatly inspired the Ukrainian people. This demonstration of leadership, courage and strength by the most senior member of government directly resulted in a huge mobilisation of large parts of Ukrainian society. A telephone poll conducted on 26/27 February, the third and fourth day of the war, showed an extraordinary 79 per cent of Ukrainians believed in victory, 90 per cent of men expressed readiness to defend their country with arms in their hand and 70 per cent of women responded in the same manner (in the east of Ukraine, at risk of possible Russian advances, the figure was 80 per cent). In addition, and from the same nationwide poll, 86 per cent of Ukrainians wanted to join the EU, and 76 per cent supported plans to join NATO.[7]

'There were two big surprises the first day', recalls the Ukrainian historian Serhii Plokhy.

> The first of them, which shocked Kyiv, was Russia's all-out attack on Ukraine and the bombing of its capital. The second stunned Moscow. Unlike Yanukovych, Zelenskyy refused to flee, and Ukrainians throughout the country, unlike those in the Crimea and many of those in the Donbas, refused to stay housebound. They fought back.

After the Russian invasion, Kuleba left New York and the United Nations to return as soon as possible to Kyiv and his homeland. His journey back home to a country now at war was complicated; he flew first to Istanbul, then to Warsaw and thereafter travelled by car into Ukraine, chased by Russian agents. But, like his President, he was determined to fight back. 'I spent the whole night of the flight from New York to Istanbul on the phone, giving instructions, following developments and receiving instructions. It was the busiest flight I have ever had,' he recalls.

> One of the instructions that I gave from the plane was to ask my parents to immediately get into the car, to take my son, Yegor, and our two dogs and start driving towards Poland. My wife at that time, Zhenya, and my daughter Lyuba were on vacation outside Ukraine, so they were safe. As a precaution, I had already some

weeks earlier told my parents that they should be ready for any development, and I told them to pack their luggage and be ready for an urgent evacuation. So, when I called them and told them to leave, they were indeed ready. My parents grabbed Yegor, the dogs, all their luggage and jumped into the car and started driving towards the border between Ukraine and Poland. My plan was that when I reached the border between Poland and Ukraine, from the Polish side, they would reach the same point, but from Ukraine. It worked out very well and we met right at the border checkpoint. I ran out of my car and hugged my son Yegor.

This was the moment when I promised to myself that we must win this war; I wanted to live to see my family happy again, living with my children in peace, in a free and independent Ukraine. It was a moment that I will never forget and, in some ways, it helped me to keep going even through the most difficult moments of the war. After hugging my parents and saying hello to our two dogs, I hastened back into Ukraine. I was more determined than ever. That was the moment when I abandoned fear. I overcame my own fear and told myself, 'We are going to win!'[8]

Arriving into the city of Lviv in Ukraine by car the day after the invasion, he joined an emergency online meeting of EU Foreign Ministers in Brussels. In a strong and emotional appeal to EU leaders, Kuleba underlined that 'the armed forces of Ukraine are fighting and will not surrender', a very important message at a time when many outside Ukraine had not yet fully understood the unquestionable determination and will of the Ukrainian people to fight the invading Russians. He also explained that the Ukrainians now understood that the ultimate goal of Russia was 'to siege Kyiv, to terminate the government and the President of Ukraine personally.' In this context, he found it imperative to give his European colleagues an update on the ongoing fighting, highlighting the progress and powerful responses of the Ukrainian military forces. Kuleba also emphasised that the Russian forces 'have seized control of the Chernobyl nuclear power plant' and that the exceedingly high levels of radiation posed a major threat not only to Ukraine, but to the whole of Europe. He also felt it necessary to warn about the 'huge amount of disinformation' that was being distributed throughout the internet and social media, which was only likely to increase. Here he obviously also had in mind the ongoing Russian disinformation campaign portraying President Zelenskyy as a 'Nazi' and 'war criminal,' as well as groundless Russian allegations of 'genocide' against Russian-speaking people in Ukraine, possibly used as a desperate attempt by Russia to justify the invasion of Ukraine.

Kuleba also warmly welcomed the sanctions and restrictive measures that the EU immediately imposed on Russia after the invasion, believing they would have 'massive and severe consequences' for Russia. In a press conference right after the speech by Kuleba, Josep Borrell, High Representative of the Union for Foreign Affairs and Security Policy, explained that a complete package of EU sanctions had indeed been agreed the previous night – the EU's first package of restrictive measures – in coordination and cooperation with both the US and the UK. The sanctions targeted the Russian financial sector, the energy and transport sectors, dual-use goods, export control and export financing, visa policy, as well as sanctions against Russian individuals – including Putin, Foreign Minister Lavrov, as well as members of the Duma and the Russian Security Council. Borrell also explained that the EU would sanction those in Belarus who collaborated with Russian military aggression against Ukraine. He emphasised that the sanctions will 'cut Russian access to the most important capital markets' and will hit '70 per cent of the Russian banking system and key state-owned companies, including in the field of defence.'[9]

For the EU foreign policy chief, Josep Borrell, it was important to highlight the intense ongoing diplomatic efforts within the United Nations, where both Ukraine and the EU were very active in mobilising support for indispensable resolutions on Russian aggression against Ukraine in the UN General Assembly, as well as in the UN Security Council, despite Russia's veto rights.

'We are mobilising support for the vote in the UN Security Council this evening, although we know Russia will veto it,' Borrell said. 'But then it will go to the UN General Assembly. To prepare this I have spoken to the Foreign Ministers of China, India and others to explain to them that this is not about Ukraine. This is about the respect for international rules and the UN Charter.'[10]

All in all, Dmytro Kuleba gave a quick and moving account of what was happening on the ground in Ukraine. He spoke of 'the heroic resistance of the Ukrainian forces', and warned that 'the next three days will be decisive for Ukraine, the region and the entire globe'. As a matter of fact, the coming days would be extremely critical, as they would determine if the Ukrainians were able to halt the Russian assault, which again would be a clear indication of how the war might end.

'Since the first days of the full-scale invasion, Dmytro Kuleba has been a guest at the Foreign Affairs Council [FAC] of the European Union,' recalls Gabrielius Landsbergis, former Foreign Minister of Lithuania.

> In the beginning, his words conveyed the horror the Ukrainian people were enduring in the face of all-out war. His message rang

true, keeping us alert and preventing us from drifting into the stream of other global affairs.

Over time, it became routine to start FAC meetings with the agenda item on Russia's war against Ukraine – so much so that Dmytro began to feel like one of the European ministers discussing everyday European issues. At one of the last FAC meetings he attended before finishing his tenure, we discussed Ukraine and smoothly transitioned to the next item on the agenda. It took a while for the chair to realise that our guest, Dmytro, was still politely sitting in the room, minding his own business and waiting for a signal to leave. Among the ministers, we remarked that it might be the perfect time to invite Ukraine to the EU – because, at least as far as FAC meetings were concerned, nothing much would change.[11]

Aside from the United Nations, we were also witnessing the first reactions to the Russian invasion in other major international organisations. The very same day that Kuleba was addressing EU Foreign Ministers in Brussels, the Council of Europe in Strasbourg, the most important human rights organisation on the continent, decided to suspend Russia's rights of representation in the organisation. It took only a few more weeks before the Russian Federation was formally expelled as a member, after being a full member for nearly twenty-six years. This marked the first time a member state had been expelled in the 75-year history of the Council of Europe.

STATEMENT BY DMYTRO KULEBA

EU FOREIGN AFFAIRS COUNCIL, BRUSSELS, 25 FEBRUARY 2022

Dear colleagues,

The armed forces of Ukraine are fighting and will not surrender. We are proud of our defenders.

Today we understand the fundamental scenario of the aggressor state – to siege Kyiv, to terminate the government and the President of Ukraine personally. This is the ultimate goal of Russia.

Only one hour ago the village Antonivka near Kherson and Vorzel was shelled by MRLS [multiple rocket launchers]. In Antonivka, the rockets hit the orphanage and some kids were killed. This is a crime against humanity. In Vorzel, the rockets hit the street near one of the biggest orphanages in Ukraine. At the moment of the strike, there were fifty kids inside. There were no casualties.

The main fight occurs at the moment in the direction of Dymer and Ivankiv north of Kyiv, Gostomel, Vorzel and Bucha – the Russian army is trying to attack, but our army provides a powerful response; a few helicopters of the enemy were destroyed and at least one column of ammunition was destroyed by Javelins.

Kyiv is preparing for defence. All men of Kyiv are invited to join the defence and to arm. In Chernihiv region, our army could stop the attack. At the moment, no military actions are held in this direction, but we understand that the enemy is regrouping. The same situation is in the Sumy region.

Kharkiv defends and only individual artillery battles are happening. Numerous enemies were destroyed in this direction; there are also prisoners of war from the Russian side.

The situation in Melitopol, eastern Ukraine, is difficult. On one side of the city stands the Russian army, but the Ukrainian army does not allow it to proceed to Mariupol. In Kherson, the Russian army will attempt to cross the Dnipro River but is searching for other ways due to the fact that Andriivski Bridge was destroyed to stop them. The army of Ukraine is holding the right bank of the river. Several air strikes occurred at night, including in Kyiv in the morning and also in Kharkiv for the second day in a row.

Russian military forces have seized control of the Chernobyl nuclear power plant. At this moment, the radiation levels have been 'exceeded' in a number of places in the area. This poses a threat not only to Ukraine but the whole of Europe. We are disappointed by a weak practical response to this fact by the international community.

It is important to mention that a huge amount of disinformation is being distributed on the internet, and it is understandable that its number will increase.

The next three days will be decisive, both for Ukraine and the entire globe. Thus, your support is crucial. We welcomed yesterday's decision to adopt restrictive measures that imposed massive and severe consequences on RF [Russian Federation] for aggression, including financial, energy, transport sector, dual-use goods as well as expert control and export financing, visa policy and additional listing of RF individuals.

It was the right decision to impose sanctions against Belarus, which is also involved in military invasion in Ukraine. I also welcome the EU to provide additional political, humanitarian, financial and logistical support, as well as further strengthening cyber resilience.

But we are disappointed that the EU could not reach consensus on blocking any operations of Russian financial and banking institutions performed using the SWIFT system.

Annalena, Luigi, Peter, Ioannis [the Foreign Ministers of Germany, Italy, Hungary and Cyprus], you are friends, you are good people. But how can your governments be against SWIFT when we are bleeding and the order you stand for is falling apart because of Russia?

There are also some urgent needs for Ukraine:

As I know, the US supports the supply of FIM-92 Stingers to Ukraine. I call upon all member states in possession of this man-portable air-defence system to transfer them to us immediately.

Blocking or interfering with the operation of satellite navigation systems in the air and at Black Sea and Sea of Azov.

Use all available means of the EU and its member states to block the work of Russian satellite navigation system GLONASS. Jam its signal over the Black Sea and Sea of Azov and airspace of Ukraine, as well as on the territory of Belarus.

Cancel the standard procedure of export control of all weaponry and military ammunition.

Make it possible for Ukraine's military forces to choose weaponry and military ammunition upon request.

Urgently reduce dependence on Russian nuclear, fuel and decommissioning services.

The EU Civil Protection Mechanism must meet the urgent humanitarian needs of citizens and the region affected by RF military invasion.

Ukraine already made a request; there are some member states who already replied positively (Croatia, Spain, Germany, Italy and Lithuania). I express great appreciation to Poland and Slovakia for their readiness to open hubs for delivering humanitarian and military assistance for Ukraine.

To find proper options for providing Ukraine with gasoline and diesel. Belarus blocks fuel transfer from Baltic States to Ukraine; proper functioning military forces depend on uninterrupted delivery of gasoline and diesel.

Ukraine urgently needs extra defensive equipment such as anti-tank weapons, air defence systems, including anti-UAV, as well as personal protective equipment.

We are planning to deploy a UN peacekeeping mission to Ukraine, but until now, the UNSC [United Nations Security Council] has failed to take necessary decisions.

Full embargo on RF oil and gas.

Expel Russian ambassadors worldwide and sever diplomatic relations with Russia.

Ban flights for any Russian air carriers. I call upon Latvia and Lithuania to consider this request, if these countries adopt such a decision, it will increase the time of arrival of Russian military aircrafts to the Ukrainian borders.

Immediately remove Russia from UN Security Council.

I will stop here.

Thank you for your attention.

CHAPTER 3

THE BIGGEST LIE OF THEM ALL

Putin's invasion of Ukraine was hardly a spur-of-the-moment decision. In an article by the Russian President published on 12 July 2021, seven months before the invasion, he made it very clear, without saying it directly, that the current government in Kyiv was deemed illegitimate and Ukraine had no right to exist from a historical point of view.[1]

Even autocrats seem obliged to justify their actions, especially their more brutal acts, to their citizens if not to themselves. Considering Moscow's renewed imperial ambitions, Putin may have felt that he was running out of options. Russia's blatant attempts at interfering and meddling in Ukrainian internal affairs had severely backfired, both in 2004 when it triggered the 'Orange Revolution' and nine years later, in 2013, when it set off another popular movement in Ukraine, the 'Revolution of Dignity'. In short, the Orange Revolution was a series of peaceful protests, sparked by allegations of widespread corruption, voter intimidation and direct electoral fraud, that successfully overturned a rigged presidential election, leading finally to a re-vote won by the pro-Western candidate Viktor Yushchenko. The Revolution of Dignity, also known as

'Euromaidan', was a sizeable protest movement that was sparked by President Viktor Yanukovych's sudden refusal to sign an anticipated political association and free trade agreement with the European Union. The protests finally led to the ousting of Yanukovych, who fled to Russia. As Dmytro Kuleba explains,

> The people of Ukraine made a choice in 2013, after Ukrainian President Viktor Yanukovych, acting at Putin's behest, sought to contravene public opinion and integrate the country with Russia instead of the EU. In November of that year, Ukrainians took to the streets in the so-called 'Euromaidan protests'. Yanukovych tried to suppress the demonstrations with brute force, but he underestimated the will of the Ukrainians, who responded with fury, not fear, and eventually ousted him.[2]

As political measures of Russian intimidation failed, Putin frantically turned to military means, with Russia seizing Crimea and destabilising eastern Ukraine in 2014. Hal Brands, of the Johns Hopkins School of Advanced International Relations, summarises Putin's failure: 'In conquering a peninsula and roiling a region, he lost a country.'[3]

In his article, Putin also tried to construct a false narrative around the 'historical unity' of Russians and Ukrainians. He wrote, 'The wall that has emerged in recent years between Russia and Ukraine, between the parts of what is essentially the same historical and spiritual space [is] a great common misfortune and tragedy.' But what he failed to mention is that this 'wall' had been imposed by the Russians themselves, in particular through their illegal annexation of Crimea in 2014 and the subsequent war they started in eastern Ukraine. In the article, Putin initially concedes that 'these are, first and foremost, the consequences of our own mistakes made at different periods of time'. But here he is not referring to events in 2014, but rather to developments that go further back in history, to the time of the Russian Revolution and the 'Bolsheviks', who, according to Putin, regrettably established 'quasi-state formations that emerged across the Russian empire at the time of the Civil War'. He additionally claimed that 'in 1954, the Crimean region of the RSFSR [Russian Soviet Federative Socialist Republic] was given to the Ukrainian SSR [Soviet Socialist Republic], in gross violation of legal norms that were in force at the time.' Putin further stated that the 'wall' was the 'result of deliberate efforts by those forces that have always sought to undermine' the unity between Russia and Ukraine.

It's deeply disturbing that Putin questions the right of Ukraine to exist as a sovereign and independent state. He claimed that 'modern Ukraine is entirely the product of the Soviet era' and asserted that 'we know and remember well that it was shaped – for a significant part – on the lands of historical Russia'.

'Lenin was indeed central to the formation of the USSR, as Mr Putin has claimed,' explains Serhii Plokhy.

> But Lenin's main contribution to the history of Russo-Ukrainian relations was not the formation of a modern Ukrainian state but the endowment of the Russian Federation – the name under which it entered the Soviet Union – with a territory and institutions of its own, distinct for the first time in centuries from the territory and institutions of the empire that it was seeking to preserve. If anything, Lenin laid the foundations for the formation of modern Russia, not Ukraine. Boris Yeltsin, Mr Putin's patron, took that state, the Russian Federation, out of the Soviet Union in 1991. It is over that state, not pre-revolutionary Russia, that Mr Putin presides.[4]

In the article, Putin also claimed that 'Ukraine's ruling circles decided to justify their country's independence through the denial of the past,' and that 'radicals and neo-Nazis were open and more and more insolent about their ambitions'. 'Step by step,' he wrote, 'Ukraine was dragged into a dangerous geopolitical game aimed at turning Ukraine into a barrier between Europe and Russia, a springboard against Russia.'

In addition to these disquieting and unsubstantiated accusations, he also made the outrageous allegation that Ukraine's leaders

> are facing the creation of a climate of fear in Ukrainian society, aggressive rhetoric, indulging neo-Nazis and militarising the country. Along with that we are witnessing not just complete dependence but direct external control, including the supervision of the Ukrainian authorities, security services and armed forces by foreign advisers, military 'development' of the territory of Ukraine and deployment of NATO infrastructure.

Finally, Putin warned that 'we will never allow our historical territories and people close to us living there to be used against Russia.' As the historian Anne Applebaum stated a few days after Putin's article was published, the piece was 'essentially a call to arms, laying the groundwork for a Russian invasion of Ukraine'.

'Not only is a new large-scale invasion of Ukraine now on the table,' Kuleba wrote at the end of 2021, but 'Putin also hopes ultimately to rearrange Europe's security architecture to the detriment of the West'.[5] This was in many ways confirmed by the Russian Foreign Minister Sergey Lavrov, who in an interview with Russian news agency TASS on 16 March 2022, only a few weeks after the Russian invasion of Ukraine, stated that 'this is not about Ukraine at all, but the world order. The current crisis is a fateful, epoch-making moment in modern history. It reflects the battle over what the world order will look like'. Similarly, Putin had on several occasions underlined the need to dramatically alter the world order. In a speech on 30 September 2022, he claimed that

> the current neocolonial model is ultimately doomed; this much is obvious. But I repeat that its real masters will cling to it to the end. They simply have nothing to offer the world except to maintain the same system of plundering and racketeering. They do not give a damn about the natural right of billions of people, the majority of humanity, to freedom and justice, the right to determine their own future. They have already moved on to the radical denial of moral, religious, and family values.[6]

On 21 February 2022, three days before the invasion, Putin repeated several of the most controversial messages from his article in a televised speech to the Russian people:

> I would like to emphasise again that Ukraine is not just a neighbouring country for us. It is an inalienable part of our own history, culture and spiritual space. [...] Since time immemorial, the people living in the south-west of what has historically been Russian land have called themselves Russians and Orthodox Christians. [...] Modern Ukraine was entirely created by Russia or, to be more precise, by Bolshevik, Communist Russia. [...] It should be noted that Ukraine actually never had stable traditions of real statehood. And, therefore, in 1991 it opted for mindlessly emulating foreign models, which have no relation to history or Ukrainian realities.[7]

Again, the main point of this misleading and lengthy speech, which could in the best case be qualified as an extremely biased Russian interpretation of history, is to question the right of Ukraine to exist as an independent and sovereign nation, while portraying the country as a recent and artificial creation without a rightful tradition and history. Not only does Ukraine lack the right to exist as a sovereign country, but its independence threatens Russia's very existence. In response to the speech, Kuleba stated, 'As Putin declared three days before the invasion, Ukraine's very existence is a mistake – the Soviet Union, he said, "created" Ukraine by casually drawing boundaries on a map – and our country must be erased.'[8] And this is the biggest lie of them all.

• • •

In fact, the history of Ukraine is an extraordinarily rich narrative spanning several millennia, with the nation characterised both by its geographical position as a crossroads between Europe and Asia and its cultural diversity and ethno-political complexities. Geography is no doubt central to understanding Ukrainian history. The frontier between the southern and eastern parts of Ukraine – known as the steppes – with their fertile farming soil, and the northern and western regions, which are more forested, were settled by important Slavic tribes. The wider region also became the frontier between Christianity and Islam.[9]

The foundations of modern Ukraine can be traced back to the establishment of the Kyivan Rus' – a conglomerate of peoples ruled by a warrior elite that traced its ancestry to Scandinavia and the Vikings – which emerged on the banks of the Dnieper River in the late ninth century.[10] Its principalities laid the origins of the political system, dynasties, law and language of Ukraine, as well as of Russia and Belarus. This was the first significant East Slavic state, with Kyiv as its capital, heralding a golden age of cultural development and the spread of Christianity in 988 AD under Prince Volodymyr the Great. Various Ukrainian polities followed, including the principality of Galicia-Volhynia and the kingdom of Ruthenia in the medieval period. The Kyivan Rus' was a major cultural and political centre until its decline in the twelfth century, which was hastened by the Mongol invasions in 1240.

Following the fall of Kyiv, Ukrainian territories were subjected to a long period of foreign rule, but the region also saw the emergence of the great Ukrainian Cossack state in the seventeenth and eighteenth centuries. By the nineteenth century, the territory of Ukraine was largely divided between the Russian and Austro-Hungarian empires. Still, Ukrainians did not surrender their cultural identity to this imperial domination. Just as other Eastern European intellectuals turned to national liberation and self-determination in the nineteenth century, Ukrainian thinkers and writers also sought to revive their nation by constructing a modern language and a master narrative of their nation's history.[11]

The nineteenth century therefore marked a resurgence in Ukrainian national identity, a celebration of the Ukrainian language, folklore and customs which had been suppressed under foreign rule. Important figures such as Taras Hryhorovych Shevchenko – the great Ukrainian poet, writer, artist and public and political figure – emerged, whose literary works and activism helped lay the groundwork for modern Ukrainian nationalism. Moreover, there were important developments taking place in strategic cities like Kharkiv, which had been the centre of Cossack settlements in the region known as Sloboda Ukraine since its founding in the mid-seventeenth century. The historian Serhii Plokhy writes,

> At the turn of the nineteenth century, while the Romanov dynasty remained in power, the first university in Russian-ruled Ukraine was founded in Kharkiv. In the 1830s the city became the centre of Ukrainian literary Romanticism, whose adherents formulated the cultural foundations of the modern Ukrainian project. In the 1920s Kharkiv became the capital of Soviet Ukraine and witnessed a Ukrainian cultural renaissance, passing on to subsequent generations the constructivist architectural masterpiece of the government centre and the work of modernist writers. The cultural revival, however, was short-lived, becoming known as the 'executed renaissance' – quite a few Kharkiv authors either committed suicide or were killed by Stalin's terror machine in the 1930s. After the declaration of Ukrainian independence in 1991, Kharkiv became the publishing capital of Ukraine and home to some of the country's leading cultural figures, such as the poet, novelist and performer Serhii Zhadan.[12]

Overall, the cultural revival set the stage for a modern, independent Ukraine to join the family of nations in the twentieth century. In 1903, Mykhailo Hrushevsky, an academic based in Lviv, published an article titled 'The Traditional Scheme of "Russian" History and the Problem of a Rational Organisation of the History of the East Slavs' that remains relevant to this day. The essay insisted that Ukrainian history was not a mere province of an overarching Russian story – and that Ukraine was *not* Russia. A coherent and distinct Ukrainian national history, he argued, stretched back over a millennium. As Georgiy Kasianov, professor at Maria Curie-Sklodowska University in Lublin, Poland, notes, 'Hrushevsky's vision of Ukrainian identity had much in common with similar schemes in Eastern Europe: It was ethnocentric, teleological (insofar as it treated Ukrainian nationhood as the inevitable outcome of centuries of history), and powerful in its ability to mobilise broad swaths of people.'[13]

Hrushevsky became not only the father of modern Ukrainian nationalism and history but also a key political actor, the inaugural President of the first Ukrainian Parliament from 1917 to 1918, as well as the spiritual leader of the national revolution that led to the creation of an independent Ukrainian republic between 1917 and 1920.[14] The turmoil of the twentieth century saw Ukraine briefly achieve independence after the collapse of the Russian Empire, only to be consumed by the ensuing chaos of the First World War and the Russian Civil War, when most of the Ukrainian region became a republic of the Soviet Union and parts of western Ukraine were divided between Poland, Romania and the former Czechoslovakia.

'Ukraine paid a high price for its independence,' explains the Ukrainian historian Yaroslav Hrytsak.

> It emerges as a sovereign state – from 1914, that coincided with a period of extraordinary bloodshed. It featured a civil war, so chaotic and confusing that it resembles the plot of Verdi's opera 'Il Trovatore'. About 4.5 million Ukrainians died in the Stalin-engineered famine of 1932–3, and the peasantry was broken and the intelligentsia was wiped out. Ukraine was at the centre of further violence during the Second World War, and an estimated 1.5 million of the six million Jews who perished in the Holocaust died in Ukraine. The Nazis executed 34,000 Jews in a single day on 29 September 1941. There were also waves of 'interconnected violence' with massacres carried out by Ukrainian partisans

> against Polish villages, and terrible pogroms. Against the odds, Ukraine emerged in the late twentieth and twenty-first centuries as a democracy, and it has become a fully-fledged civic nation.[15]

However, Russian elites and state-backed historians have over a long period of time attempted to trace a chronology that could reinforce the notion that Russians and Ukrainians are one people. These Russian historians, who Putin has eagerly studied, have insisted that there should be no schism between the Russian and Ukrainian people, as they both descend from the Kyivan Rus', and their union was reaffirmed by the 1654 Pereyaslav treaty. The Russian account demonises or downplays historic figures and events that suggest the uniqueness of Ukraine. For example, Russians vilify the seventeenth-century Cossack leader Ivan Mazepa, who sided with Sweden against Muscovy. They also dismiss the Ukrainian revolution of 1917–20, and the accompanying independent republic, as a fleeting and unfortunate civil conflict within a single community. They portray the Great Famine of 1932–33, which killed as many as four million Ukrainians, as a shared tragedy of all peoples of the Soviet Union. This view is, of course, contrary to that held by the Ukrainians, who call the tragedy the Holodomor ('death by starvation') and see it as a genocide perpetrated against them by the Russian-dominated Soviet Union.

In Putin's Russia, the Ukrainian nationalist movement that followed in the 1930s and 1940s is seen merely as the work of anti-Russian collaborators who colluded with Nazi Germany. It is worth noting that in 2003 a joint Russian/Ukrainian commission of historians attempted to discuss these historical events with the goal of 'harmonising' their narratives. The debate ended up underscoring the gulf between both sides. The same year, Ukrainian President

Leonid Kuchma, whose political opponents consistently accused him of being pro-Russian, published a book titled *Ukraine is not Russia*. The volume was written in Russian, printed in Moscow and addressed to Russian readers. Kuchma wanted to underline that Russians and Ukrainians have separate historical experiences, identities, languages and cultures.[16]

To a large degree, the Soviet era in Ukraine was marked by forced collectivisation, 'The Great Terror', deportations, genocide and the aforementioned mass starvation. During the Second World War, Ukraine became one of the most conflict-scarred areas, suffering immense losses not only on the battlefield (with the related civilian deaths) but also as a result of the Holocaust. Post-war, Ukraine remained under a totalitarian Soviet regime, experiencing a mix of industrial development and political repression, as well as the Chernobyl nuclear disaster in 1986.

Following the disintegration of the USSR, Ukraine quickly declared its independence on 24 August 1991; this was confirmed by an overwhelming majority in a national referendum in December of that year. Developments in Ukraine in subsequent years were marked by ongoing efforts to forge a path towards a stable, democratic society replete with economic reforms, but also struggles with corruption and political instability. As already mentioned, the 'Orange Revolution' (2004–5) and the 'Revolution of Dignity' (2013–14) sparked widespread public discontent in light of intense Russian meddling and interference, while demonstrating that freedom is the definitive choice and expression of the Ukrainian people. In 2019, European and Euro-Atlantic integration was ultimately incorporated into Ukraine's Constitution as a vision of national development – a strategic course that has since become fundamental to a large majority of Ukrainians.

Overall, and especially since 1991, Ukraine has gone through profound political changes, leading to a broad commitment to democracy and independence and a distinct Ukrainian identity. But Russia has reacted violently against these trends, initially culminating in the illegal 2014 occupation and annexation of Crimea, a direct intervention intended to destabilise Ukraine's Donbas region. 'Russia planned a blitzkrieg with the ultimate goal of dividing Ukraine in half and establishing a puppet state called Novorossiya in Ukraine's eight eastern regions,' wrote Kuleba.

> But Putin greatly underestimated Ukrainian resolve. Tens of thousands of Ukrainians from all regions and all walks of life raced to the frontlines to take up arms in defence of their country. They were backed by hundreds of thousands of civilian volunteers, ordinary Ukrainian citizens who supplied the army with everything from food to do-it-yourself armoured vehicles. It became clear that Putin hadn't attacked the defenceless state he had imagined; the Ukrainian people, however poorly equipped, were highly motivated. Putin's grand designs quickly fell apart, leading to a years-long stalemate on a tiny fraction of land near the Ukrainian border.[17]

Consequently, over 14,000 Ukrainians were killed during the period 2014–22. And, as we have seen, after eight years of war in eastern Ukraine a full Russian invasion triggered a large-scale mobilisation of Ukrainian resistance and an unyielding determination to stop the Russian onslaught.

Today, Ukraine's history continues to be written amid an ongoing total war. Its path is characterised by the resilience and enduring spirit of its people, who strive to safeguard their sovereignty and foster a distinct national identity. Historically situated at the intersection between powerful cultural and political forces, Ukraine's past tells us a compelling story of endurance, national unity and an unending pursuit of self-determination. As Kuleba explains,

> Millions of young Ukrainians have not lived a single day in the Soviet Union, and many of them now have children of their own. The idea of a 'common Soviet past', already fading among older generations, means little to them. These young people have lived through two revolutions – first the Orange Revolution and then the Revolution of Dignity – and an ongoing war with Russia. For them, Ukraine has never gained independence; it has always been independent.[18]

Analysts are rightly very distrustful of politicians who use history as a manipulative tool for pursuing political, social or military ends. History, however, remains an inescapable part of how people see themselves and the world; how they structure their beliefs and determine their actions. History shapes and affects the lives of millions in this conflict and cannot be dismissed.[19]

This is why an important initiative has been launched by over 115 international historians and scholars in the humanities, social sciences and sciences, with the goal of establishing a scholarly and accessible account of the remarkable history of the lands of contemporary Ukraine and the peoples who have inhabited them. Its goal is to rewrite the narrative of Ukrainian history by placing it at the centre of global and European history, rather than viewing it entirely through the lens of Russian and Soviet influence. The initiative to undertake this major project, titled the 'Ukrainian History Global Initiative', was taken by the Ukrainian philanthropist and businessman Victor Pinchuk and led by three distinguished historians: Timothy Snyder at Yale University, Serhii Plokhy at Harvard University and Yaroslav Hrytsak at Lviv National University.

Snyder explains that

> the history of the twenty-first century looks different if you understand the reasons why Ukraine resisted the Russian invasion. So, this is not a project about the war. And it's not a reaction to the war. Every time you look at some portion of European history and you add Ukraine, it shifts the whole modern history of colonialism and Empire.[20]

The project will cover roughly seventy different themes over the course of three years. In an overview of the project, the following initial reflection is highlighted:

> Ukrainian history is not marginal, but central, to an extent that can be hard to bear, and hard to acknowledge. This can be seen at every stage, from the role of the Yamna in the spread of what will become Indo-European languages; the synthesis of Scythia and the Bosporus Kingdom with ancient Athens in the development of classical culture; the formation of Rus as a unique yet exemplary medieval state with Slavic, Viking, Byzantine, Khazar, and west European elements; the appearance of the Cossacks as an early anti-colonial or proto-national entity; and the centrality of Ukraine to both Soviet and Nazi views of global transformation. In this light, the connections between the present war and larger developments in global economy and politics are no surprise.[21]

• • •

Putin concluded his speech to the Russian people on 21 February 2022 by referring to the ultimatum that Moscow issued in December 2021. It demanded 'reliable and firm legal guarantees' that NATO would not expand eastward; that it would 'refrain from deploying assault weapon systems on Russian borders'; and that it would begin 'rolling back the bloc's military capability and infrastructure in Europe to where they were in 1997, when the NATO-Russia Founding Act was signed'. These demands were deemed completely unacceptable and entirely unrealistic to NATO countries and many others. It is important to remember that NATO had not canvassed new members. Rather, countries that have historically borne the brunt of Russian savagery have actively sought NATO membership to help ensure their own security.

Finally, Putin declared that he considered it 'necessary to take a long overdue decision and to immediately recognise the independence and sovereignty of the Donetsk People's Republic and Luhansk People's Republic'. The declaration met with overwhelming international criticism and condemnation. A strongly worded formal statement by the Ukrainian Ministry of Foreign Affairs stated,

> Ukraine condemns the Russian Federation's decision to recognise the 'independence' of the quasi-entities it had created in the temporarily occupied territories of Ukraine, the so-called 'Luhansk People's Republic' and 'Donetsk People's Republic'. With this action the Russian side has blatantly defied the fundamental norms and principles of international law, the UN Charter, violated the sovereignty and territorial integrity of Ukraine within its internationally recognised borders.[22]

As we have discussed, in the early hours of the invasion, on

Thursday 24 February 2022, Putin once again delivered a speech to the Russian people, this time announcing a '*special military operation*' against Ukraine, a euphemistic term to disguise his full-fledged invasion of a neighbouring country. He continued,

> The purpose of this operation is to protect people who, for eight years now, have been facing humiliation and genocide perpetrated by the Kyiv regime. To this end, we will seek to demilitarise and denazify Ukraine, as well as bring to trial those who perpetrated numerous bloody crimes against civilians, including against citizens of the Russian Federation.[23]

Plokhy summarised the general Ukrainian response to Putin's remarks:

> Despite Putin's illusions about his mission of 'liberation' in Ukraine and the propaganda used to portray the Ukrainian government as a Nazi band, many Ukrainians saw the Russian invaders as the true Nazis. The Russian occupation of Ukrainian cities and villages was reminiscent of scenes of the Nazi occupation of Ukraine during World War II. Those memories never faded away in Ukraine, as they were passed from one generation to the next.[24]

The Russian invasion would shatter the last vestiges of the belief that Ukrainians and Russians are fraternal peoples, let alone the same people. This is ironically evident even in the aspects of shared heritage – historical and cultural roots and religious traditions – that Putin referenced in his articles and speeches.

CHAPTER 4

MOSCOW'S FALSE NARRATIVES

Dictators often make and maintain falsehoods to hold on to power. Stalin had official photos crudely altered to remove associates who had fallen out of favour. In recent years, authoritarian regimes around the world have learned to conscript social media platforms and artificial intelligence to turn their own populations against groups they don't like, whether political opponents, journalists, ethnic minorities or the LGBTQ+ community. And, of course, the leadership in Moscow have used these platforms as a strategic weapon against democratic countries they consider a threat, most ominously in the case of Ukraine.[1] As we have discussed, Russia has for decades disseminated false narratives about Ukraine. Its main aim has been to marginalise Ukraine and Ukrainians and to deny their distinct identity. Moscow has repeatedly tried to portray the nation as a failed state, roiling with ethnic and political divisions. In addition, Russia has persistently claimed that Ukraine is intractably divided into a distinct western and eastern part – and has done its best to reinforce such a division. Successive Kyiv governments have been accused of ethnic intolerance, particularly against the Russian-speaking people. Finally, Russia has deliberately tried to take advantage of and amplify Ukraine's historical inferiority complex and narrative of victimhood.

Before and after the invasion of Ukraine, numerous false narratives have persistently been promoted by the Russian government-controlled media and pro-Russian websites, as well as various cyber-actors, social media trolls, official diplomatic and pro-Kremlin X/Twitter accounts and on other social media platforms. This chapter will highlight five of the most blatant of these false narratives.

FABRICATION 1: THE MYTH OF NATO EXPANSION

One of the earliest fabricated excuses used by the Kremlin to justify the invasion was the groundless assertion that NATO and the West pose a threat to Russia's security, with a need to prevent further NATO enlargement.

To start, Putin and the Russian leadership repeatedly accused NATO and individual NATO countries of making empty promises. In the speech three days before the invasion on 21 February 2022, the Russian President repeated the claim that American leaders promised not to expand NATO to the east in the period after the fall of the Berlin Wall:

> In 1990, when German unification was discussed, the United States promised the Soviet leadership that NATO jurisdiction or military presence will not expand one inch to the east and that the unification of Germany will not lead to the spread of NATO's military organisation to the east.[2]

This is a myth, as such a promise was never made. The idea of NATO enlargement beyond a united Germany was not even on the agenda in 1989–90, particularly as the Warsaw Pact still existed until 1991. This is also confirmed by the former Soviet leader Mikhail Gorbachev, who in an interview in 2014 stated that 'the topic of NATO expansion was not discussed at all, and it wasn't brought up in those years. I say this with full responsibility. Not a single Eastern European country raised the issue, not even after the Warsaw Pact ceased to exist in 1991. Western leaders didn't bring it up either'. Furthermore, and as a matter of principle, individual NATO countries cannot make agreements on NATO's behalf. Even though Russian President Boris Yeltsin, Putin's mentor, tried several times to get US President Bill Clinton to make a commitment to exclude future NATO membership to former Soviet Republics. President Clinton replied, 'I can't make commitments on behalf of NATO, and I'm not going to be in the position myself of vetoing NATO expansion with respect to any country, much less letting you or anyone else do so. [...] NATO operates by consensus.'

Russia's frequent tactical use of the term 'NATO expansion' is in many ways a misnomer, deliberately designed to give the wrong impression. It is not that NATO hunted, or continues to hunt, for new members for the purpose of expanding eastward or in any other direction. But NATO respects every nation's right to choose its own path. NATO membership is therefore a joint decision between those countries which express a wish to join and the NATO alliance and its member countries. NATO's door has been open to new members since it was founded in 1949; it has been a defensive alliance for all of the last seventy-five years. Furthermore, no treaty or agreements signed by NATO allies and Russia included provisions on NATO membership – and it is highly unlikely they will ever do so, or at least not in the foreseeable future. A decision on NATO membership is always taken by consensus among all allies, and for obvious reasons the Russian Federation, as a non-member, does not in any way have any right to veto any issue related to NATO or NATO enlargement.[3]

In the months before the full-scale invasion of Ukraine, Russia demanded security guarantees, including limitations on NATO membership, thereby trying to undermine the sovereign rights of Ukraine and other nations to determine their foreign and security policies. Moreover, as Russia positioned up to 200,000 troops along the Ukrainian border, the Russian Ministry of Foreign Affairs continuously disseminated disinformation to obscure its intentions, falsely claiming there were no troops on the Ukrainian border and accusing the United States and its allies of creating hysteria. In his infamous article of 21 July 2021 and the subsequent televised speeches to the Russian people, Putin wrongly blamed NATO for rising tensions, including 'an impudent development of Ukrainian territory as a theatre of potential military operations', and accused the United States of using Ukraine as a 'tool to contain Russia'. Official Russian media and disinformation outlets linked to Russian intelligence services, such as the FSB and GRU, have only amplified these deceitful claims, framing the United States' and NATO's warnings of a possible Russian military offensive as 'Western hysteria' aimed at drawing Ukraine into war.

Over the course of the war, the Kremlin has further modified its false narratives, suggesting that Ukraine has absolutely no future in NATO and that promises of a membership have been a hoax. The spokesperson of the Russian Ministry of Foreign Affairs, Maria Zakharova, stated on 12 July 2024,

> Every year since the Bucharest summit in 2008, when the door to the bloc was half-opened for Ukraine, the leaders of NATO

> countries, primarily the United States, invented new formulas to hide the fact that Kyiv has no future in the bloc. They did it this time again. The Washington summit declaration mentioned Ukraine's 'irreversible path to full Euro-Atlantic integration, including NATO membership' and said that it would 'extend an invitation to Ukraine to join the alliance when allies agree and conditions are met'.

The military support to Ukraine from NATO countries, the EU and others has also been described as only prolonging or escalating the conflict. Russian Foreign Minister Sergey Lavrov and others have repeatedly accused NATO and NATO allies of encouraging Ukraine to continue the war, as part of a cynical plan that only victimises the Ukrainians. On top of this, there have been numerous Russian statements alleging that NATO and NATO countries are 'Russophobic'. In July 2024, the Russian Ministry of Foreign Affairs stated,

> Overall, the [Washington] summit showcased NATO's continuing aggressive Russophobic approach and cynical plans to continue the hybrid war against our country at the hands of Ukrainians and at the cost of their lives. Kyiv is being encouraged to fight without regard for casualties. The main thing is to prevent Russia from winning.[4]

Despite the various false Russian claims and narratives, one thing remains an undeniable fact: NATO has not been and is not the aggressor. The aggressor is without any doubt the Russian Federation. As a matter of fact, after the fall of the Berlin Wall and disintegration of Soviet Union, the West invited Russia 'to join the party' – as

Sarah Paine at the US Naval War College puts it. But Russia opted for a path towards suppression of human rights, widespread corruption and aggressive nationalism. Along the way, Russia abused Western liberal attitudes in their attempts to plant sympathy, or at least create confusion, among European and US citizens. The truth of the matter is that not once did NATO countries amass troops along the Russian border, as Russia did along Ukraine's from 2021, nor did any Western country illegally annex any European territory or start a violent conflict, as Russia did in 2014. Quite simply, the war in February 2022 was *Russia's* choice, a choice driven by obscure ideas of rebuilding a Russian empire and justified by false narratives. As the US Secretary of State Antony Blinken stated at the United Nations Security Council on 22 September 2022, 'If Russia stops fighting, the war ends. If Ukraine stops fighting, Ukraine ends.'

FABRICATION 2: UKRAINIAN PROVOCATIONS

A second predominant false Russian narrative has been allegations of serious 'Ukrainian provocations' and the claim of a genocide ensuing in Donbas.

While Russia accused NATO of aggression, it also falsely claimed Ukraine was preparing military strikes against ethnic Russians in Donbas. One month before the invasion, in January 2022, Russian officials alleged that Ukraine had deployed significant military forces to Donbas and increased attacks on the self-declared 'Donetsk and Luhansk People's Republics'. The Kremlin suggested an imminent Ukrainian incursion. Moscow also repeatedly accused Ukraine of planning to use chemical weapons in the conflict area.[5] These claims intensified after the United States exposed a Kremlin plot to orchestrate a false flag operation in Donbas, involving fabricated videos of violence to justify an invasion. Russia's disinformation and propaganda machinery also falsely accused Ukraine of terrorism, alleging it was preparing a 'chemical disaster'[6] and planted rumours that Ukraine would conduct a 'crushing strike' on the Zaporizhzhia nuclear power plant.[7]

Putin used these false narratives about Ukraine's internal situation as another pretext for the invasion, overtly claiming a genocide was ensuing in Donbas in a statement on 15 February 2022. Russian media has most willingly continued to promote these false genocide accusations, amplified by government-backed websites targeting Ukraine, NATO and EU countries, as well as others.

Furthermore, in his televised address on 21 February 2022, Putin announced the deployment of 'peacekeeping' troops to Donbas, while recognising Donetsk and Luhansk as independent countries:

> Meanwhile, the so-called civilised world, which our Western colleagues proclaimed themselves the only representatives of, prefers not to see this, as if this horror and genocide, which almost 4 million people are facing, do not exist. But they do exist and only because these people did not agree with the West-supported coup in Ukraine in 2014 and opposed the transition towards Neanderthal and aggressive nationalism and neo-Nazism which have been elevated in Ukraine to the rank of national policy.[8]

There is absolutely no evidence to back these allegations, and independent media, counter-disinformation experts and international human rights bodies have repeatedly exposed and discredited them. In spite of this, these false narratives periodically re-emerge, notably in Russian-language social media channels.

While Putin's Russia has cited the alleged need to protect Russian-speakers in Ukraine from 'genocide', it is, in fact, the

Russian military and special forces that have inflicted devastating damage and ruthless suffering on people living in Russian-occupied areas of Ukraine. This has forced millions to flee, mostly westward, while over two million have gone to Russia (although it is unclear how many have done so voluntarily and how many have been subject to forced relocation). The illegal issuing of Russian passports in temporarily occupied areas of eastern Ukraine, frequently putting people under severe pressure, has also raised tension. In addition, through various independent reports, there is considerable evidence of war crimes by Russia, such as civilian deportations and the operation of so-called 'filtration camps/operations'.[9] By February 2023, a year into the invasion, there was considerable evidence of crimes against humanity, including torture, rape and executions.[10]

The UN-based Independent International Commission of Inquiry on Ukraine has for more than three years documented a wide range of violations of international human rights law and humanitarian law. Many of the violations amount to outright war crimes, such as wilful killings, attacks on civilians, unlawful confinement, torture, rape and sexual violence, as well as the forced transfer and deportation of children. It has also found that attacks with explosive weapons against civilians were indiscriminate and disproportionate, with an abject failure to take necessary precautions, all in breach of humanitarian law. Attacks against Ukraine's energy infrastructure have also been considered unlawful.[11] Weighing up all of this evidence, the Commission concluded in October 2024 that the Russian authorities have committed crimes against humanity in all provinces of Ukraine under the control of Russian authorities and in detention facilities the Commission investigated in the Russian Federation.[12] The Commission has also documented the devastating impact of the violations and crimes on victims, their families and communities.

It is worth noting that in its reports, the independent Commission has consistently promoted a broad notion of accountability. As regards criminal accountability, it has emphasised the importance of holding perpetrators, including commanders and other superiors, accountable. At the same time, non-judicial accountability includes truth-seeking initiatives, reparations for victims and guarantees of non-repetition, which are essential for the rehabilitation process of the victims and their families.

In addition to the valuable reports of the independent Commission, individual testimonies of Russian war crimes are many. Andriy Turas and his wife Lena were captured while defending the city of Mariupol in 2022. Andriy was brought home in a prison swap with Russia in September 2024. 'They beat us mercilessly, with their fists, sticks, hammers, anything they could find,' Andriy recalls in an interview with the BBC.

> They stripped us naked in the cold and forced us to crawl on asphalt. Our legs were torn up, and we were terrified and freezing. The food was horrifying – sour cabbage and spoiled fish heads. It was just a nightmare. It's like waking up from a bad dream in the middle of the night, drenched in sweat, terrified.

'They held lectures with us about how Ukraine never existed,' explains Lena. 'They tried to exterminate our Ukrainian identity in our heads.' Lena was released after two weeks of captivity, but the psychological scars of what she experienced in a Russian detention centre remain. 'We constantly heard screams, we knew the men in our unit were being tortured.'[13]

Moreover, Russia's measures extend to a deliberate policy designed to undermine Ukrainian sovereignty by erasing its cultural legacy and identity. On 31 July 2024, UNESCO issued an independent report that verified damage to 432 sites since the start of the invasion, including 139 religious sites, 214 buildings of historical and/or artistic interest, thirty-one museums, thirty-two monuments, fifteen libraries and one archive.[14] Several such incidents of deliberate destruction of Ukrainian cultural and religious sites as well as artefacts have been reported in international media, including in Kherson, where Ukrainian literature was removed from libraries during the occupation and museums looted. In addition, the historic home of Ukraine's treasured poet and philosopher Hryhorii Skovoroda was destroyed by a Russian artillery strike, along with a museum dedicated to his work.

'Skovoroda's home was in a tiny village not far from Kharkiv – nowhere near any obvious military targets such as a railway or ammunition depot. The attack appears to have been a deliberate act of cultural vandalism,' a CNN report stated.[15] 'In general, it is most regrettable to observe a process of "russification" in all of its aspects, in all the temporarily occupied areas of Ukraine, including Crimea,' it was noted.[16]

Last but not least, the Russian invasion has deprived Ukraine's 7.5 million children of their normal life. More than 20,000 Ukrainian children have been illegally deported to Russia or Russian-occupied areas of Ukraine for so-called 're-education' or adoption, thereby also risking permanent loss of their Ukrainian heritage. So far, only a few hundred Ukrainian children have successfully returned to their parents in Ukraine. 'They base their strategy on deception, indoctrination of children and genocide of the Ukrainian nation,' observes Mykola Kuleba, the leader of a Ukrainian charity working to return the children, adding 'Russia is stealing our future'.[17]

These developments led the International Criminal Court (ICC) in The Hague to issue an arrest warrant on 17 March 2023 for two individuals: Vladimir Putin and Maria Alekseyevna Lvova-Belova, the Russian Commissioner for Children's Rights in the Office of the President of the Russian Federation.[18] The warrant invoked reasonable grounds to believe that each bears responsibility for the war crime of 'unlawful deportation of population (children) and of unlawful transfer of population (children) from occupied areas in Ukraine to the Russian Federation'.[19] Significant efforts have been launched to try to facilitate the return of children to Ukraine, an extremely difficult task due to non-cooperation by Russia. A welcome development has, however, been the creation, at the initiative of President Zelenskyy, of an International Coalition for the Return of Ukrainian Children, co-chaired by Canada and Ukraine, officially launched in Kyiv in February 2024. An important ministerial conference on the follow-up was held in Ottawa, Canada, in late October 2024.

Over seventy countries and international organisations, including the UN, the EU, the Organization for Security and Co-operation in Europe (OSCE) and the Council of Europe, participated and pledged to support Ukraine in the reintegration of returnees. In addition, information about Russia's unlawful detention and ill-treatment of Ukrainian civilians and prisoners of war, deportation and forcible transfer of children was spread through strategic communication campaigns, as well as a number of other relevant initiatives outlined in the so-called 'Montreal Pledge'. The Minister of Foreign Affairs of Canada, Mélanie Joly, who hosted the conference, highlighted that Qatar, the Vatican, the Republic of South Africa, Lithuania and the United Arab Emirates had made specific commitments on the return of deported children and captives to Ukraine. She said:

> I want to thank Qatar, the Vatican and South Africa for their role as intermediaries in negotiating the return of children. I also thank Qatar and Lithuania for serving as transit countries in returning these children home. I am grateful to the UAE for continuing as a mediator in the negotiations on the exchange of prisoners of war.[20]

In support of these international efforts, the Secretary-General of the Council of Europe, Alain Berset, announced in February 2025 the appointment of the former Foreign Minister of Iceland, Thórdís Kolbrún Reykfjord Gylfadóttir, as his special envoy on the situation of the children of Ukraine. 'I will do my utmost to contribute to securing and protecting the rights of children of Ukraine and to serving the wider cause of its people,' Gylfadóttir said. 'We have a collective duty to stand by those children who were hit the hardest by Russia's full-scale invasion.'[21]

A Leaders' Summit was held in New York in September 2025, in the margins of the 80th session of the UN General Assembly, co-chaired by President Zelenskyy and Canada's Prime Minister Mark Carney. It focused on increasing sanctions against those involved in abductions of children.

A Yale Humanitarian Research Lab report, published on 3 December 2024, uncovered Russia's systematic deportation and adoption of Ukrainian children. The report exposed Russia's deliberate and systematic programme of forcibly deporting Ukrainian children into coerced adoption and fostering, a programme that researchers describe as one of the largest missing persons crises since the Second World War. Oona Hathaway, a professor of international law at Yale Law School, said in an interview,

> The evidence compiled by the Humanitarian Research Lab researchers could lead to additional charges against Russian President Vladimir Putin; Maria Lvova-Belova, presidential commissioner for children's rights; and other officials involved in the extensive forced relocation program in the International Criminal Court for war crimes and crimes against humanity.

A recent report from the Yale Humanitarian Research Lab, from September 2025, concluded that Ukrainian children have been taken to at least 210 facilities across Russia and the Russian-occupied areas, that 60 per cent of these facilities were used for 're-education' and at least 18 per cent for military training, aiming to Russify the children. The report also concluded that more than half of the facilities which children from Ukraine were taken are managed by the Russian government.[22]

On the Russian side, all allegations of deportation of Ukrainian children have been denied and ridiculed (together with the Russian massacre of 509 Ukrainian civilians in Bucha in March 2022). In July 2024, the spokesperson of the Russian Ministry of Foreign Affairs claimed,

> This scheme is a vivid demonstration of the rotten and cynical essence of the Kiev regime, whose representatives climb international platforms to shed tears about children allegedly abducted by Russia. However, they can't provide a list of these children, just like they can't provide a list of those who were allegedly killed in Bucha, which we have requested publicly on numerous occasions. The explanation is very simple: Russia has not abducted children or killed anyone in Bucha.

Ukraine has rallied the world on this issue, building international coalitions to try to push Russia to cooperate. But its success has been limited. Less than a quarter of the 2,000 children who have returned so far came back through official chennels: eighty-three with the help of Qatar and nineteen through a scheme spearheaded by US First Lady Melania Trump.

FABRICATION 3: 'DEMILITARISING' AND 'DENAZIFYING' UKRAINE

A third false and absurd Russian narrative has been claims of the need to 'demilitarise' and 'denazify' Ukraine, as well as allegations of Ukrainian 'Satanism'.

In his February televised speech announcing the attack on Ukraine, Putin revived the Kremlin's persistent narrative that Russia aimed to protect people from an alleged eight-year genocide by Kyiv and to 'demilitarise and denazify' Ukraine. He also accused Ukraine's democratically elected government of being a 'gang of drug addicts and neo-Nazis'.

Using the absurd claim of 'neo-Nazism' against Ukraine's Jewish President and his government, is most likely part of a calculated campaign by Russia to link 'Russophobia' with neo-Nazism. It has also been a segment of a broader Kremlin strategy using the history of the Second World War to stoke nationalist sentiments in Russia and thereby increase domestic support for the war. This is, however, a dangerous and very cynical claim, casting the Russian invasion of Ukraine as a continuation of the Soviet Union's struggle against Hitler and Nazi Germany. It also implies a desire to overthrow the existing and democratically elected Ukrainian President and his government. Russian Foreign Minister Lavrov has equated Western support for Ukraine with the action of the Nazis by claiming the West's assistance is similar to Nazi Germany's invasion of the Soviet Union.[23] This is yet another example of absurd Russian attempts to manipulate history, all for the purpose of trying to justify the extreme suffering inflicted upon Ukraine and its people. Timothy Snyder, who was invited in 2023 to address the United Nations Security Council, pointed out that

> the notion that Ukrainians were 'Russophobes' was part of the Russian state's campaign to destroy them. The claims that Ukrainians were vermin, beasts, Nazis, and so on were made by a media monopoly controlled by an oligarchic dictatorship. There was no person, no truth, and no risk. The lies were told not only to preserve power, but to allow the power to commit genocide.[24]

In a two-hour televised 'State of the Union' speech on 21 February 2023, Putin again repeated his outrageous allegation, referring to 'the neo-Nazi regime that set up in Ukraine after 2014'.[25] In this context, it's important to note that in Ukraine's last parliamentary election in 2019, support for far-right candidates was 2 per cent – far lower than in many other European countries. One can certainly find extremist groups with Nazi sympathies in all European countries, including in the Russian Federation, but to brand the whole political leadership of a country as 'neo-Nazis' is completely unacceptable and utterly shameful.

In the same speech, Putin also claimed that

> quite recently, a brigade of the Armed Forces of Ukraine was named Edelweiss after a Nazi division whose personnel were involved in deporting Jews, executing prisoners of war and conducting punitive operations against partisans in Yugoslavia, Italy, Czechoslovakia and Greece. We are ashamed to talk about this, but they are not. Personnel serving with the Armed Forces of

> Ukraine and the Ukrainian National Guard are particularly fond of chevrons formerly worn by soldiers from Das Reich, Totenkopf (Death's Head) and Galichina divisions and other SS units. Their hands are also stained with blood. Ukrainian armoured vehicles feature insignia of the Nazi German Wehrmacht.

According to a fact-check by the BBC, the truth is that

> the Edelweiss flower – which grows in Alpine regions – has been used as a symbol by other European mountain military divisions, including the Croatian Mountain Rescue Service, Swiss Army generals and the 21st Rifles Brigade of Poland. Even Russia had a special unit called Edelweiss. The 17th special purpose detachment of Rosgvardia was given this title in 2011. The name was changed to Avanguard in 2016.[26]

As the war took its heavy toll, the Kremlin further ramped up its baseless claims, alleging that it was combating 'Western Satanism'. Kremlin propagandists have also labelled Ukrainians as 'Satanists'.[27] This narrative gained official status when President Putin, in a speech on 30 September 2022, labelled societal developments in Western countries regarding its values as 'pure Satanism':

> Let me repeat that the dictatorship of the Western elites targets all societies, including the citizens of Western countries themselves. This is a challenge to all. This complete renunciation of what it means to be human, the overthrow of faith and traditional values, and the suppression of freedom are coming to resemble a 'religion in reverse' – pure Satanism.

The Kremlin has been keen to position itself broadly as a defender of 'traditional values', opposing what it considers corrupt Western influence in Ukraine (and Russia). This viewpoint emerged prominently in April 2022, after news of Russia's war crimes in Bucha surfaced. Patriarch Kirill, a firm advocate of the '*Russkiy mir*' (Russian world) ideology, has depicted Russia's military involvement in Ukraine as a sacred fight for the 'Russian world', claiming that it represents the last defence against an immoral West – and that Russia has 'God's truth' on their side.[28] He further claimed that this crusade has divine support in countering the 'Antichrist'. Kirill insists that Ukraine must remain within the 'canonical territory' of the Russian Orthodox Church, despite the fact that Ukraine has formed an independent Orthodox Church.

FABRICATION 4: UKRAINE WANTS NUCLEAR WEAPONS

In the same speech delivered in September 2022, Putin repeated a previous false allegation that Russians 'also remember the attempts of the Kyiv regime to acquire nuclear weapons, because they talked about it publicly'. There is absolutely no evidence that Ukraine has at any time attempted to acquire nuclear weapons, and Putin – who has made this baseless claim on more than one earlier occasion – has never provided any form of verification for such an allegation. As a matter of fact, Ukraine inherited a large number of nuclear weapons after the break-up of the Soviet Union but agreed to give all of them up; thereafter, Ukraine signed up to the Nuclear Non-Proliferation Treaty in return for a set of what proved to be hollow security guarantees, as specified in the infamous Budapest Memorandum from 1994. The extraordinary story surrounding these historic events will be dealt with in a later chapter.

FABRICATION 5: DEFENDING TERRITORIAL INTEGRITY

As Russia was facing a Ukrainian counter-offensive in September 2022, the Kremlin shifted its rhetoric, framing its war as a necessary defence of Russia's sovereignty. Within a year of presenting its security demands in December 2021, Russia shifted its emphasis back to the initial claim that the West is aggressively seeking to destroy Russia via a proxy war in Ukraine. Such messages have since been repeated on numerous occasions. In a video by Putin, posted on the Kremlin's website on 30 September 2023, he claimed that with the invasion of Ukraine he is 'defending Russia itself' and 'fighting together for the Motherland, for our sovereignty, spiritual values and unity, for victory'.

Putin has also claimed that the controversial internal mobilisation and referenda in the autumn of 2022 were crucial for Russia's 'sovereignty, security, and territorial integrity'. Defence Minister Shoigu and Duma Chairman Vyacheslav Volodin have reiterated that the mobilisation in Russia was essential, as Russia was not only combatting Ukraine but also NATO and the 'collective West'.

In his 2022 New Year's Eve address, the Russian President contextualised the military operation as a vital fight for Russia's 'sovereignty' and 'true independence', while employing old narratives about Western hypocrisy and aggression. Putin also underscored the defence of the Motherland as a 'sacred duty' for all Russians. The former Russian President and current member of the Russian Security Council, Dmitry Medvedev, has been blunt in describing the extreme anti-Ukrainian goals of the invasion, stating on Telegram,

> The existence of Ukraine is deadly for Ukrainians [...] no matter how much they aspire to the mythical European Union and NATO. When choosing between eternal war and inevitable

> death and life, the absolute majority of Ukrainians will eventually choose life. They will realise that life in a big common state, which they do not love much now, is better than death. Their death and the death of their loved ones. And the sooner Ukrainians realise this, the better.[29]

• • •

At the Cyber Policy Centre (CPT) at Stanford University in April 2022, Barack Obama told students,

> People like Putin understand it's not necessary for people to believe this information in order to weaken democratic institutions. You just have to flood a country's public square with enough raw sewage. You just have to raise enough questions, spread enough dirt, plant enough conspiracy theories that citizens no longer know what to believe. Once they lose trust in their leaders, in mainstream media, in political institutions, in each other, in the possibility of truth, the game's won.[30]

This is exactly how Russia has diligently worked when it comes to the false narratives and broader disinformation campaigns. Although a majority of people in the United States and in European countries still support Ukraine, in the US at least, such support has waned over the course of the war. Although some of this may be caused by a certain degree of 'war weariness', the effects of disinformation are certainly at play here, evidenced not least by partisan splits in the US and in Europe. The well-known American TV personality Tucker Carlson – still a prominent voice for right-wing groups in the US, despite his ousting from Fox News – has for many become a shameless apologist for Putin and Russian aggression against Ukraine. He has also given a voice to guests on his show who echo claims that Nazi Germany's mass murder of Jews during the Second World War was an unintended consequence, something akin to poor planning instead of the methodical extermination that it was.[31]

All this underscores the power of false narratives and disinformation – through promoting false content online and in traditional media – that regrettably has helped shape public opinion on the Ukraine war and many other issues. This is potentially a most severe threat not only to the survival of Ukraine, but also the future of our democracies. In the next chapter we will look at this crucial issue in more detail.

CHAPTER 5

LIES, FAKE NEWS AND DISINFORMATION

Every time we read a newspaper article, either online or in print, anywhere on this globe, we risk being manipulated or being spoon-fed blatant lies. When we are constantly hit with different stories, cognitive dissonance becomes a daily struggle. And with so much information coming at us and no sure way to know what's true, we can start feeling overwhelmed, lose interest and, sometimes, stop paying attention to what's going on in the world. New technologies no doubt make it easier than ever before to make and spread lies, including disinformation (false information deliberately and often covertly dispersed in order to influence public opinion or obscure the truth) and misinformation (incorrect information that is shared unwittingly). It is, however, not always possible to distinguish between misinformation and disinformation, as content can be created as disinformation and unknowingly shared as misinformation.

According to a risk analysis by the World Economic Forum in Davos, Switzerland, in 2024, disinformation and misinformation are defined as the biggest global risks over the next two years, even more dangerous than war, extreme weather or pollution. This is primarily due to disinformation's potential to undermine democratic elections, promote social unrest and increase censorship through counter-disinformation measures.[1] Indeed, the global outlook for democracy is clouded, if not downright disheartening.

Political extremism, polarisation and distrust have been on the rise even in long-established liberal democracies. 'We have to understand how changes in the contemporary political environment make people want to believe negative information about the opposition,' stresses Darrell M. West, senior fellow at the Brookings Institution. 'In a highly polarised world, where people are divided into competing political tribes, millions of Americans admit they themselves have intentionally spread information they know to be false. If that continues, it will lead to disaster for our country's politics and governance.'[2] What is deeply worrying is that statements made by senior political leaders and officials are frequently a key source of disinformation.[3] In 2020, the Oxford Internet Institute reported findings that government agencies have used disinformation in attempts to shape public attitudes in sixty-two of seventy countries surveyed.[4] An analysis of 55,000 media stories, five million tweets and 75,000 Facebook posts illustrated that a mainstream American media organisation was central to spreading the unevidenced claim made by Donald Trump that election fraud was a 'major concern' with mail-in ballots.[5] And finally, in a 2021 Reuters Institute survey of UK adults, 66 per cent said they were concerned about what was 'real' and 'fake' on the internet, but the most common concern was mis/disinformation from domestic political actors (and journalists).[47] Respondents were also more concerned about misinformation coming from their government than foreign governments.[6]

Free and fair elections are fundamental to any representative democracy. They are also unique opportunities to defend and renew democracy. But when elections are manipulated or distorted, the very fine fabric of our democracy is ultimately destroyed. In 2024, voters across some eighty countries, home to an estimated 4 billion people – roughly half of the world's population – headed to the polls to cast their vote, making it the year of elections. According to a 2025 report by Freedom House,

> censorship and content manipulation undermined voters' ability to make informed decisions in elections around the world over the past year, and people in a growing number of countries faced retaliation for their online expression. Both factors were major contributors to the 14th consecutive year of decline in global internet freedom.[7]

And according to an analysis of the elections in 2024 by the *Financial Times*, 'the results show widespread anger and frustration at incumbents, and growing support for populists on the left and right'.[8]

A noteworthy study by the Brookings Institution in Washington DC, on both the Presidential and Congressional elections in the United States in 2024, points out that

> there were many reasons for the stunning election victories of Donald Trump and congressional Republicans: inflation fears, concerns about border security, worries about cultural issues related to race, gender, and sexuality, and feelings that President Joe Biden and the country as a whole were headed in the wrong direction. But one cannot ignore the ways in which disinformation shaped views about the candidates, affected how voters saw leader performance, and generated widespread media attention.

Some of these measures included 'the infamous stories about immigrants eating cats and dogs, hurricane disaster relief funding going to undocumented immigrants, Kamala Harris in a swimsuit hugging convicted sex offender Jeffrey Epstein, and the supposed case of Tim Walz abusing a young man thirty years ago'.

Disinformation – particularly from the Russian Federation, but also China and Iran – has matured into a consistent and pernicious threat, as the countries test, iterate and deploy increasingly nuanced tactics, according to various intelligence and defence officials, tech companies and academic researchers. Foreign state-backed disinformation often aims to provoke confusion, aggravate political polarisation, undermine democracy and/or sow distrust in societies.

Today, regrettably, Kremlin-produced talking points are frequently repeated by politicians in both Europe and America. On top of this, opinion polls have also shown that groups of European and US citizens tend to agree with Russian lines of disinformation, which suggests that Moscow's campaign to sow doubt about the truth might be working. 'Russian propaganda has made its way into the United States, unfortunately, and it's infected a good chunk of my party's base,' admitted Representative Michael McCaul, the Texas Republican who chaired the House Foreign Affairs Committee in March 2024.

'Russia has built networks and an infrastructure to mislead, to lie and to destabilise,' underlined the EU High Representative Josep Borrell in his opening statement at a European External Action Service (EEAS) conference in Brussels on disinformation in February 2023.

> I want to use these strong verbs: to mislead, to lie and to destabilise in an industrial manner. To erode trust in institutions. This is a major threat for the liberal democracies, which are based on

> information. Democracy is a system that is based on the information that people have, because they make their choices – their political choices – according to their own perceptions and information that they receive about what is happening in the rest of the world. If the information is toxic, democracy cannot work. If information is manipulated, people don't have a clear idea of what is going on. So, their choices are biased, and the information is the oil of the engine of democracy. We have to take care of the quality of information because it is the sap, the blood, the oil, the thing that makes democracy work.[9]

Amil Khan, a former journalist and current research fellow at the UK's Foreign Policy Centre (FPC), explains,

> For many years the standard way of doing things was to use hundreds or thousands of social media accounts, controlled by a single piece of software, to pump out the same message or link, or to 'like' or reshare particular posts. On a large scale this 'co-ordinated inauthentic behaviour' (CIB) can fool the curation algorithms on a social media network such as Facebook and X into thinking there is a groundswell of interest in, or support for, a particular viewpoint. The algorithm then promotes those posts to real users, who may then share them with their own followers.[10]

However, CIB operations have been fairly easy to identify and Meta, the tech firm behind Facebook, has until recently identified and shut down such networks quite quickly (see below). X, on the other hand, has been slower, and with Elon Musk's ownership matters have no doubt further deteriorated.

Amil Kahn has noted how in 'poor countries with few opportunities for young, tech-savvy men and women, there is an industry of building up "spreader" accounts and then selling them to malicious actors once they reach 100,000 followers'. The challenge with identifying spreaders is that their behaviour is genuine, at least to begin with, and they are not *originators* of disinformation, but merely *distributors* of it.[11]

It was Aeschylus, the first great dramatist of classical Athens, who correctly observed that 'in war, truth is the first casualty'. And there is no doubt that both before and during the Russian invasion of Ukraine in February 2022, truth was deliberately manipulated and distorted in ways that were unimaginable just a few years ago. According to a previous study by the Rand Corporation,

> the current Russian approach to propaganda builds on Soviet Cold War-era techniques, with an emphasis on obfuscation and on getting targets to act in the interests of the propagandist without realising that they have done so. In other ways, it is completely new and driven by the characteristics of the contemporary information environment. Russia has taken advantage of technology and available media in ways that would have been inconceivable during the Cold War. Its tools and channels now include the Internet, social media, and the evolving landscape of professional and amateur journalism and media outlets.[12]

It is interesting to note that early CIB networks targeting Ukraine were simple and could be traced to Russian intelligence services. *The Economist* has pointed out that

> Since 2022, disinformation campaigns have taken on a new form. Run by 'deniable entities' such as marketing companies and troll

farms without direct state links, they post on a range of social networks and blogging platforms and create entire fake websites. Since March 2023 the number of AI-generated news outlets peddling misleading information has risen from 49 to 802, according to NewsGuard, an American organisation that monitors disinformation. These sites mostly feature innocuous articles, generated by AI, but with disinformation mixed in.[13]

An instructive example is DC Weekly, an apparently American website dispersing Russian-produced disinformation, such as alleging that the wife of President Zelenskyy, Olena Zelenska, Ukraine's First Lady, spent no less than $1.1 million on jewellery during a shopping spree at New York's Fifth Avenue. It featured a 'video interview' with an alleged Cartier intern describing her encounter with Zelenska, while the 'intern' flashes a false receipt on the screen. It was shared 20,000 times on X and viewed by millions of people. Another story that originated on DC Weekly claimed that Ukrainian officials bought yachts with US military aid, a lie that was thereafter regrettably repeated by several members of the US Congress, including Senator J.D. Vance and Representative Marjorie Taylor Greene.[14]

Several European countries, and especially the German government, have uncovered specific techniques that are often applied in promoting false narratives and disinformation, in particular in the context of the Russian invasion.

The first technique, 'dismiss', involves agents of disinformation refuting unfavourable objective information with dubious arguments to undermine the source's credibility and create doubt. For example, the Russian government denies any responsibility for military escalation, claiming it was compelled to act defensively, thus portraying itself as a victim and fabricating baseless justifications for its actions. As we have seen in previous chapters, this includes a plethora of unfounded accusations against Ukraine.

The second technique, 'distort', sees agents altering the perception of facts, as demonstrated by Russia's labelling of its invasion of Ukraine as a 'special operation', avoiding the term 'war' domestically. This narrative contradicts the reality of a large-scale aggressive war, violating international law, and is supplemented by false claims like the US and Europe waging war on Russia, likening it to fighting a fascist alliance.

The third technique, 'distract', involves shifting attention from unfavourable information. Russia does this by falsely depicting Ukraine as the aggressor and an unjust regime, diverting from its unlawful attack on a democratic state and covering up its war crimes, such as the documented abuses in Russian-occupied Ukraine.

The fourth and final technique, 'dismay', aims to instil fear and hinder action in target countries. Russia threatens further escalation, including nuclear attacks, and spreads warnings of economic crises in countries like Germany to create fear and influence public opinion. Despite these tactics, Germany and its allies maintain their stance with strong sanctions and measures against Russia, advocating that international law violations, not 'Russophobia', motivate their actions.[15]

In 2019, Dmytro Kuleba published a book entitled *The War for Reality*, examining fake news, disinformation and propaganda. 'The book summarises seven years of my career in communication and my experience in fighting Russian propaganda,' Kuleba explains.[16] 'And it quickly became a bestseller in Ukraine.'

'My own survival in this cruel world has taught me the rule of four *don'ts*,' he continues.

Don't be surprised by anything; don't trust information at first glance; don't take anything personally; and don't jump to conclusions. Whether you are a politician or a public servant, in business, an artist, or an ordinary citizen surfing on the internet, there are basically five simple rules of engagement that are equally applicable to any communication battle:

- Keep a firm grip on reality.
- Use critical thinking.
- Control your emotions.
- Sense the community.
- Engage with the government.

As regards the last point, there is an absolute need to be open to cooperate with the government when it comes to fighting enemy disinformation and rely on official sources always. This is really one of the most important lessons from the war in Ukraine. So, if you see something on social media telling you interesting things about your government's actions or the situation in your country or around your country, do not believe it instantly. Go and check what official sources are saying. Check also where this information comes from and then make your choice.

When the war started, when the full-scale Russian invasion of Ukraine began, the first information campaign that the government rolled out was about trusting official sources. And every TV channel in Ukraine and every news outlet spread this information to all our citizens, reminding all of them that there are the official sources, like the official website of the President, as well as his accounts on social media. Then there are the websites and social media accounts of the Ministry of Defence, the Ministry

> of Foreign Affairs and so on. Consume information about the war from these official sources only, otherwise you will drown in Russian disinformation, we told them. To many people's surprise, Ukraine has been successful both as regards the ground war and in the information battles against a much more powerful adversary.

In Ukraine, a vital aspect of countering disinformation emerged through the rapid response of online groups skilled in open-source investigation. These groups acted with remarkable speed, often debunking false narratives within an hour of their publication. This immediate action was crucial, as it prevented disinformation from seeping into and becoming part of the usual media ecosystem.[17] At the same time, Ukrainian strategic communication has been fast, creative and skilful. It has consistently reached its audience at any time, day or night. But what is the secret behind this success?

'Ukraine applies the same rules for successful strategic communication known to all, but it has done it in an exemplary manner throughout the war,' explains Nico Lange, a former senior adviser at GLOBSEC and currently a senior fellow at the Center for European Policy Analysis and the Munich Security Conference.

> It all starts with regularity and routines: the president, for instance, records a statement every evening and the Ukrainian general staff gives a written briefing every day. All official information is immediately played out on different channels: telegram, TV, press releases, TikTok, Instagram, Twitter, Facebook, even LinkedIn. Everyone knows that this is how it should be done – but Ukraine does it every day in a disciplined and consistent manner. This is the secret to its success.[18]

Dmytro Kuleba explains that

> this came as no surprise to the Ukrainians themselves. We know how much blood, sweat and tears went into these successes. We never relied on a 'lucky ticket'. We got our kicks and gained skills, and we employed them to win battles. I only regret that it took a devastating total war to make people outside of Ukraine realise how calm and cool Ukrainians are. And in terms of communication, it's particularly true since 2014, when we first faced Russia's arsenal of hybrid warfare. Sadly, few across our borders were interested in our experience until 2016, when Russia heavily interfered in the US elections. And even after that, our know-how remained largely in the shadow of the great US battle for reality. The bottom line is: deal with your problems, but put arrogance aside, and listen to those who already have experience. It is never too late to start listening to Ukraine. Learn from what we have to say and trust our experience.

Disinformation, misinformation and lies, if left unchecked, are not just a challenge at this moment, but a mounting crisis for the future. It is a war we cannot afford to lose. The question is how are we going to combat this fundamental threat to our societies and our democracies?

Firstly, some ongoing projects aim to stop fake information once it's already out there. This can include deleting false content or marking it as untrue. Another very modest and yet effective way to reduce fake news is to prompt users to confirm they have read something before they share it.[19] This step alone has already helped to improve the quality of information shared on some social networks. But as pointed out by Bellingcat, the Dutch investigative journalism group that specialises in fact-checking and open-source intelligence,

> addressing the root causes of disinformation requires a grassroots approach. And education stands at the forefront of this strategy. The idea is simple yet transformative: integrate open-source investigation and critical thinking into the curriculum. Equip youth with the skills to navigate the labyrinthine digital realm, to question, analyse and verify before accepting or sharing information.[20]

Several civil society organisations are already active in this field, including The Student View, a group that trains young people to be critical consumers and creators of both online and offline media. Amnesty International's Digital Verification Corps brings students from all over the world together to investigate human rights violations; it has shown how impactful such initiatives can be, when students and universities together apply skills and develop new methodologies.[21] Other important initiatives include the 'Journalism Trust Initiative' by Reporters Without Borders (RSF), which is a helpful mechanism for curbing disinformation and providing tangible rewards for ethical and professional journalism. 'This initiative was born from a simple realisation: journalism is undergoing direct and massive unfair competition from manipulative content that proliferates in the digital space,' explains Antoine Bernard, Director at RSF. The Council of Europe in Strasbourg has identified concrete approaches to help combat disinformation, focusing primarily on building societal resilience, assisting forty-six member states in developing national strategies that cover areas such as education, culture and media policies. The organisation also places a significant focus on empowering citizens – particularly students and youth – with critical thinking skills, as well as supporting quality journalism as a crucial antidote to disinformation.

The EU in Brussels also does valuable work in meeting this challenge; at a meeting in Brussels on 16 March 2026, leaders from twenty-seven EU countries reaffirmed the need to

> strengthen public resilience to FIMI [Foreign Information Manipulation and Interference], including through measures to foster a well-informed and critically engaged public, improve media literacy and digital skills, and promote fact-checking initiatives, in full respect of human rights and fundamental freedoms and with continued strong emphasis on promoting freedom of expression, independent media, and the protection and safety of journalists and human rights defenders.

Secondly, organisations that check facts play a crucial role. These groups often follow standards and principles set by the International Fact-Checking Network (IFCN). The adherence to the Code of Principles has grown significantly globally, and has so far been signed by 182 organisations from eighty-one countries. Signatories include Full Fact, Africa Check, Chequeado, Factcheck.org, PolitiFact, Snopes and the *Washington Post*'s Fact Checker. The European Fact-Checking Standards Network (EFCSN) has published a Code of Professional Integrity for European fact-checkers, developed in cooperation with fact-checking organisations and approved by them.[22] While some fact-checkers work independently, others are hired by social media companies. Major news outlets like Reuters and the BBC have started their own fact-checking sections where journalists show how they verify information. However, studies have shown mixed results on how effective fact-checking is. Sometimes, even after seeing the corrected information, people might still choose to believe the false stories. In addition, expanding fact-checking can be costly, requiring trained journalists. At the same time, research has shown that state-driven fact-checking must be evaluated with caution as it brings with it potential threats to the independence of media actors in democracies.[23]

Thirdly, social media companies themselves could do more to stop the spread of fake information. 'There needs to be meaningful content moderation by social media platforms. Right now, many leading platforms are cesspools of rumours, false information and outright lies,' underlines Darrell M. West, senior fellow at The Brookings Institution. 'They are widely disseminated and seen by millions of people. If that continues, it will become increasingly difficult to discern fact from fiction – endangering our country's ability to address major problems. Companies need to get far more serious about content moderation.'[24]

But things are certainly happening. Until recently, Meta (the parent company of Facebook, Instagram and Threads) used external fact-checkers and closed accounts that showed 'coordinated inauthentic behaviour (CIB)' which involved using fake profiles to hide a person's or group's real identity. In January 2025, however, Meta said it would stop using third-party fact-checkers and instead rely on Facebook and Instagram users to add notes or corrections to posts. This is a highly regrettable move. In a comment, the Nobel Peace Prize Winner Maria Ressa, a co-founder of the Rappler news site, said that Meta's decision to end fact-checking on its platforms and remove restrictions on certain topics means 'extremely dangerous times' lie ahead for online journalism, democracy and social media. 'Journalists have to set standards and ethics,' Ressa said in an interview with the AFP news service. 'What Facebook is going to do is get rid of that and then allow lies, anger, fear and hate to infect every single person on the platform.'[25]

'It's time to get back to our roots around free expression,' Mark Zuckerberg said in a video announcing the changes, as reported in the *New York Times.* The company's fact-checking system, he added, had 'reached a point where it's just too many mistakes and too much censorship'. Zuckerberg conceded there would be more 'bad stuff' on the platforms as a result of the decision. 'The reality is that this is a trade-off,' he said. 'It means that we're going to catch less bad stuff, but we'll also reduce the number of innocent people's posts and accounts that we accidentally take down.'[26]

The other reality is that under such conditions, citizens' right to access a plurality of trustworthy sources of information (those promoted by RSF and recognised for the first time in the new European Media Freedom Act) won't survive platform algorithms, unless democratic countries stipulate that platforms amplify reliable sources of information. This can be done through self-regulated ISO-type standards such as the 'Journalism Trust Initiative' mentioned above or authoritative, domestic, self-regulated journalistic standards. Antoine Bernard from RSF notes, 'After years of calls on platforms to voluntary commitments obviously have failed, enacting the principle of due prominence, a must-carry and must-be-found obligation on platforms, has become ever more urgent to protect journalism, democracy and social media users, as well as citizens, from the consequences of the manufactured flow of disinformation.'[27]

Another concern is the lack of transparency and accountability surrounding social media companies; this extends to explanations of how the social media platform's algorithmic systems work, as these no doubt have a significant effect on the dissemination of disinformation. Such a lack of public understanding makes it almost impossible to assess the effectiveness of measures adopted by the platforms themselves in addressing mis- and disinformation, as well as the possible impact of any measures on human rights.[28]

Companies like OpenAI, Amazon and Google are developing ways to mark AI-generated content clearly. At the same time, some will argue that social media's very business models, which thrive on user engagement, can in many ways stimulate disinformation, as many of these false news items are highly popular and generate huge interest, thereby increasing the companies' income by making the sites more attractive to advertisers. Advertising already makes up the majority of Meta's annual revenues, which were nearly $135 billion in 2023.[29] As long as spreading lies is lucrative, it will be hard to get a serious handle on the flood of disinformation that plagues our current global system.[30]

Joseph Nye, the former dean of the Kennedy School at Harvard University, says, 'Social media models, some controlled by Trump and Musk, are based on algorithms that profit from polarising extremism, and artificial intelligence makes all social media subject to manipulation by conspiracy theorists. The problem of polarisation is far from solved, and there is much to worry about in democratic terms.'[31]

In addition, there is a growing need for media literacy, to ensure people know how to be critical with what they read, see or hear on social and traditional media. Studies have found that media literacy effectively helps people spot false information and makes them less likely to spread it. Many European governments already see this as a key step in fighting disinformation and several countries work actively in developing various education programmes. In Finland, media literacy has been part of the national core curriculum starting in preschool. Similarly, the Council of Europe, the oldest and most important inter-governmental organisation on safeguarding democracy and human rights in Europe, is, as already mentioned, actively working in this field. The organisation has developed relevant Europe-wide educational programmes, providing young people with critical skills to handle disinformation, fake news and blatant lies, both online and offline. At the same time, research has shown that media literacy programmes are still failing to reach some of the most vulnerable groups, including elderly people. Creativity in shaping new measures is therefore desperately needed. In this regard, it is worth mentioning that the Dutch company Tilt Studio has worked with the British government, the European Commission and NATO to create educational games that help identify misleading content – one example of the creative approach we sorely need.[32]

Stronger and smarter laws are of course needed, as well as better oversight of social media platforms. In this context, lawmakers should look carefully into the various aspects of dis- and misinformation, including how it spreads, its sources and the balance between controlling it and preserving free speech. The EU's Digital Services Act, which came into force in February 2024, is an important step forward, as it requires platforms to make data available to researchers who are working on measures to combat disinformation. But as we have seen with 'SLAPPS' – targeted lawsuits against journalists – those studying disinformation have been subject to lawsuits and attacks from various political groups. Following these challenges, some researchers have now stopped alerting platforms about suspected suspicious accounts or posts. This is a deeply worrying development that needs to be addressed.

Individual countries have taken concrete action to limit the influence of disinformation on elections around the world. 'Taiwan offers the gold standard,' says Reneé DiResta, who studies information flows at the Stanford Internet Observatory. Taipei's model involves close cooperation between civil society, internet platforms, the government and media, and when disinformation is spotted by fact-finding organisations, they inform the tech platforms – and, where appropriate, government ministries – and rapid rebuttals and corrections are issued. The Taiwanese government also promotes media literacy in school curriculums. Other countries have taken different approaches. In Brazil, in the run-up to the elections in October 2022, a Supreme Court judge ordered the immediate suspension of the social media accounts of politicians and influencers whose posts were seen to be threatening the integrity of the election process.

At the same time, AI is making fake information seem more real and therefore harder to detect, such as with 'deepfakes'. This highly advanced technology also collects extensive data on individuals, targeting them with tailored content. Consequently, there is no doubt that AI will pose new and significant challenges. At the same time, however, AI can help detect disinformation and enhance fact-checking efforts.

Lastly, research shows that people who regularly follow independent, professional journalism are better at resisting disinformation and identifying false content when they explore a variety of news sources.[33] This is also something to keep in mind when identifying relevant measures to counter disinformation.

• • •

'All these points are very important,' Dmytro Kuleba underlines.

But there is one issue that I think we have to be more open-minded about and bolder in discussing. It's the issue of freedom of expression. Freedom of speech is fundamental and sacred and must be protected. But we currently have a situation where freedom of speech is being abused by those who do not share our democratic ideals and the respect for human rights, because they know how this principle functions in democracies; they have learned how to abuse it by manipulating people's opinions and emotions. So, we have to think about ways and instruments to protect our freedom of speech. Let me give you one very concrete example. Freedom of speech implies access to multiple opinions, which then boils down to a journalistic standard that you must present the opinions of both sides in one report. So, what if a journalist is making a report about the war between Russia and Ukraine, and Russia says that Ukraine staged the massacre in Bucha, and Ukrainians counter it and say, 'No, it's Russia who did it'? According to the current standard, the journalist must make both points available to the audience. Then the journalist will certainly explain to the readers that, according to third parties, it's Russia who did it, but Russian lies will still make it to those people and reach those who want to believe Russia.

And second, if we are serious about it, self-regulation of social media is dystopian. Social media must be regulated; if social media poses a threat to national security, it should of course be shut down. But when Ukraine first shut down a Russian social media channel some years ago, we were mildly criticised by some Council of Europe experts for doing so. Look at the recent decision that the United States took against TikTok. They tried to shut down TikTok in the US because the government must recognise that the social media algorithm – not the social media platform itself, but the algorithm it is based on – can pose a threat to national security and people's mental health, but, of course, in January 2026, TikTok avoided a nationwide US ban by transferring control of its US operations to an American consortium. But again, I strongly believe there must be social media regulations, so as to keep them within relevant borderlines. The problem is that these organisations are so rich that they will be spending millions and millions on lobbyists, lawyers and opinion leaders, explaining why they can self-regulate better than anyone else.[34]

Finally, let us not forget what is at stake. The journalist Peter Pomerantsev has explained it well in his book *Nothing Is True and Everything Is Possible*. He makes the point that disinformation seeks to make truth unknowable and undermine public trust in the possibility of an established set of facts.[35] But at the same time – the stream of lies, fake news and disinformation – is very much a never-ending story.

'As long as humans and ideas exist, there will be a war for reality,' says Kuleba. 'And you cannot say that "I won the war" or "I lost the war". What you can say is that "I won this battle" or "I lost this battle". And the conclusion, whether you are winning or losing, is a calculation of the number of battles, the ratio between battles lost and battles won. This is my perception, and I think overall, we are winning more battles than losing.' Let us hope this is the situation not only for Ukraine in its 'war for reality' against Russia, but also for all of us as we combat lies, disinformation and misinformation, both online and offline.

CHAPTER 6

THE ART OF SPEECHWRITING

Dmytro Kuleba and his speechwriter, Heorhii 'Gosha' Tykhyi, share a deep passion for the art of speechwriting and recognise its exceptional political significance, especially in times of crisis and war. They have worked closely together over a period of several years, most importantly before and immediately after the full-scale Russian invasion of Ukraine. Altogether, Kuleba served as the Foreign Minister and Deputy Prime Minister of Ukraine for four and a half years, until his resignation in September 2024 during a large wartime government reshuffle. A popular public figure in his homeland, Kuleba also became one of the most respected and recognised Ukrainian politicians abroad, known for his strong and passionate appeals to partners to support Ukraine in its fight for survival and freedom.

'Since the war began, Ukrainian Foreign Minister Kuleba has been tirelessly and eloquently making the case for Ukrainian victory on the world stage,' explains Dan Kurtz-Phelan, the executive editor of *Foreign Affairs*.[1] Gideon Rachman, chief foreign affairs columnist for the *Financial Times*, recalls, 'I first met Kuleba in Kyiv in 2023. There were sandbags and fortifications surrounding the ministry, but he was strikingly relaxed and funny – a living refutation of old clichés about a backward country run by post-Soviet apparatchiks.'[2] Mihai Popșoi, the Foreign Minister of the Republic of Moldova, echoes such endorsements:

> Dmytro Kuleba is a force of nature in diplomacy, a colleague whose resolve strengthened us all in the face of adversity. I remember our meeting in Kyiv on 13 March 2024, when he greeted me with a steady calm despite the war pressing in around us. His passion for Ukraine's European future was infectious, but it was his clarity under pressure that left the deepest mark. During one of our talks about Russia's aggression, he shared a striking story about the valour of Ukrainian diplomats who, in the chaotic early days of the assault on Kyiv, refused to surrender their posts. Even as bombs fell, they stood firm, and throughout the war they countered Russia's lies on the global stage with unyielding courage. Dmytro embodied that same spirit: fierce, principled and unwavering. His leadership didn't just defend Ukraine – it inspired me to bolster Moldova's own stance against such threats.[3]

As for Kuleba himself, he is clear on his objectives. Sitting opposite Gosha, he reflects on the clear aim of his speeches.

> The underlying message of every single speech I delivered as Ukraine's Foreign Minister, every single interview I gave and every talk I did, can be summed up in three words: 'Ukraine can win.' This is what it's all about. Because we started with no one believing that we could survive. And regardless of all the successes and all the achievements that we had – even the setbacks we've

experienced to this day – the underlying message of every speech, every point we are making should be: 'Ukraine can win!'

We always had to convince partners that we can win if you do this and that. In other words, we can win if you believe in us! Take, for example, all that we did to source enough weapons and military aid to defend ourselves and to fight back against the Russians. Every conversation we had with our partners on weapons was met with a simple 'no', or 'it's an escalation', or 'it's not what you need', or 'it's too complicated', or 'it's going to take too much time.' But we turned every 'no' into 'yes' and unlocked these options – whether it was tanks, Patriots, howitzers or fighting jets.

Smiling, Kuleba slams his fist on the table.

But we still hear the argument of 'non-escalation'. Non-escalation is a very politicised term. When you have a country with nuclear weapons, a permanent member of the UN Security Council, which attacks its neighbour with a clear goal of destroying it – this is not called escalation. So anything the defending country does to exercise its right to self-defence cannot be considered as escalation per se. This country is fighting for its life and survival. So, when anyone says that Ukraine cannot do this or that because it will be an escalation, they basically invite Russia to finish Ukraine off. All the nice words – calls for peace, not nurturing the war, not escalating – when it applies to helping Ukraine, this is an invitation for Russia to continue destroying Ukraine.

The escalation argument is flawed for another simple reason. We see that Russia keeps escalating at any cost. Russia brought North Korean troops to the front line because it lacked its own

> resources, not in response to Ukraine's actions nor as a reaction to the actions of its partners. And now Russia is destroying our energy system and our civilian infrastructure not because Ukraine is escalating, but because Russia is committed to achieving its goals. Consequently, it's hypocritical for our key partners to think of helping Ukraine in terms of avoiding escalation.[4]

There is a detectable anger in Kuleba's voice as he speaks about the fate of Ukraine and the survival of his home country. Russia is conducting a ruthless campaign against Ukraine's cities and infrastructure using air-launched glide bombs, missiles and drones (many supplied by North Korea and Iran), while Ukraine can only use its drones and short-range missiles to strike back. The argument of fear of 'Russian escalation' is therefore inappropriate and unfair. Furthermore, while Russia has had 'free hands' on the battlefield, Ukraine's were tied. Kyiv was repeatedly advised and encouraged to respect supposed Russian 'red lines', despite Ukraine being the victim of a full-fledged military invasion with an inherent right to self-defence. As a matter of principle, Ukraine should long ago have been able to hit positions, even deep inside the Russian Federation, from which the aggressor's attacks are launched. Another argument voiced for denying the access of Ukraine to long-range missiles (such as ATACMS, SCALP and Taurus) was insufficient Russian targets within the range of such missiles. Such a claim was swiftly repudiated by the US-based Institute for the Study of War, which identified 245 targets, such as communications stations, logistics centres and ammunition warehouses that would be hard for Russia to move but off-limits to Ukraine's existing missiles. However, a change in the US position finally took effect in November 2024, when Ukraine was given the permission to fire US-made longer-range missiles (specifically ATACMS) onto Russian soil.

Kuleba explains,

> Well, if you do the breakdown and you start with 'Ukraine can win', then the next step is that you must *believe* that Ukraine can win. And if you believe that Ukraine can win, then you will most likely take the necessary decisions. And as I already said, this was the underlying, fundamental message of everything I said and did as a minister. But maybe Gosha has something to add, or perhaps he wants to challenge this.

Kuleba looks across to Gosha with a smile.

'I couldn't put it better myself,' says Gosha.

> But I will add that this message resonated differently and needed to be put differently in various contexts, to diverse audiences, and during different periods of the war. Because at some periods of the war, it was easy to say, 'Ukraine can win'. And I remember Dmytro's appearance on *The Late Show with Stephen Colbert* on US television, at the time when Ukraine had liberated the Kharkiv region in a lightning military operation. Confidence in Ukraine skyrocketed. Dmytro appeared before the US audience and said, 'We know how to win, and we will.' It was a moment when this message resonated extremely well.
>
> There were other much more difficult moments when Ukraine was losing ground, when we were on the back footing and when Russia was advancing militarily. But we still needed to deliver the key message that 'Ukraine can win', despite the harsh reality

on the ground, and some people were mockingly saying, 'Well, maybe it won't work out for Ukraine' or 'We already gave them all the weapons we could, so maybe they should start to negotiate with Russia instead of trying to win', and so on and so forth. In those dark moments when things really did not go well, it was very, very challenging to instil that faith and convey that positive message.

In this situation, you need to look for some creative and alternative ways to deliver your message. I believe it was in the autumn of 2023, when many had become more sceptical because the front line had not moved anywhere. As mentioned, the expectations of the Ukrainian counter-offensive had been very high, but it didn't deliver the results we wanted. We came to the conclusion that we should use more facts and figures – use the magic of numbers, if you like – because this is how you convince a sceptical audience: with something that sounds objective but is seen as unbiased. And I remember how we used this strategy repeatedly in speech after speech, trying in this way to get our main messages across. But we were also adjusting all the time, given the circumstances on the front line, and given the overall sentiments out there. Rest assured, the main message remained absolutely the same, but the point is that the methods we used were different and varied depending on the overall situation and what was happening in the war.[5]

Kuleba nods and adds,

I remember a more extreme situation in Toledo, Spain, in August 2023, when I was attending the informal EU Foreign Ministers' meeting. I was doing a press point against the backdrop of our

> long-awaited counter-offensive in the south of Ukraine; it had stumbled from the very beginning. And there was this barrage of loud, negative questions from the media, some were even shouting at me, 'Don't you think that your counter-offensive is failing?' And I responded with, 'Shut up.' Maybe it wasn't the most eloquent way to respond to questions, but it illustrates how we had to adjust and change our approach and method, according to the specific circumstances.

As a matter of fact, at the press conference in Toledo the Ukrainian Foreign Minister did much more than calling on those criticising the slow pace of Ukraine's counter-offensive to keep their mouths shut. In the weeks leading up to the Toledo meeting, stories had appeared in the *New York Times*, the *Washington Post* and in other media, quoting unnamed US and other Western officials who suggested that the offensive was falling short of expectations. Some had even faulted Ukraine's military strategy, including accusations that it was concentrating its forces in the wrong places. It was only natural on that occasion that Kuleba felt a strong need to be clear and direct in his reply. He bluntly told gathered officials that 'criticising the slow pace of the counter-offensive equals spitting into the face of the Ukrainian soldier who sacrifices his life every day, moving forward and liberating one kilometre of Ukrainian soil after another. I would recommend all critics to shut up and come to Ukraine and try to liberate one square centimetre by themselves.'[6]

It's worth reflecting for a moment on exactly how to communicate – and how one can most effectively convey key messages – during crisis and wars. A report by the Stockholm-based Swedish Defence Research Agency (*FOI Totalförsvarets forskningsinstitut*) on how Ukraine used strategic communication during the first year of the war is revealing. To start with, as we have seen, Russia has effectively been waging a war against Ukraine since 2014, including in the information domain. As a response, several valuable initiatives were taken between 2015 and 2021 to strengthen Ukraine's national capabilities in countering Russian disinformation. As a result, Ukraine was relatively well prepared when Russia launched its full-scale invasion in 2022. Instead of only responding and reacting to Russian lies, Ukrainian authorities 'instead focused on proactive and reliable information, often anticipating and pre-empting Russia's next move', in the words of the Swedish report.

Other factors that contributed to the high degree of success of the Ukrainian efforts were President Zelenskyy's, Foreign Minister Kuleba's and other high-ranking government officials' 'well calibrated' communication style, as well as, in the words of the report, the 'use of the many tools in today's media landscape, which stands in stark contrast to Russian communications'. Moreover, the flexibility and speed with which the Ukrainians were able to take control of the narrative at the onset of the invasion – instead of debunking falsehoods after they became widespread – was imperative. Per-Erik Nilsson, one of the researchers who prepared the Swedish study, summarises, 'The Ukrainians used humour, sarcasm, affect, bullying and defiance, packaged in memes, snappy one-liners and even trolling.' He adds that 'the political leadership and state agencies were quick in picking up communicative trends in social media and amplifying and adapting them to specific target audiences'.

The Ukrainian side was particularly successful in reaching audiences and rallying support in the West, though the picture looked different, for many reasons, in other parts of the world. 'In the Global South, the Russian portrayal of the war had a much bigger impact, depriving Ukraine of important outside support,' explains

Nilsson. As a matter of fact, in many parts of the world, especially the Global South, a different worldview was dominant. As the UK Attorney General Lord Hermer KC explained in his 2024 Bingham Lecture, 'The international rules-based order and human rights are often seen as imperialist constructs, selectively invoked by Western governments when it suits their interest.'[7] In the face of such scepticism, Lord Hermer says, 'It is incumbent upon us to, first, listen to those who feel unheard. And secondly, to demonstrate – not with warm words, but with concrete actions – that international law can deliver real benefits to all. And those actions must be consistent; we must show that we hold ourselves to the highest standards.'

'The war is still ongoing, and its outcome is far from certain,' says Ivar Ekman, co-author of the Swedish study. 'Given that Ukraine's war effort is very much dependent on continued outside support, the sustained success on the information front is of the outmost importance.'[8] In this context, it is important to mention that Ukraine took another effective initiative by establishing the Centre for Strategic Communication (SPRAVDI), through joint efforts of both the state and civil society, to help counter Russian disinformation and information attacks in a more sustainable way. The Centre has taken on numerous tasks, including to report regularly on Russian hybrid aggression, to help create messages for coordinated government communication, as well as conducting various training and information campaigns. One particularly interesting project is the handbook that gives concrete advice to every Ukrainian on practical, essential and everyday issues during war, including how to prepare for long-term power outages, cook without electricity and ensure uninterrupted mobile and internet access.

• • •

As for the fine art of speechwriting, Heorhii 'Gosha' Tykhyi has spent a good deal of time reflecting on how he and Kuleba worked on the speeches and which strategies and approaches they used.

> It's all about being close together during the working days, so that I could sit in on Dmytro's meetings, and also listen in on his phone calls and conversations. Basically, I was listening to what Dmytro had to say to his counterparts, to help understand his line of thinking. And after a while, I could easily predict what he was going to say, because I knew in detail the logic of his thinking. And when you spend years together like this, I believe it is fair to say that I became the 'reserve brain' of Dmytro.

To write good speeches for others is indeed a very demanding task. But, like Gosha, many of the legendary speechwriters who wrote for presidents and other high-level political leaders all underlined how essential it is to be close to the person you are writing for.

'I'd just say: listen. Listen to your boss when he is giving a speech and not giving a speech,' underlined Peggy Noonan, who wrote many of President Ronald Reagan's most successful speeches. 'Listen to how he talks. Take mental note of what works and what doesn't.' President John F. Kennedy and his newly hired, young and inexperienced speechwriter Ted Sorensen spent three and a half years in the 1950s travelling together across fifty US states. 'Those three and a half years of travelling the country made an enormous difference,' Sorensen later said. 'There were all kinds of press stories – some of them exaggerations – about how I was inside Kennedy's mind, could finish his sentences, knew what he was thinking before he said it. Well, I think maybe there is something to that. That's a tremendous advantage for a speechwriter to know his boss's mind as well as I did.'[9]

As for being a 'reserve brain', as Gosha puts it, there is certainly a very close, if not a unique, relationship between a speechwriter and his/her superior. President Kennedy came to use a different metaphor when describing his exceptional relationship with his speechwriter, calling Sorensen 'my intellectual blood bank'.

Gosha explains,

> It was certainly not about writing down what I believed or thought about an issue, or what I had to say about it, but rather what I believed Dmytro was thinking and what he would do in this or that situation. And I must say that this is a pretty interesting experience to have, because you're basically mimicking someone else's thinking. We became such like-minded people and we were always so close, since I could on a daily basis follow what he said and wrote and see what he did. So, in the end it was not a very difficult task for me to be his speechwriter and to mimic his thoughts.
>
> But when it comes to the actual writing process, the hard work of hammering out a speech, that process was rather like a ping pong game. Dmytro would have some suggestions on what he wanted to see in the speech, and then I would draft something, and thereafter he would edit it. And often he would then mark some places in a text where something needed to be rephrased or described more exactly, or there was a need to expand or elaborate, and then I would follow up and make the necessary changes.
>
> We have already discussed some of the most important speeches we wrote during the war, but let me underline here that successful speeches are not only about the right messages and how they are worded – although that is of course important – but also about picking the right tone. Sometimes it's *more* about the tone, as a

matter of fact, and this might be shocking to some public speakers – that in the end it's less about what you say than how you say it! To better understand this, have a word with your grandmother or grandfather about your interviews or TV appearances, because they will not focus necessarily on what you said, but much more on how you presented it and how convincing you were. So, that's what I mean by the tone and the delivery of the speech. And as for the most important speeches we prepared – be it the UN General Assembly speech on the eve of the invasion [see Chapter 1] or the address to NATO on Patriots missiles [Chapter 10] – it was much more about the tone and the delivery as the substance of the speech. As I was not together with Dmytro when he delivered the EU Foreign Affairs Council speech on the day after the Russian invasion [Chapter 2], I cannot evaluate it, but I will guess the tone of the speech was as important on that occasion. And at these types of moments, when the stakes are so high, you go deep inside yourself – to the bottom of your heart – to set the tone and find the right way to deliver the speech.[10]

For those of us who believe that speechwriters are about to be replaced by AI, Gosha has some bad news, based on his experiences in Kyiv.

'I want to tell you an amusing story about the art of speechwriting and why AI, which is a great technology, cannot fully replace speechwriters,' Gosha explains, before he quickly adds,

For now, at least. I remember a speech that I had lacked time to draft. I believe it was for an important G7 event on energy resilience, led by the US Secretary of State, Antony Blinken. I took the early draft of the speech that the department had given to me and then I tried to use AI to help improve it – to make it more elegant and fluent and ensure proper English. Consequently, the final speech was largely written, or at least fundamentally edited, by AI. But when we put that speech on the teleprompter and Dmytro started reading it, something strange happened. He read the first paragraph, the second paragraph and then the third, but then I saw that he appeared to be falling asleep. He became bored and unfocused and it felt as if he was just reading it and not focusing on the words. After the speech, he said to me very diplomatically, 'Well, you have written better speeches in your life.'

Let this serve as a warning to those who think that with AI you will automatically have brilliant speeches. This is far from the truth! It is hard to explain, but if you do it with AI, in a strange way, the speech will not connect. There isn't necessarily anything wrong with the wording of the speech and it doesn't have any obvious mistakes, but you feel that it's cold. It's the machine that did it, and there is no 'human spirit' inside.[11]

• • •

With or without the help of AI, in today's media environment short, credible and well composed video messages have a great appeal, especially considering the influence and audience of social media. A very good example of how a public speech in the twenty-first century should look is Foreign Minister Kuleba's video message on the issue of 'NATO expansion'. Laconic, fact-based and with the right balance of emotion, while at the same time hitting right at the heart of the most heated debate, the speech was published on social media for maximum outreach and it has so far reached more than 2 million people. In times of war, the fight against lies and deceptive narratives necessitates such unorthodox yet successful methods. The short speech is appended to the end of this chapter.

Brian Jenner, one of the most experienced speechwriters in Europe and the founder of the European Speechwriter Network, sees

> a definite development in the speeches of the Ukrainian Foreign Minister from the beginning of the war. He is clearly a sincere and decent man and this war has changed him and his attitudes. At the same time, he and Mr Tykhyi have developed a very terse and winning style. They have crafted an appealing narrative of how the ongoing struggle can lead to the emergence of a self-confident Ukrainian state which feels at home in both NATO and the EU. And in their speeches, they frame the war as an opportunity for renewal and reset – and that is something that appeals strongly to the younger generation in Ukraine and the citizenry of Europe, who are at ease with modernity and deeply fearful of Russian revanchism.[12]

Looking back at his own speeches since the start of Russia's invasion, there are two main observations Kuleba wants to highlight.

> First, during the hot stage of a 'war for reality', emotions totally drive out critical thinking. Those who do not succumb to this pressure will pull themselves together under the most severe pressure and fight back – just like the Ukrainians.
>
> Second, the war demonstrates just how complex the phenomenon of deep convictions is. For example, most Ukrainians, who even after 2014 had some warm feelings for Russia, completely changed their views after Russia went for its full-scale invasion.

However, some of them still don't believe that Russian atrocities have even taken place or they try to justify them. When the brain's protection mechanisms – which are based on deep convictions – function, even thousands of facts will fail to change them. And this is horrendously obvious as regards the Russians. Who would have thought that in the twenty-first century, in the era of a declared digital Enlightenment, one can brainwash millions of people to the extent that they will not believe their eyes and support an unjustified aggression, even being ready to sacrifice their dearest ones in such a war? They certainly have an alternative, they have access to a variety of information online, but they prefer to see only one perspective that feeds their convictions. Therefore, when deep convictions are established, no brilliant speeches, short video messages or alternative information will alter people's views.[13]

STATEMENT BY DMYTRO KULEBA ON NATO EXPANSION

2024

I sometimes hear people say that Russia was forced to attack Ukraine because Ukrainians wanted to join NATO. Those people also often say that NATO promised it would not expand to the east but later broke this promise. And this, allegedly, is the reason why Russia keeps attacking its neighbours. If you have ever heard people say something like that, please know that this is not true. And it will take me less than five minutes to prove with facts that both statements are false.

First, let's have a look at the timeline of events. Russia first invaded Ukraine in February 2014 by occupying the Crimea peninsula. At that moment, Ukraine was a neutral country by law and expressed no intention of joining NATO whatsoever. For instance, during the Revolution of Dignity, the protestors insisted on Ukraine joining the EU, not NATO. It was only in autumn 2014, after many months of war, that Ukraine abandoned neutrality.

So, what came first? Russia attacking Ukraine or Ukraine wanting to join NATO? The answer is clear. Had Russia not threatened Ukraine's existence, there would be no reason for our country to seek collective security. So please, do not repeat the lie that 'Russia attacked because Ukraine wanted to join NATO'. This does not correspond with the facts.

Now, let's have a look at the story of NATO allegedly promising not to expand to the east. If you ask people who say this, when exactly such a promise was made and who made it, most of them will not be able to provide a clear answer. Spoiler: because no such promise has ever been made and the whole story is a Russian fairytale.

Those more sophisticated will tell you that the promise was made to the President of the USSR, Mikhail Gorbachev. They may even refer to the 1990 US-Soviet negotiations on the reunification of Germany. Again, let's consider the timeline. In summer 1990, when the talks were held, the Soviet analogue of NATO, the Warsaw Pact, still existed. Its dissolution, let alone the Soviet Union's dissolution, was not on the cards; no one even talked about it or imagined it. It was only next year, in 1991, that the Warsaw Pact, and later the USSR, quite unexpectedly ceased to exist.

Now explain to me just how the very issue could be even discussed in the summer of 1990. It is not surprising that Mikhail Gorbachev later himself refuted this falsehood. When asked by a journalist whether any such promise had been made, he said this was a myth.

Now, let's look at it from another perspective. How could NATO even promise anything like that? Initially, it is not NATO that decides which country joins it. Countries themselves need to want it and, actually, the membership criteria are very difficult. It requires a lot of political will and reform. All the NATO members that joined it after 1991 really wanted to be part of it. Their people wanted this.

And here comes the most uncomfortable question for Russia. Why were all of the nations that had been part of the Soviet Union or the Socialist Bloc so eager and desperate to join NATO? Well, maybe because in three decades Russia has invaded or incited war in at least three of its neighbours: Moldova, Georgia and Ukraine? At the same time, Russia has not dared to invade any of its NATO neighbours. See the pattern?

The only reason for countries in the vicinity of Russia to seek NATO membership has always been and remains the need to protect their people from Russia. Therefore, Moscow has only itself to blame for the fact that all of the Central European and Baltic nations ran away from it and hid under the NATO umbrella as quickly as they could.

Don't let Russian officials or their supporters in the West fool you. Russia attacked Ukraine not because NATO 'expanded to the east' or because Ukraine 'wanted to join NATO'. Russia attacked because it denies Ukraine's right to exist and wants to conquer our land and kill our people. It is through our shared strength that we can and must stop Russia and put an end to its aggressive plans for the rest of Europe. For this to happen, keep supporting Ukraine and don't buy Russian lies.

CHAPTER 7

THREE STRATEGIC MISTAKES

Those who fail to learn from history are condemned to repeat it.

Sir Winston Churchill

In a remarkable speech delivered at Harvard University on 23 February 2023, almost exactly a year after the Russian invasion of Ukraine, Dmytro Kuleba sought to pass on to students the lessons learned by Ukraine and the international community from three crucial strategic mistakes over a three-year period, from 1991 to 1994. In a fundamental way, these strategic failures set the stage for the Russian invasion on 24 February 2022.

'Instead of cementing Ukraine's place in the West, our state was disarmed and abandoned in the grey zone to see what would come out of it. The Cold War was over, but Ukraine was left outside in the cold,' Kuleba points out.

What essentially took place and what conclusions can one draw from these three incidents?

First of all, in 1991, after the fall of the Berlin Wall, the disintegration of the Soviet Union and the dissolution of the Warsaw Pact, the whole of Europe lived through a period of rapid, deep and profound change. In 1995, the renowned American diplomat and historian George F. Kennan wrote,

> I find it hard to think of any event more strange and startling, and at first glance more inexplicable, than the sudden and total disintegration and disappearance from the international scene, primarily in the years 1987 through 1991, of the great power known successively as the Russian Empire and the Soviet Union. [...] How then to explain the extreme abruptness, the sharp quick ending, and not least the relative bloodlessness with which the great Soviet Empire came to an end in the four years in question, bearing with it those attributes of the earlier Russian Empire which it had contrived to incorporate into itself?[1]

At the time, there was no doubt that the Russian President was prepared to use force against autonomous republics within the Russian Federation should they attempt to secede, but evidently not against similar aspirations of Soviet Union republics such as Ukraine. Moreover, the Soviet Army was evidently short of resources and Russians serving in it were not eager to fight.[2]

On 1 August 1991, after visiting Moscow and Mikhail Gorbachev only days before, the President of the United States, George W. Bush, paid a visit to Kyiv and Ukraine. He was invited to speak in the Ukrainian Parliament – known then as the Supreme Soviet of the Ukrainian SSR, as Ukraine was still a Soviet republic. He was going to deliver what would later be known as the not very flattering 'Chicken Kyiv' speech.

Bush voiced his strong support for President Gorbachev and, remarkably, expressed the view that the Soviet Union would continue to be the main counterpart for the United States. The Soviet republics, including Ukraine, would have to find their place therein. Bush told the Ukrainian parliamentarians that

> some people have urged the United States to choose between supporting President Gorbachev and supporting independence-minded leaders throughout the USSR. I consider this a false choice. In fairness, President Gorbachev has achieved astonishing things, and his policies of *glasnost*, *perestroika* and democratisation point toward the goals of freedom, democracy and economic liberty. We will maintain the strongest possible relationship with the Soviet government of President Gorbachev. But we also appreciate the new realities of life in the USSR. And therefore, as a federation ourselves, we want good relations – improved relations – with the republics.[3]

But then the American President came to the worst part of his speech: the warning against independence, or what he referred to as 'suicidal nationalism'. He declared that 'freedom is not the same as independence. Americans will not support those who seek independence in order to replace a far-off tyranny with a local despotism. They will not aid those who promote a suicidal nationalism based upon ethnic hatred.'[4]

Bush was essentially lecturing the Ukrainians against self-determination, while imprudently placing Washington on the side of Moscow's centralism and against the tide of history. These were messages that were not convincing or appropriate to convey to Ukraine, a country anxiously longing for its independence.

'He had just met Gorbachev in Moscow. Now he is in Kyiv, cautioning against what he called "suicidal nationalism"', Kuleba told the students in his speech at Harvard University (appended to this chapter), before he pointed out that President Bush 'told tens of millions of Ukrainians who wanted their own country to give up their dreams and stay with Moscow. In just three weeks, tanks will enter central Moscow. The Soviet Union starts to collapse, leading to Ukraine proclaiming independence.'

It's likely President Bush was 'badly advised by the stability-obsessed "realist" Brent Scowcroft [his National Security Advisor],' wrote the highly respected American columnist William Safire in the *New York Times*. It was Safire who dubbed this the 'Chicken Kyiv' speech, a decision that, in Safire's words, 'so infuriated Bush, who mistakenly saw the phrase as imputing cowardice rather than charging colossal misjudgement, that he has not spoken to me since.'[5]

Overall, it's fair to say that the speech and the main messages conveyed represented a rare foreign policy blunder of extraordinary proportions. Bush's discourse would indeed be criticised both in Ukraine and elsewhere in Europe as well as in the US. Several Ukrainian parliamentarians quickly responded to the speech, including the Chairman of the People's Movement of Ukraine, Ivan Drach, who told journalists that 'President Bush seems to have been hypnotised by Gorbachev.'[6] The pro-independence politician Stephan Pavluk pointed out that 'Bush does not understand that we are fighting against a totalitarian state' and that the American President 'talks a lot about freedom, but for us, it is practically impossible to conceive of freedom without independence.'[7]

Several years later, and to his defence, Bush explained in his memoirs that

> whatever the course, however long the process took, and whatever its outcome, I wanted to see stable, and above all peaceful

> change. I believed the key to this would be a politically strong Gorbachev and an effectively working central structure. The outcome depended on what Gorbachev was willing to do. If he hesitated at implementing the new agreement [i.e. the Union of Sovereign States Treaty] with the republics, the political disintegration of the Union might speed up and destabilize the country. [...] If he appeared to compromise too much, it might provoke a coup – although there were no serious signs of one. I continued to worry about further violence inside the Soviet Union, and that we might be drawn into conflict.[8]

On a visit to Kyiv in 2004, Bush again commented on the speech delivered thirteen years earlier, insisting that both the Ukrainian and Western press missed his main point. The message he wanted to send is that Ukrainians should not do 'something stupid'. 'If your leaders hadn't acted smartly, there would have been a crackdown,' he claimed, referencing the potential threat of retribution from Moscow.[9]

'It's more than natural for a politician to defend his legacy but history is merciless – Bush framed the US policy towards Ukraine for years to come,' explains Kuleba.

> All mistakes emanate from the 'Chicken Kyiv' speech. Metaphorically speaking, this chicken became the egg of America's general attitude to Ukraine. Had Bush taken a more embracing stance on Ukraine, Clinton would likely have taken Ukraine's concerns and fears more seriously during the denuclearisation talks, Bush Junior would have tried to integrate Ukraine in NATO before his last year in office, Obama would not have given Ukraine to Russia's mercy in 2014 and Biden would not have been so constrained

> by the non-escalation argument while helping Ukraine to repel the Russian invasion. Would Russia ever have dared to invade at all, had history been more generous to Kyiv?[10]

As Kuleba also discussed in his Harvard speech, the Soviet Union collapsed only a few weeks after the American President's infamous speech in Kyiv. This leads us to the second of the key strategic mistakes highlighted by the Ukrainian Foreign Minister.

A coup d'état in Moscow against Soviet President Mikhail Gorbachev took place on 18 August 1991. The period leading up to the coup was characterised by two major trends: attempts by the fifteen Soviet republics to gain more autonomy vis-à-vis Moscow and counter-attempts by Gorbachev to hold the union together.[11] Essentially, Gorbachev wrongly believed he could reform the Soviet system. For various reasons, the coup failed, quickly leading to the demise of the Soviet Union. After the three Baltic countries of Estonia, Latvia and Lithuania declared their independence, the remaining twelve republics had proclaimed their independence in turn by the end of 1991. On 24 August 1991, shortly after the failed coup attempt in Moscow, Ukraine's Supreme Council voted to declare Ukraine's independence. The declaration stated that henceforth, only the Constitution, laws, resolutions and other legislative acts of Ukraine were valid on its territory. It called for a referendum on 1 December 1991 to 'support the Act declaring independence'. A national referendum was held as planned, with more than 90 per cent of the population voting for independence, including 54 per cent of the voters in Crimea, a largely Russian-populated peninsula; in the Donbas region of eastern Ukraine, support for independence exceeded 80 per cent.[12]

At a tripartite meeting of Russia, Ukraine and Belarus held in

Minsk on 8 December 1991 and subsequently at a meeting of eleven republics on 21 December 1991 in Alma-Ata, Kazakhstan, former republics declared that the Soviet Union had ceased to exist as a subject of international law and that they would henceforth constitute the Commonwealth of Independent States (CIS). It's interesting to note that in the preamble to the two declarations by the leaders of Belarus, Russia and Ukraine, the three signatories stated that 'the USSR, as a subject of international law and a geopolitical reality, is ceasing its existence'.[13] Likewise, the eleven participating republics at the Alma-Ata conference stated in the fifth operative paragraph of the first of five declarations that 'with the formation of the Commonwealth of Independent States, the Union of Soviet Socialist Republics ceases to exist'.[14] Furthermore, in Article 1 of the fifth declaration, entitled 'On UN Membership', the eleven signatories agreed (though the legality was questionable) that 'Member states of the Commonwealth support Russia in taking over the USSR membership in the UN, including permanent membership in the Security Council'.[15]

On 25 December 1991, President Mikhail Gorbachev resigned and the fate of the Soviet Union was finally sealed. Just a day earlier, however, the Permanent Representative of the USSR to the United Nations, Ambassador Y. Vorontsov, transmitted a letter to the Secretary-General of the United Nations from the President of the Russian Federation, Boris Yeltsin. The letter stated, 'The membership of the Union of Soviet Socialist Republics in the United Nations, including the Security Council and all other organs and organizations of the United Nations system, is being continued by the Russian Federation (RSFSR) with the support of the countries of the Commonwealth of Independent States.' This was obviously a reference to the declaration from Alma-Ata. Yeltsin's letter continued,

> In this connection, I request that the name 'Russian Federation' should be used in the United Nations in place of the name 'The Union of Soviet Socialist Republics.' The Russian Federation maintains full responsibility for all the rights and obligations of the USSR under the Charter of the United Nations, including the financial obligations. I request that you consider this letter as confirmation of the credentials to represent the Russian Federation in United Nations organs for all the persons currently holding the credentials of representatives of the USSR to the United Nations.[16]

The UN Secretary-General thereafter circulated Yeltsin's request among UN members. In the absence of any objection in New York, the delegation of the Russian Federation took over the Soviet seat in the UN General Assembly, the Security Council and in other organs of the United Nations, with the necessary changes of the name plates and flag being undertaken by the UN Secretariat. No new credentials were presented by Ambassador Vorontsov in his new capacity as the Permanent Representative of the Russian Federation. On 31 January 1992, during a visit to New York and the UN at a summit meeting of the Security Council, attended by several heads of state and government, President Yeltsin took the seat previously held by the USSR, but now as the Russian Federation.[17]

According to relevant parts of the UN Charter and its interpretation – as defined by the United Nations General Assembly's Sixth Committee (covering legal issues) back in 1947 – with the demise of the Soviet Union itself, Soviet 'membership in the UN should have automatically lapsed and Russia should have been admitted to membership in the same way as the other newly independent republics (except Belarus and Ukraine)', in the words of legal scholar Yehuda Zvi Blum.[18] (Belarus and Ukraine, as longstanding members of the

UN, did not need to apply.) But, curiously, a very different procedure was applied on this occasion by the UN Secretary-General and its Secretariat. And, as Blum states in his analysis,

> The correct legal path to this end would have been for all the republics of the Soviet Union except Russia to secede from the union, thus preserving the continuity between the Soviet Union and Russia for UN membership purposes. For reasons of Soviet domestic politics, such a solution was apparently not feasible. Thus resulted a practical solution which, while politically the only realistic one, remains legally suspect.

In his speech at Harvard, Kuleba summarised the legality of such a decision:

> Russian leader Boris Yeltsin sends a letter to the UN Secretary-General. He is claiming Russia's right to the Soviet seat on the UN Security Council. No legal procedures defined by the UN Charter are upheld. [...] A simple letter, legally null and void, becomes the reason for the UN Secretariat to change name plates at the table. Russia usurps the seat with the silent consent of the other members.

This is no doubt a very important institutional issue, particularly in light of the UN's critical role in global affairs. It seems several missteps were made in the process leading up to the UN Secretary-General's decision. Kuleba is correct in raising the issue from a legal, but also political, point of view. According to rigorous legal analysis, the UN did not follow its own rules and the relevant principle of the UN Charter when the name plates of the Soviet Union were expeditiously changed to the Russian Federation. In particular, it is appropriate that Kuleba raises this issue as a Ukrainian; as Ukraine was a founding member of the United Nations in 1945, it could have claimed the seat held by the Soviet Union in 1991, as Ukraine saw its legal status as a successor to the Soviet Union on a par with Russia.

The third strategic mistake regards the infamous and inept Budapest Memorandum, signed on 5 December 1994. As a result of the rapid collapse of the Soviet Union – a military superpower – Ukraine suddenly inherited the world's third largest nuclear arsenal. It included 176 intercontinental ballistic missiles, forty-four strategic bombers armed with cruise missiles, as well as close to 2,000 strategic nuclear warheads and 2,600 tactical nuclear weapons.[19] Belarus and Kazakhstan also inherited nuclear weapons but not nearly as many as Ukraine. Kyiv had physical rather than full operational control over the nuclear arms on its territory, since the power to launch them was still partially or fully in Moscow's hands. Or to be more precise, what was required when it comes to the launch of the intercontinental ballistic missiles was a joint launch order by the Russian Strategic Rocket Force headquarters and the President of Ukraine.[20]

It's important to note that a year earlier, on 16 July 1990, while Ukraine was still a Soviet republic, the Ukrainian Parliament adopted a historic declaration stating its intention to become a non-nuclear country. The background for this decision was the truly devastating accident at the nuclear power plant in Chernobyl in 1986, giving rise to widespread anti-nuclear sentiments in Ukraine. Such sentiments became an integral part of Ukraine's pro-independence movement, as the Soviet system's negligence, incompetence and failure to act in a timely and adequate way to the accident reinforced the criticism of the system, so that 'anti-nuclear' became in many ways synonymous with 'anti-Soviet'.[21] The sudden rise of Ukraine as a major military nuclear power naturally raised several complicated questions, if not concerns, among the political elite in Kyiv at the time, but also outside Ukraine. These questions were raised most urgently in Washington – the capital of the only remaining superpower after the demise of the Soviet Union. But Ukraine faced a real dilemma: the fastest (and possibly only viable) way of gaining international recognition of Ukraine's independence was to give up nuclear weapons but the most effective (and possibly only plausible) way of assuring the country's long-term security was to keep them.[22] Washington's position on this issue was unambiguous, however, as defined by the US Secretary of State at that time, James Baker, who took the very firm view that only Russia should succeed the Soviet Union as a nuclear state, lest the unravelled Soviet Union could become a 'Yugoslavia with nukes'.[23] He outlined this position in an interview with the *New York Times* on 9 December 1991:

> The important thing is that they proceed in a positive and peaceful fashion, because we really do run the risk, in my view, at least, of seeing a situation created there not unlike what we have seen in Yugoslavia with nukes, with nuclear weapons thrown in, and that could be an extraordinarily dangerous situation for Europe and for the rest of the world – indeed for the United States.[24]

As a remarkable result, Washington's and Moscow's interests became to a great extent identical, as they both sought for all the nuclear weapons of the former Soviet Union to be destroyed or relocated to Russia.[25] But gradually, Ukraine adopted a guarded and pragmatic approach to its new nuclear weapons status, concerned that a possible Russian monopoly on nuclear arms in the post-Soviet area would be conducive to Russia's resurgence as a dominating force in the region. Ukraine, therefore, preferred to denuclearise gradually through treaties with other nuclear powers.[26]

Four concrete questions or requests were articulated in Kyiv and shared with the government of the US.

- First of all, by what means would the warheads, missiles and bombers be dismantled so they did not end up in the Russian arsenal?
- Secondly, and given the very difficult economic situation in Ukraine in the middle of the 1990s, who would cover the costs of eliminating the missiles, the bombers and the missile silos in Ukraine?
- Thirdly, given that those nuclear warheads that might potentially be transferred to Russia had an economic value due to their highly enriched uranium, how would Ukraine be compensated for such a loss? (On this topic, a special arrangement was worked out whereby Russia blended down the highly enriched uranium and sent back to Ukraine an equivalent amount of low enriched uranium in the forms of fuel rods for Ukrainian nuclear power plants.)
- And finally, fourth, and by far the most important question, what will provide for Ukraine's security after the nuclear weapons were gone?[27]

When Ukraine acceded to the Treaty on the Non-Proliferation of Nuclear Weapons (NPT) in 1994 as a non-nuclear state, certain specified 'security assurances' were given to Ukraine in the Budapest Memorandum, signed by the United States, Russia (!) and the United Kingdom. In the memorandum, the three nations 'reaffirm[ed] their commitment to Ukraine' and vowed to 'respect the independence and sovereignty and the existing borders of Ukraine'. They also 'reaffirm[ed] their obligation to refrain from the threat or use of force against the territorial integrity and political independence of Ukraine' and they 'reaffirm[ed] their commitment to seek immediate United Nations Security Council action to provide assistance to Ukraine, if Ukraine should become victim to an act of aggression or an object to a threat of aggression in which nuclear weapons are used'. The memorandum was later circulated to the UN Security Council member states at their forty-ninth session on 19 December 1994 by the four relevant ambassadors, including Madeleine K. Albright and, most noticeably, Sergey Lavrov, the current Russian Foreign Minister.[28]

One may ask what the actual results were of this extraordinary manoeuvre by the three great powers.

Foreign Minister Kuleba sums it up in his Harvard speech:

> Budapest, December 1994. Russia and the US join forces to denuclearise Ukraine. In exchange for abandoning its numerous nukes, Ukraine gets security 'assurances', the most significant of which is the commitment to convene consultations in case Ukraine should become a victim to an act of aggression, or an object of a threat of aggression in which nuclear weapons are used. Russia, the US and the UK also pledge to ensure there will be no use of force or threat of use of force against Ukraine. Nukes in return for consultations and promises. That's what it was.

Today, there is no doubt that the Budapest Memorandum is seen as a naïve and serious diplomatic blunder with severe consequences for Ukraine, especially given the brutal war the Russian Federation has been waging against Ukraine in stark violation of it since 2014.

A basic lesson is that the 'security assurances' it provided rested on the good-will and self-restraint of the guarantors, an arrangement that can certainly work between allies but not potential adversaries. The illegal annexation of Crimea and the war in eastern Ukraine in 2014, followed by the full-scale invasion of Ukraine in 2022, exposes how quickly self-restraint dissipates when a guarantor becomes a revisionist aggressor.[29] But despite not getting the appropriate 'security guarantees', Ukraine anyhow decided to sign the memorandum, likely because Kyiv had a weak hand. The country was on the verge of economic collapse and with both the United States and Russia 'allied' against it on the issue, Ukraine faced the prospect of international isolation if it did not sign. Signing the agreement seemed therefore to be a way to escape isolation and also to receive much-needed financial assistance.[30] It is telling, however, that in September 2014 at an international conference in Kyiv, former President Leonid Kuchma, who signed the Budapest Memorandum on behalf of Ukraine, bluntly stated that Ukraine was 'cheated'. He recalled, 'In 1994 when I signed the Budapest Agreement, the United States, Great Britain, and then also China (in a separate national declaration) guaranteed security for us. It seemed to me that we were going to live as in God's bosom. We don't need an army.' He also admitted that when he visited Paris, after signing the memorandum in Budapest, the French President, François Mitterrand, bluntly said to him, 'Don't believe them, they will cheat you.'[31]

• • •

It is these mistakes, according to Kuleba, that prepared the ground for the invasion of Ukraine and the current war. As he said,

> These were strategic mistakes. From 1991 to 1994, this chain of mistakes set the stage for the war. Instead of cementing Ukraine's place in the West, our state was disarmed and abandoned in a grey zone to see what would come out of it. The Cold War was over, but Ukraine was left outside in the cold.

As Kuleba also indirectly refers to, we could conceivably add to the list a fourth major strategic mistake: the infamous decision made at the NATO summit in Bucharest in 2008 (for a more detailed discussion of this decision, see Chapter 10). During the summit it was declared that 'NATO welcomes Ukraine's and Georgia's Euro-Atlantic aspirations for membership in NATO'. The Allies subsequently agreed that 'these countries will become members of NATO'.[32] As we know, however, these decisions have to a large degree remained words only, without any real will to follow up. This is an ambiguity Putin was quick to take advantage of. Only a few months after the NATO summit, Russia launched a war against Georgia, occupying a good part of the country, before deciding to keep control over the two Georgian regions of South Ossetia and Abkhazia. In Moscow, they undoubtedly calculated that the territorial division of Georgia would likely undermine Georgia's chances of ever joining NATO.

'But what about Ukraine?' Kuleba asked the Harvard students towards the end of his speech. 'We have made our mistakes, too,' he admitted.

> But whatever flaws we have had, one thing has always made us fundamentally different from Russia. The core of the Ukrainian project has always been freedom, whereas the core of the Russian project has always been obedience: obedience of citizens of

> Russia to the Tsar and obedience imposed by Russia on other nations, most importantly its neighbours.

He then explained to the students what he sees as the essence of today's Ukraine.

> Modern Ukraine is not only a state; it's a project in the making. The Ukraine we want to be is always ahead. We are essentially a collaboration of people of all ages, all walks of life, all ethnic backgrounds and all faiths, united in our determination to make Ukraine a success and put an end to Russia's imperial frenzy.

As a matter of fact, what unites Ukrainians is far more important than what divides them, and it is ordinary Ukrainians and not the political elite that are at the centre of this unity.[33] These ordinary Ukrainians seem to have a strong attachment to Ukraine as their homeland regardless of their nationality or language.[34]

In the mid-1990s, Russia and Ukraine parted ways in a very fundamental manner: Russia became more authoritarian with each passing year, while Ukraine stayed democratic despite the repeated efforts of the Presidential office in Kyiv to follow the Russian model and subordinate the Parliament under itself. But despite this, in Ukraine the political elite enhanced rather than undermined democratic institutions born out of the chaos of Gorbachev's political and economic reforms. In other words, Russia's democratic moment became in many ways an era of democracy in Ukraine.

Ukrainian democracy would in itself present a major threat to the Russian political regime, as it provided an example of a functioning democratic political system with a strong parliament.[35]

There were other factors that contributed to these two very different outcomes, outcomes which have strongly influenced relations between the former senior partners of the Soviet project.[36] It's important to recognise that Ukraine is very much divided by history, culture, political orientations and the instincts of its people, in ways the Russian Federation never was.[37] There is also a very strong regionalism that fragments the Ukrainian political space and makes politics much more competitive than it has ever been in Russia. The east and south of Ukraine were once the industrial heartland of the Soviet Union and are highly Russified in culture, with millions of ethnic Russians among the inhabitants. The centre is largely rural and Ukrainian-speaking, a product of the Soviet Ukrainian national project of the 1920s, which tolerated Ukrainian cultural, but not political, identity. Then there is the west, which for a long time was part of Central European states and empires. Its strongly exclusivist national identity was strengthened by the interwar nationalist movement, as well as the lengthy guerrilla war against Soviet rule waged by the Ukrainian Insurgent Army in the late 1940s and early 1950s.[38]

'Things are different today,' Kuleba underlined at the end of his speech.

> We are almost done breaking the cycle and making sure that the Russian imperial project will fail. A Ukrainian victory is essential to this end. As history teaches us, Ukrainian independence and Russian imperialism are irreconcilable, just as freedom and obedience are irreconcilable.

Importantly, he reassured those students eager to learn more about the background to the most devastating military conflict in Europe since the Second World War that Ukraine is 'determined to prove that, this time, we will not only struggle but actually win'. 'Because Ukraine's victory is in everyone's interest. To put it simply: it is far less expensive to support Ukraine now and allow us to defeat this evil than to face it later,' he concluded.

STATEMENT BY DYMTRO KULEBA ON STRATEGIC MISTAKES AND THE FORCES OF HISTORY

HARVARD UNIVERSITY, 23 FEBRUARY 2023

Dear ladies and gentlemen,

I am thankful for the invitation. It's an honour to address you today. I wish I could be present in person, as I sincerely wanted to personally experience the greatness of your university and directly pass on to you the thoughts and feelings of the great people of Ukraine.

The UN is to blame for my online appearance. Apparently, it's always easy to blame international institutions, but jokes aside – yes, I had to stay in New York to address the UNGA [United Nations General Assembly] and hold additional bilaterals to persuade some members that it's worth supporting the resolution.

Let me begin by taking you back to 1991.

August 1, 1991. President of the US George W. Bush visits Kyiv and delivers the famous 'Chicken Kyiv' speech in the Ukrainian Parliament. He had just met Gorbachev in Moscow. Now he is in Kyiv, cautioning against what he called 'suicidal nationalism'. He told tens of millions of Ukrainians who wanted their own country to give up their dreams and stay with Moscow. In just three weeks, tanks will enter central Moscow. The Soviet Union starts to collapse, leading to Ukraine proclaiming independence.

Fast forward four months. December 1991. The USSR legally ceases to exist. Russian leader Boris Yeltsin sends a letter to the UN Secretary-General. He is claiming Russia's right to the Soviet seat on the UN Security Council. No legal procedures defined by the UN Charter are upheld. A simple letter, legally null and void, becomes the reason for the UN Secretariat to change name plates at the table. Russia usurps the seat with the silent consent of the other members.

Fast forward three years. Budapest, December 1994. Russia and the US join forces to denuclearise Ukraine. In exchange for abandoning its numerous nukes, Ukraine gets security 'assurances', the most significant of which is the commitment to convene consultations in case Ukraine should become a victim to an act of aggression, or an object to a threat of aggression in which nuclear weapons are used. Russia, the US and the UK also pledge to ensure there will be no use of force or threat of use of force against Ukraine. Nukes in return for consultations and promises. That's what it was.

These were strategic mistakes. From 1991 to 1994, this chain of mistakes set the stage for the war I just came from. Instead of cementing Ukraine's place in the West, our state was disarmed and abandoned in the grey zone to see what would come out of it. The Cold War was over, but Ukraine was left outside in the cold.

We were not left alone, though. Ukraine was held at a distance of a firm, friendly handshake. The strategic failure to start Ukraine's accession to NATO at the 2008 Bucharest summit has become just the first level of this house built upon all previous mistakes.

While the West exercised short-sighted cautiousness, Russia was growingly persistent and self-assured. Unlike the West, it has always had a Ukraine strategy.

Think of this. There hasn't been a decade in which Russia hasn't threatened Ukraine's territorial integrity. Attempts to claim rights in Crimea in 1993, the crisis around the tiny island of Tuzla in 2003, the occupation of Crimea in 2014, the war in the east of Ukraine and then the full-scale invasion of Ukraine in 2022. There has not been a single decade when Russia has not betrayed the willingness of its partners to be friends with it and pardon it for its sins. Recall the Obama Reset as an example.

But what about Ukraine? We have made our mistakes, too. Economic model, the rule of law and the state of the army. But whatever flaws we have had, one thing has always made us fundamentally different from Russia. The core of the Ukrainian project has always been freedom, whereas the core of the Russian project has always been obedience. Obedience of citizens of Russia to the Tsar and obedience imposed by Russia on other nations, most importantly its neighbours.

Freedom is what makes Ukraine part of the West. But there is also something else that has united us: lack of self-confidence. Neither we nor you have had confidence that we can prevail in a standoff with Russia. And that is why the conclusion has always been that we need to make concessions.

Russian imperialism has been overlooked for decades. Moldova, 1992. Chechnya, 1996 and 1999. Georgia, 2008. Ukraine, 2014. Russia was invited to the table, pleased, appeased and pardoned. Its imperial influence has spread easily through academia, the media, culture, politics, sports and business in the West.

This is how we got to the Bucharest 2008 mistake, the invasion of Georgia, the annexation of Crimea, the interference in the 2016 US election and other troubles and tragedies.

I remember the moment when I began to believe in Ukraine without a second thought. Early hours of February 25th, 2022. I was driving from Poland into my dark and war-ravaged homeland. My car was the only one driving in; everyone else was driving out. That was the moment when I abandoned fear. I overcame my fear and told myself: we are going to win. That was when I crossed the border.

I also know when we abandoned fear as a nation. After one week of resistance. Because this was the maximum that even our closest friends gave us.

As Foreign Minister, I always fight for a change of perspective. Stop looking at Ukraine through the prism of Russia. Don't assume that peace is only achievable through Ukraine's concessions. Don't say that Russia shouldn't win. Set a positive goal instead: Ukraine must win. Don't be afraid to arm us with whatever weapons we require. At the end of the day, don't be scared of Russia's collapse or the future without Russia as we know it today.

It takes these slight shifts of perspective to start making correct policy decisions. In my tenure as Foreign Minister, I have realised time and again that it's not about asking someone to take certain decisions but rather asking to change the perspective so that certain decisions become possible.

What will a Ukrainian victory look like? Ukraine restoring its territorial integrity.

Why are those who advocate for the cessation of security assistance to Ukraine hypocrites? Because what they really want is not peace but Russian victory.

What is the answer to the question, 'How long will this war last?' The right answer is: Don't ask how long this war will last; ask what you can do to bring Ukraine's victory closer.

Why does it make no sense to fear escalation? Because Russia's decisions to escalate depend on their decisions, not on yours.

What to do with Russia? Change it so that it no longer poses a threat to anyone.

This is not a war for compromise as an endgame. This is a war for Ukraine's victory. Because Ukraine's victory is in everyone's interest. We cannot allow Russia to get away with what it has done and get even more emboldened. This will also embolden the world's other evil forces. To put it simply: it is far less expensive to support Ukraine now and allow us to defeat this evil than to face it later.

Only on the battlefield can a just and lasting peace be achieved in this war. And it will then be fixed by diplomats. In such a case, the goal of our wartime diplomacy is to help achieve it. With supplies of weapons, new sanctions, financial support and building strong coalitions.

Things are different today. We are almost done breaking the cycle and making sure that the Russian imperial project will fail. A Ukrainian victory is essential to this end. As history teaches us, Ukrainian independence and Russian imperialism are irreconcilable, just as freedom and obedience are irreconcilable.

We are far better off today than we were during all previous attempts to break free and bring down the empire. Nowadays, we are winning the information war, unlike in 2014. We have one of the strongest armies in Europe and strong support from the rest of the world, including military aid. This is different from the beginning of the twentieth century. We have President Zelenskyy, an inspirational wartime leader who has become the hero of our time and galvanised global attention. Today, our core idea of freedom is universally shared, unlike in the seventeenth and early twentieth centuries.

We now have the first generation of Ukrainians in their thirties who have not lived in the Soviet Union and have never attended a Soviet school. They are already part of the resistance on many levels, holding important posts and leading units. For them, Ukraine has never gained independence; it has always been independent.

Modern Ukraine is not only a state; it's a project in the making. The Ukraine we want to be is always ahead. We are essentially a collaboration of people of all ages, all walks of life, all ethnic backgrounds and all faiths, united in our determination to make Ukraine a success and put an end to Russia's imperial frenzy. We are determined to prove that this time, we will not only struggle but actually win.

Last year, a few weeks before the full-scale invasion began, the Secretary of State, my friend Antony Blinken, visited Kyiv and we sat down for a talk, just the two of us. I told him, 'Tony, I know we may face some dreadful challenges soon. But one thing I am confident about is that I don't want to be writing my memoirs in exile, as many Ukrainian politicians of the past did. I will be writing my memoirs in Kyiv.' And that is still my retirement plan.

This is the feeling that drives us forward through these darkest of times. We have gotten our kicks. We have made our mistakes. We will not give up or fail this time. We will win. I encourage you to learn from past mistakes and prevail together.

Let me recap five key takeaways.

1. Forces of history need to be followed, not opposed.
2. Short-sighted cautiousness yields opposite results.
3. Evil must be defeated, not pardoned or appeased.
4. It takes a change of perspective to change policy.
5. To win, we have to abandon fear and believe in our joint cause.

I thank you!

CHAPTER 8

THE BEST WAY TO PREDICT THE FUTURE IS TO CREATE IT YOURSELF

The trust and confidence of partner countries have been vital to Ukraine's resistance to the Russian invasion. Equally important has been the Ukrainians belief in themselves and in their ability to resist and win. In a captivating speech in Kyiv at the end of 2022 to all of Ukraine's ambassadors, appended to the end of this chapter, Foreign Minister Kuleba clearly spelled out what he defined as 'the three rules' for Ukrainian diplomats' future work. These rules were summarised as: 'Ukraine is a legend'; 'I work for Ukraine'; and 'Nothing is impossible.' These were rules that strove to combat Ukraine's historical inferiority complex and the narrative of victimhood which neighbouring Russia has persistently used to its advantage and deliberately tried to amplify.

'For centuries, Russia has fostered contempt for us and imposed contempt upon us,' Kuleba told the ambassadors. 'They have erased us from the history of Europe – everything from the Viking voyages to the building of a common European home. They made us a nation that sincerely believes that we are losers, objects, that we "never miss an opportunity to miss an opportunity"'. This, he stressed, is now set to change. 'Today we are proud of ourselves. The world is proud of us. [...] I am a Ukrainian, and Ukraine is a legend. This is our new positioning in the world. Ukraine has become a legend – this is the starting position.'

Kuleba's speechwriter, Heorhii 'Gosha' Tykhyi, explains the message well:

> Ukraine has had this inferiority complex for a very, very long time and the Russians have certainly played a huge role in boosting such negative sentiments. But living in Ukrainian society, you would always hear from experts, from journalists, from the media, from everywhere, that we are worse than everyone else. We really cannot grab the chance. We really cannot realise the opportunities. This inferiority complex is the reason that we're not so strong; we basically started believing all of this, that you're a loser and your country is a loser! Dmytro is one of the most prominent fighters of this narrative. This deeply, deeply disgusts him and he spends all of his time fighting this narrative – and of course, he wants his ambassadors to do the same.[1]

As regards Kuleba's third rule, that 'nothing is impossible', this is something that President Zelenskyy has often repeated. Gosha explains,

> I think Dmytro actually got it from Zelenskyy, because this is the President's style of work. He hates the words 'impossible' or 'I can't do that'. And he hates it when he hears it from people; he just gets furious. He really thinks nothing is impossible – and Dmytro tries to convey this in his speech to the ambassadors.[2]

As for the first rule, that 'Ukraine is a legend', Gosha explains the origins of Kuleba's belief:

> It is something that Dmytro got from his son, Yegor. He attended university this year and, as a teenager, he is really into slang and TikTok language, words like 'You're a legend'. I mean, this is the highest form of recognition a teenager is going to hear from a friend, so it's very cool. I believe Dmytro chatted with his son, who may have said something like 'Ukraine is a legend', and Dmytro must have liked it very much and found it a very good way to fight the Ukrainian inferiority complex.[3]

In the speech Dmytro Kuleba not only clarified the three rules but he also shed light on the reasons behind selecting five fundamental principles for the work of all Ukrainian envoys during the war.

The first principle was the indivisibility of territories, community and interests. 'Ukrainian land, up to the last piece within its internationally recognised borders, will be returned to Ukrainian control and sovereignty,' he underlined, adding, 'Square metres cannot and will not be the subject of diplomatic concessions.' As regards the 'indivisibility of the community', Kuleba informed the ambassadors that the government would launch a

> new policy towards Ukrainians in the world. Our nation of millions is a single entity, both at home and abroad. We will start developing and implementing this policy immediately, otherwise, in no less than ten years, we will lose a large number of people whose identity will simply dissolve in the countries to which they have moved both this year and earlier.

Regarding 'indivisibility of interests', he said, 'There is no place on the map where Ukraine is not interested. So, we just haven't found it yet, and we have to find it. From Latin America to Oceania, from the Arctic to the Antarctic. This search is primarily our task; we are the diplomatic Google of Ukraine.'

During his time as Foreign Minister, Kuleba paid a number of visits to African countries, as well as meeting repeatedly with several leaders from other parts of the world, including the Global South. 'Going to Africa was a professional revelation to me,' he points out after giving his speech.

> After I came back from the first tour, I said to my diplomats: listen, if you really want to excel – the way you argue, the way you speak, the way you discuss – it's not about going to Washington, Brussels, Berlin, Paris or any other place. You have to go to Africa. You will meet completely different perceptions, completely different lines of arguments. You have your profession as diplomats, but professionally you can grow only there. And for me, it was challenging, but very exciting. And I always enjoyed these conversations, because I was walking out from them stronger than I was walking in. And with every conversation, with every visit, I felt how we are taking one brick after another from the wall built by the Russians to separate Ukraine from Africa. That was rewarding.

On the other hand, he stresses the inherent difficulties that some foreign leaders see when opposing Russia.

> Every leader asks himself, 'What is going to happen to me if I openly oppose Russia?' African leaders were particularly concerned about that. Some of them literally were afraid that Russia

> will stage a coup or kill them if they openly support us. And then there was always the other elephant in the room – China. Because Africa is Chinese territory with very few exceptions.[4]

The second principle Kuleba stressed in his speech to ambassadors is that Ukraine is part of the West. 'In the three decades of modern history, we have lost time, then integrated into the West, then hesitated, then turned around, then approached again, then begged to be taken in, hitting the wall of Western misunderstanding,' Kuleba explained. 'Enough of this. This dilemma has been resolved once and for all. And this is not a matter of a negative choice: not to be with Moscow. It is a matter of making a positive choice for a better future for Ukraine.'

Overall, Ukraine has taken major steps towards a full-fledged membership of the European Union. 'I have to commend the EU for really speeding up the process of Ukraine's accession and actually being able to make some very ambitious and complicated decisions,' Kuleba underlined.

> We will find the solutions. Listen, two years ago, Ukraine was not even a candidate for membership in the EU. And the time gap between granting Ukraine candidate status and opening accession talks with Ukraine, it's arguably the shortest for any country that has applied for membership in the EU in recent decades.[5]

That Ukraine is part of the West 'is not something you need to preach to Ukrainians because they basically understand it', Gosha explains.

> But it's rather a point which we emphasise to a foreign audience, especially in the West. Because we really need to change

> the perception, which is still out there, that Ukraine is part of the post-Soviet state. And for many in the West, it's not so clear whether Ukraine is in the West, whether it's a Western country or not. But our view is very clear and simple. Ukraine has always been part of the West, before we were captured by the Russian Empire and we came under Moscow's influence. And what we are doing right now is a very natural and historic process of returning to where we always belonged. That's how we see it from Kyiv. It will take time to shift the perspective in the West, but at the same time I believe it has already shifted a lot over the last years, since the war started.[6]

The third principle highlighted by Kuleba is that Ukraine is becoming the strongest military power on NATO's eastern flank, with a military further bolstered by the unique insights and practical knowledge gained from its wartime experience.

'Frankly speaking, we used to desperately need to join NATO precisely to prevent Russia from attacking us,' Kuleba explained to the ambassadors.

> Then Moscow intimidated the NATO allies in 2008 and we were denied protection. But today the situation is fundamentally different. With the strong support of the same allies, but now it is our army that is beating the aggressor. It is our army that, while overcoming its own internal problems, is building up weapons and tactical muscles that Ukraine has never had in its history and that it has yet to learn to use.

He discussed the fact that

> having overcome the Russian threat not only for ourselves but also for the Euro-Atlantic area, we will become a participant in collective security on fundamentally different terms than could have happened between 2008 and 2022. Ukraine will no longer be a 'poor cousin' hidden under the wing of Article 5 [Article 5 provides that if a NATO Ally is the victim of an armed attack, each and every other member of the Alliance will consider this act of violence as an armed attack against all members and will take the actions it deems necessary to assist the attacked]. Our country will be, and already is, a strong military power that fundamentally changes the military balance in the region and acts as a security donor for NATO.

As the fourth principle, Kuleba stressed that Ukraine is creating new economic opportunities through significant investments to rebuild the nation. According to an updated joint Rapid Damage and Needs Assessment (RDNA5) released on 23 February 2026 by the government of Ukraine, the World Bank Group, the European Commission and the United Nations, it is estimated that as of 31 December 2025, the total cost of reconstruction and recovery in Ukraine would be $588 billion over the next decade. As the war continues, this estimate will increase considerably. As has been emphasised by various G7 countries, the Ukrainian efforts to combat widespread corruption will be essential. In a statement issued by the Italian chairmanship of the G7 countries in May 2024, it was said that

> Ukraine, which is now a candidate country to join the European Union, has continued throughout the years as a resilient

> democracy to develop an anti-corruption framework including by gradually aligning with relevant EU legislation, and elaborating a new national anti-corruption strategy with a focus on relevant sectors. This framework should now be further strengthened. Several recommendations and opinions from relevant international anti-corruption monitoring mechanisms, including UN, GRECO and OECD, have only been partly implemented.[7]

Finally, Kuleba's fifth principle is that Ukraine is the guarantor of global food security. 'Food is politics,' he began.

> Our task is to create political and economic added value of Ukraine's powerful agricultural exports. President Zelenskyy's 'Grain from Ukraine' initiative is the first step in a strategically unalterable direction. [...] The establishment of Ukraine as a guarantor of global food security will also have a special ideological meaning for us. The people who faced the Holodomor [a famine that spread through the Soviet Republic of Ukraine from 1932 to 1933, peaking in the late spring of 1933] ninety years ago not only survived but are now feeding the world. This is what restoration of historical justice looks like and the most important victory we can win over our own past. This is liberation from the victim complex and the transition to the status of a saviour.

Kuleba elaborated on these five principles:

> The five principles were practical issues for me; they were points on how you transform or break down some fundamental principles into practicalities. But it was interesting to see their [the ambassadors'] reactions, because they had never heard anything

> close to what I told them. So, silence was hanging in the air for a moment, but then they gave me a round of applause. And the very same afternoon and evening many texted me, or reached out to me in other ways, saying that this was a completely new experience for them, because they never heard Foreign Ministers speak in this way about these things. But for me it was the demand of the moment. You know, we had to. We had to change their way of thinking, and it left them shocked, but in a positive way![8]

One such expression of admiration came from Thórdís Kolbrún Reykfjord Gylfadóttir, the former Foreign Minister of Iceland. Looking back on Kuleba's speech, she explains, 'Dmytro Kuleba is a modern giant of diplomacy. He not only possesses superior experience and knowledge of the craft but also the confidence and creativity to break obsolete traditions and create new rules that are fit for our time.' She perfectly sums up the role played by Kuleba's diplomacy in the war with Russia: 'Under his leadership, the Ukrainian diplomatic service became an unmatched weapon in the battle for the world's support against the Russian Federation's imperialistic aggression.'[9]

At the end of his speech, Kuleba urged the ambassadors to remain optimistic regarding the future of Ukraine, concluding,

> We have to believe and move forward. We have no other way. The future I have outlined will become our reality at the end of this difficult journey. But the ambitiousness of the goal should not discourage us. After all, the best way to predict the future is to create it ourselves.

STATEMENT BY DMYTRO KULEBA

23 DECEMBER 2022, CONFERENCE OF AMBASSADORS OF UKRAINE

Dear Ambassadors,

It has been ten months since we were supposed to be here. But we are here, against all odds, to the dismay of our enemies and the happiness of future generations of Ukrainians.

The biggest war in Europe since the Second World War is underway. The greatest battle of good and evil in this century. Ukraine, led by President Zelenskyy, did not cower and did not fall. We accepted the battle. Despite the fact that no one in the world gave us a chance. And we are winning.

The vast majority of you are bringing the victory closer with your struggle on the diplomatic front. Some of our diplomats went to the front from the very first days of the war, saw the deaths of their comrades and killed the occupiers. Some of them are still at the front. They deserve special respect. They are warrior diplomats in the literal sense of the word.

There is no doubt that Ukraine will win. But three questions remain unanswered: when, what and how? When will Ukraine win? What exactly will the victory be? How will Ukraine act after the victory?

Of these three questions, I have no answer to the first one. When you are fighting for the right to exist, deadlines are inappropriate. The basic answer to the second question is simple: anything that involves the full restoration of Ukraine's territorial integrity will be a victory. Other victories will follow: compensation, convictions for crimes, expulsion of Russia from the UN Security Council, and so on.

We are diplomats, and we understand what to do now to bring

this basic victory closer: weapons, sanctions, energy, strengthening the international coalition, finance, your concern, the concern of the countries and organisations you work for. You know what you have to do.

My task with you today is to outline the answer to the third question: how will Ukraine act after the victory?

For centuries, Russia has fostered contempt for us and imposed contempt on us. They have erased us from the history of Europe – everything from the Viking voyages to the building of a common European home. They made us a nation that sincerely believes that we are losers, objects, that we 'never miss an opportunity to miss an opportunity'.

All this is now in the past. Today, we are proud of ourselves. The world is proud of us. We hug our friends. We are unyielding with our partners. We beat the enemy.

I am a Ukrainian, and Ukraine is a legend. This is our new positioning in the world. Ukraine has become a legend; this is the starting position.

As the President said in his historic speech to Congress, the outcome of this war will determine the history of the world and its face for generations to come. The contours of a world in which a victorious Ukraine will take its rightful place must be outlined today.

With this in mind, here are five key principles that I believe we must now and in the future develop in our daily professional, patriotic and decent work.

The first principle: indivisibility of territories, community and interests.

Ukrainian land, up to the last piece within its internationally recognised borders, will be returned to Ukrainian control and sovereignty. Square metres cannot and will not be the subject of diplomatic concessions. After the victory, a long political and social integration of the occupied territories will begin.

You may remember how for many years we were told that we first had to win the hearts of the people behind the front line, and then they would want to return. We were deceived. First, we need to remove the front line by force of arms and negotiations and then rebuild lives. And there is work for us here.

Indivisibility of the community. The state will launch a new policy towards Ukrainians in the world. Our nation of millions is a single entity, both at home and abroad. We will start developing and implementing this policy immediately, otherwise, in no less than ten years, we will lose a large number of people whose identity will simply dissolve in the countries to which they have moved both this year and earlier.

Indivisibility of interests. Ukraine will open new horizons and go where our national interests are in the world. We will turn the logic of the question, 'Who is waiting for us there?' In fact, we are waiting everywhere. And in Africa, by and large, they are waiting for our return. We just need to find common ground, common interests, common benefits.

Ukraine has interests in all corners of the world. There is no place on the map where Ukraine is not interested. So, we just haven't found it yet, and we have to find it. From Latin America to Oceania, from the Arctic to the Antarctic. This search is primarily our task. We are the diplomatic Google of Ukraine.

The second principle: Ukraine is part of the West.

Today, we are paying with blood not so much for allowing the conventional Pereyaslav [Russian imperial historiography propagates the notion that the 1654 Pereyaslav Agreement was a 'voluntary reunification' of Ukraine and Russia] to bring us back under

Moscow's control, but for failing to achieve the success of Hadiach [the Treaty of Hadiach in 1658 aimed to create a Polish-Lithuanian-Ruthenian Commonwealth, while creating an independent 'Grand Duchy of Ruthenia'; at the following battle of Konotop a year later, a coalition of Cossacks, Crimean Tatars and Polish forces dealt a stunning defeat to the Muscovite army]. The problem of subjectivity is not in the wrong choice. The problem and lack of subjectivity begins when you cannot change your choice. And today, we can change everything.

However, the other extreme of this policy is the constant change of choice. In the three decades of modern history, we have lost time, then integrated into the West, then hesitated, then turned around, then approached again, then begged to be taken in, hitting the wall of Western misunderstanding. Enough of this. This dilemma has been resolved once and for all. And this is not a matter of a negative choice: not to be with Moscow. It is a matter of making a positive choice for a better future for Ukraine. No one cares where you are running from. Everyone is interested in where you are running to and who you want to be.

As a result of the war, Ukraine will be cemented in all political and security structures of the West, whatever they may be, present or future. It is as part of the West and guided by the indivisibility of our interests in the world that we will actively develop mutually beneficial and deep relations with the countries of Asia, the Middle East, Africa, Oceania and Latin America. In no case will diplomacy in these regions be secondary. Ukraine needs first-class diplomacy everywhere in the world.

The third principle: Ukraine is becoming the strongest military power on NATO's eastern flank.

Frankly speaking, we used to desperately need to join NATO

precisely to prevent Russia from attacking us. Then Moscow intimidated the NATO allies in 2008, and we were denied protection. But today the situation is fundamentally different. With the strong support of the same allies, but now it is our army that is beating the aggressor. It is our army that, while overcoming its own internal problems, is building up weapons and tactical muscles that Ukraine has never had in its history and that it has yet to learn to use.

Having overcome the Russian threat not only for ourselves but also for the Euro-Atlantic area, we will become a participant in collective security on fundamentally different terms than could have happened between 2008 and 2022. Ukraine will no longer be a poor cousin hidden under the wing of Article 5. Our country will be, and already is, a strong military power that fundamentally changes the military balance in the region and acts as a security donor for NATO.

The world is dynamic. We cannot accurately predict the future security architecture of Europe and the world. But we can confidently say that we will be one of its key and integral components.

Today, do not listen to those who talk about the impossibility of Ukraine's membership in NATO. We have already been through this. If we do our job well, tomorrow these same people will be singing the praises of a Euro-Atlantic Ukraine.

Ukraine's military potential will become an instrument of our foreign policy. We diplomats and the security and defence sector are already facing an ambitious task: to learn how to conceptually and practically project Ukraine's military power in the world. We used to do this by selling weapons and participating in peacekeeping operations. Now this is no longer enough.

The fourth principle: Ukraine is creating new economic opportunities, both for foreign investors and Ukrainian companies.

Ukraine's victory and the national reconstruction programme

will attract multi-billion-dollar investments to our country. At the same time, we are already using the resources available to the Ministry of Foreign Affairs to create an exporter class as a systemic phenomenon, not a unique one. The Ukrainian exporter will become the new core of the nation, just as the wealthy peasantry was in the nineteenth and twentieth centuries.

That is why the MFA [Ministry of Foreign Affairs] has created the NAZOVNI platform. We are already assisting in entering foreign markets, and in the future, we will launch the Academy of Ukrainian Exporters as part of the platform. We will attract the best specialists who will share their experience and teach. Ukrainian exports will become one of the engines of our country's economic renaissance after the war.

The fifth principle: Ukraine is the guarantor of global food security.

Food is politics. But we will no longer be a raw material appendage of global food policy. Our task is to create political and economic added value of Ukraine's powerful agricultural exports. President Zelenskyy's 'Grain from Ukraine' initiative is the first step in a strategically unalterable direction.

The establishment of Ukraine as a guarantor of global food security will also have a special ideological meaning for us. The people who faced the Holodomor ninety years ago not only survived but are now feeding the world. This is what restoration of historical justice looks like and the most important victory we can win over our own past. This is liberation from the victim complex and the transition to the status of a saviour. We will never again allow anyone to use hunger as a weapon, neither against ourselves or against others.

In a broader sense, it is about turning Ukraine into a donor of aid. It is a slow, difficult process but we have to psychologically adjust.

You heard the President of Ukraine say today that the Ukrainian International Aid Agency will be established.

We have to believe and move forward. We have no other way. The future I have outlined will become our reality at the end of this difficult journey. But the ambitiousness of the goal should not discourage us. After all, the best way to predict the future is to create it ourselves. I am convinced that together we can create the best possible diplomatic future for Ukraine.

And today I would like you to remember, in addition to the five principles I have already mentioned, three rules of your work, which I also follow – your daily diplomatic 'Our Father':

1. Ukraine is a legend.
2. I work for Ukraine.
3. Nothing is impossible.

Glory to Ukraine!

CHAPTER 9

THE ROAD TO EU MEMBERSHIP

This is Europe's moment, and we must live up to it.

URSULA VON DER LEYEN, PRESIDENT, EU COMMISSION

For several decades, the European Union has been a driving force for closer economic and political integration in Europe. In response to the full-scale Russian invasion of Ukraine in 2022, the EU and its institutions, led most vocally by EU Commission President Ursula von der Leyen, have demonstrated commitment, leadership and, most importantly, a willingness to act with determination. The support to Ukraine has been massive; so far, the EU and its member states have contributed approximately €194.9 billion in financial, humanitarian, refugee and military assistance to Ukraine, including roughly €69.7 billion in military support and €104.5 billion in financial, economic and humanitarian support. At the same time, the EU Military Assistance Mission to Ukraine (EUMAM Ukraine) has trained over 86,000 members of the Ukrainian Armed Forces in both combined arms training and specialised training.[1] By 2024, Europe had committed twice as much aid to Ukraine as the United

States, excluding the costs of the continent welcoming five million refugees.

In many ways, we experienced a mobilisation and strengthening of the EU as a direct response to the return of a major war in Europe, the continent's largest, deadliest conflict in generations. Some observers, such as Mark Leonard at the European Council on Foreign Relations (ECFR), have argued that we have seen a fundamental shift from the European Union as a peace project to a war project, forcing Brussels and European governments to reconsider priorities and policies. There is no doubt that the unprovoked, illegal and completely unacceptable Russian invasion of Ukraine has had the most severe and serious consequences, leading to a rude awakening, to put it bluntly.[2]

As for the possible emergence of a geopolitical Europe, capable of defending itself against threats and pursuing its fundamental interests throughout the continent and even beyond, we see encouraging trends. It would, however, be premature to draw firm and definite conclusions at this point. On the other side, within the European Union, but also throughout the broad membership of the Council of Europe – encompassing all European countries except Russia and Belarus – we are facing the rise of political forces seeking to undermine the European project, its institutions and a rules-based international order. Nationalists, populists and anti-rights movements are all part of the mix. Add Russian campaigns of disinformation, 'fake news' and hate speech, and the 'cocktail' becomes toxic.

In any event, in light of Russia's war of aggression against Ukraine, Europe now conceives of itself as a more coherent unit. As French President Emmanuel Macron has underlined, the next steps are to ensure that 'Ukraine and Moldova are part of our European family and should join the European Union, when the time comes, as should the Western Balkans'.[3]

Ukraine's future EU membership holds paramount importance from a political, economic and security perspective. As we touched on above, the ambiguity of where countries like Ukraine belong has led to Russian opportunism and aggression, a message which Foreign Minister Kuleba has repeatedly conveyed. Shortly after Ukraine applied for EU membership on 28 February 2022, it received the European Commission's opinion (or, more correctly, an assessment of the application) on 17 June 2022. In this report, the Commission recommended that Ukraine should be granted candidate status on the understanding it takes seven steps, mainly regarding the rule of law. Less than one week later, on 23 June 2022, the European Council – the highest decision-making organ in the EU – decided to grant Ukraine the status of candidate country, while it invited 'the Commission to report to the Council on the fulfilment of the seven steps as part of the regular enlargement package'.[4]

'We are determined to implement the steps defined by the European Commission in its conclusions,' Kuleba clarified three weeks later, in a historic speech to all the EU Foreign Ministers in Brussels, appended to this chapter. Kuleba was delighted, as he declared that Ukraine had

> elaborated a special road map and an action plan of legislative and executive steps towards the membership criteria. We will further bring our legislation closer to the EU legislation at an accelerated pace and in accordance with the list of priority European Integration bills for 2022. We proceed with implementing crucial reforms, in particular to strengthen rule of law and anti-corruption institutions. We keep working on integrating into

> the EU internal market and advancing sectoral integration. Our priorities are removing all barriers in the customs, industrial and transport areas, integrating into the energy, digital, roaming and payment areas of the EU, as well as implementing the Green Deal.

After the meeting in Brussels, Josep Borrell explained in his press remarks that the Ukrainian Foreign Minister had briefed EU ministers on the latest developments as regards the Russian aggression against Ukraine, which 'showed that the situation on the ground continues being dramatic, worsening day by day'.[5] Borrell declared, 'Russia is trying to destroy Ukraine and the Ukrainian nation, and is, at the same time, unleashing a global food and energy crisis.' He also explained that EU Foreign Ministers had been discussing 'the battle of narratives around who is guilty of what, and which are the causes of the war, and about reasons for the high increase of energy and food prices'. Borrell emphasised that ministers 'were unanimously agreeing on the need to continue standing firmly with Ukraine and lending Ukraine all our support', clearly stating, 'Ukraine needs more arms; we will provide them.' All in all, this was a most welcome response to the Ukrainian Foreign Minister, particularly as regards military aid, as Kuleba spent a lot of his time strongly appealing for more ammunition and weapons.

Borrell also mentioned that they discussed the new sanctions he and the EU Commission had presented to close loopholes and avoid existing measures being circumvented. Borrell underlined that the 'sanctions are working, and that the Russian economy is severely affected'. In response to Russia's military aggression against Ukraine, the EU has put in place unprecedented sanctions, representing some of the toughest measures the Union has ever enacted. These sanctions are designed to reduce the Kremlin's ability to finance the war, impose clear economic and political costs on Russia's political elite and diminish Russia's economic base.

All in all, the EU has so far introduced nineteen packages of sanctions against Russia, coordinated among the EU's allies. They cover a wide set of areas: on individuals, companies and organisations; on visa measures; on import and export bans; on financial and business service measures; sanctions on energy – including Putin's shadow fleet; on transport; on dual-use goods; and on asset recovery and confiscation. The EU, often in coordination with other G7 countries like the US, Canada and the UK, regularly assesses and adjusts the sanctions to enhance their effectiveness and address any emerging issues. In a comment on the latest set of sanctions, EU foreign policy chief and current Vice-President of the European Commission Kaja Kallas said, 'We are putting more pressure on Russia's military industry, Chinese banks that enable sanctions evasion and blocking tech exports used in drones.'[6]

The effective and diligent implementation of sanctions is primarily the responsibility of EU member states. The EU Commission, however, works closely to provide support in this work. It does this through regular expert group meetings on sanctions implementation; the 'Freeze and Seize Task Force', tasked with ensuring better coordination of asset freezes against Russian and Belarussian individuals and entities; a high level group, chaired by an EU commissioner, which allows all twenty-seven member states to share information together with representatives of EU industry and businesses; and ad hoc stakeholder meetings held by the Commission that provide guidance and enable a discussion on sanction implementation with operators. In addition, the EU has taken steps to avoid the circumvention of sanctions, including through the establishment of a special monitoring commission.

National systems differ significantly regarding the criminalisation of the violation of EU sanctions, including as regards the nature of the offence (criminal or administrative) and the penalties applied. Andriy Zayats, the head of the Council of Europe's office in Brussels, explains, 'To make it easier to investigate, prosecute and punish violations of EU restrictive measures and ensure their uniform implementation in all member states, the Commission adopted on 2 December 2022 a proposal for a directive to harmonise criminal offences and penalties for such violations.'[7] An EU directive on the definition of criminal offences and penalties for the violation of EU restrictive measures was adopted on 24 April 2024 and entered into force on 19 May 2024.

In his speech, Foreign Minister Kuleba welcomed the announcements of new sanctions but insisted that 'all Russian television channels must be banned from European cable and satellite networks'. He explained that 'this is not about the freedom of speech, but about depriving Russia of tools to spread disinformation and state propaganda'. He also made a more subtle point for EU ministers to reflect upon:

> Russia keeps saying sanctions don't work. At the same time, they use every opportunity to try to lift them. Why? Because sanctions *do* work –they weaken Russia's ability to wage the war. We need to maintain and step up the pressure until Putin's war machine malfunctions. With higher pressure, he will have to back down.

Through various conflicts, it has been a difficult exercise to assess the real impact of international sanctions but Russian officials have publicly acknowledged that they were surprised by the scope and depth of the sanctions that were imposed against the Russian

Federation after the invasion. According to Daniel W. Drezner at the Fletcher School of Law and Diplomacy at Tufts University,

> While sanctions may not have deterred Russia, it remains possible that they succeeded as a more general form of deterrence. If other actors contemplated similar irredentist violations of territorial sovereignty but were persuaded by the punitive nature of the Russia sanctions, that would be a significant policy accomplishment. Relatedly, sanctions also serve as a means of norms enforcement. Violations of Westphalian territorial sovereignty are among the most transgressive acts in modern world politics. It makes sense that states defending those norms would need to use sanctions. Finally, the sanctions might accelerate – on both sides – a degree of necessary economic autonomy. The less dependent that Europe is on imports of Russian energy, for example, the less anxiety there is on the continent about the future.[8]

Addressing international media, Josep Borrell also highlighted that the EU will continue to support Ukraine in implementing 'the reform agenda on its European perspective, after Ukraine has been considered and granted the status of candidate country'. The advice and assistance provided by the EU and EU countries are crucial for Ukraine. Due to Kyiv's accelerated reform efforts, EU leaders officially acknowledged at the special European Council meeting on 9 February 2023 the 'considerable efforts that Ukraine has demonstrated'. They also encouraged Ukraine to do even more to progress further in fulfilling the conditions specified in the Commission's opinion of 17 June 2022.

The next milestone in Ukraine's journey to becoming an EU member came on 8 November 2023, when the EU Commission issued its annual Ukraine Report for 2023. In the report, the Commission concluded that Ukraine had completed four out of the seven requirements, but that more needs to be done in the following areas:[9]

- 'Further strengthen the fight against corruption, in particular high level, through proactive and efficient investigations, and a credible track-record of prosecutions and convictions; complete the appointment of a new Head of the Specialised Anti-Corruption Prosecutor's Office through certifying the winner of the competition and launch and complete the selection process and appointment of a new Director of the National Anti-Corruption Bureau in Ukraine.' It's worth noting that G7 countries have strongly emphasised the importance of combating corruption in Ukraine, also in light of the extraordinary efforts needed to rebuild and reconstruct Ukraine after the war. According to the World Bank, as of 31 December 2025, the total cost of reconstruction and recovery in Ukraine over the next decade is estimated at $588 billion.
- 'Implement the anti-oligarch law to limit the excessive influence of oligarchs in economic, political, and public life; this should be done in a legally sound manner, taking into account the forthcoming opinion of the Venice Commission on relevant legislation.' The recommendations of the Venice Commission of the Council of Europe were issued in June 2023.
- 'Finalise the reform of the legal framework for national minorities, currently under preparation as recommended by the Venice Commission, and adopt immediate and effective mechanisms.'

On 4 November 2023, Ursula von der Leyen was invited to address the Ukrainian Parliament (the Verkhovna Rada), during an official visit to Kyiv. She gave an extraordinary and rather detailed overview of the long and complex road to Ukrainian EU membership, focusing on the Ukrainian achievements thus far:

> I remember very well when, one year ago, we presented the seven necessary steps to accompany Ukraine's candidate status on its way towards the European Union. Some said they were too ambitious. But your reaction was extraordinary. All your democratic institutions have mobilised at maximum to fulfil the desire of the Ukrainian people. As President Zelenskyy said, you did not ask for discounts or shortcuts. Instead, you have shown that Ukrainian democracy can deliver. The breadth and depth of the reforms you have passed is amazing and astonishing. The constitutional justice reform. The selection of the High Council of Justice. The Anti-Corruption Programme. Progress against money laundering. Important measures to curb the oligarchs' grip on your public life. The new media law. And progress on national minorities. We know that this has not always been easy. But this is the normal path of any democracy. We discuss. We disagree. We discuss even harder. Then, we find solutions. And then, we deliver. [...] And you have made great strides, much greater than anyone expected from a country at war. You are undergoing deep reforms, while fighting a full-scale war. The goal is truly within reach. Continuing to strengthen even further your anti-corruption efforts, passing the law on lobbying, strengthening the asset declaration framework in two aspects and addressing the remaining recommendations of the Venice Commission on national minorities, including education – these are measures that are necessary to fulfil completely the seven steps.

Then she came to her rallying call:

> You can make it. And you can make it swiftly. You have already completed way over 90 per cent. And we will continue to provide all the technical and political support you need. I am confident that you can reach your ambitious goal: that is, for the historic decision to open the process of accession negotiations to be taken already this year.[10]

The European Commission President proved to be entirely correct in her wishes and expectations in Kyiv. At the end of the year, on 14 December 2023, EU leaders decided to open accession negotiations with Ukraine; they invited the European Council to adopt the negotiation framework, once the relevant steps set out in the Commission's annual report on Ukraine, adopted on 8 November 2023, had been taken. Only three months later, on 21 March 2024, the European Council adopted the draft negotiation framework for Ukraine, as well as for Moldova.

In a moving statement on the same day, Kuleba declared,

> This is a big day for Ukraine, Moldova and the European Union. All twenty-seven EU member states have approved negotiating frameworks, and practical EU accession talks are scheduled to begin next week. We thank the European Council and the Belgian Presidency in the European Union for making history. [...] Ukraine's path to today has not been easy, involving a revolution and a war. But, thanks to the Ukrainian people's bravery, we have not let anyone or anything derail our historic trajectory. Ukraine is a nation on the move. Nothing can stop it from realising its European dream or the wheels of history from turning.

He went on to say that

> Ukraine has also set a record by moving from the EU membership bid to the start of negotiations in just over two years, faster than any other candidate in history. At the same time, no discounts were given. Ukraine diligently met all of the requirements and implemented critical reforms to enable this historic day. We accomplished this despite fighting a total war for our survival. As an EU member, Ukraine will strengthen security and prosperity for all Europeans while also making significant contributions to our shared European defence, foreign policy, green transition, digitalisation, innovation, culture, economic development, and other areas. What happens next is the process of negotiations. It will take time. But we are certain that we will accomplish this path. Most importantly, today's decision reinforces the EU's position as a global player and a powerful political force, realising Europeans' dream of living on a continent of freedom, prosperity, and peace.

The next step, as Kuleba suggested, was to start the official negotiations on Ukraine's future membership. The so-called 'accession negotiations' take place in an intergovernmental conference between ministers and ambassadors of the EU member states and the candidate country. Ukraine's was held in Luxembourg on 25 June 2024. The delegation of Ukraine was led by Olha Stefanishyna, Deputy Prime Minister for European and Euro-Atlantic Integration. The EU delegation was led by Hadja Lahbib, Belgium's Minister of Foreign and European Affairs, who underlined in her opening statement that this was 'a historic day for Ukraine and the EU' and that 'the accession negotiations will be rigorous and demanding. With determination and commitment, we are confident that Ukraine can bring them to a successful conclusion. The future of Ukraine and its citizens lies within the European Union.'[11]

At the conference, the EU side also presented the negotiating framework, taking into account the experience of past enlargements and ongoing accession negotiations, as well as the evolving EU acquis (the accumulated legislation, acts and decisions that form EU law). It also duly reflected Ukraine's own merits and specific characteristics, and most importantly outlined key aspects of the process and methodology. As a future member state, Ukraine was expected to adhere to the values set out in Article 2 in the Treaty of the European Union, namely respect for human dignity, freedom, democracy, equality, the rule of law and respect for human rights, including the rights of persons belonging to national minorities.[12]

For the purpose of screening and the subsequent negotiations, the EU acquis was broken down into a number of chapters, each covering a specific policy area, with the chapters categorised into six groups. One group, known as the 'fundamentals', included chapters on: Judiciary and Fundamental Rights (Chapter 23); Justice, Freedom and Security (Chapter 24); Economic Criteria; Functioning of Democratic Institutions; Public Administration Reform; Public Procurement (Chapter 5); Statistics (Chapter 18); and Financial Control/External Audit (Chapter 32).[13] Ukraine was invited to prepare and adopt a 'road map' for both the functioning of democratic institutions and for public administration reform. In addition, Ukraine was invited to adopt an 'action plan' on the protection of the rights of persons belonging to national minorities and implement in good faith relevant bilateral agreements with EU member states.[14]

In parallel with the enlargement process, the EU and Ukraine would continue to cooperate to strengthen their political and economic relations, including through the Eastern Partnership (2009). Since 2017, an Association Agreement (AA) between the EU and Ukraine, which includes a far-reaching Deep and Comprehensive Free Trade Area (DCFTA), is in force. Partners have been continuously working on its implementation, aimed at further deepening Ukraine's political association and economic integration with the EU.

On 27 June 2024 in Brussels, the Joint Security Commitments between Ukraine and the European Union were signed by Zelenskyy, Charles Michel (President of the European Council) and Ursula von der Leyen. These agreements enshrined a multilateral, long-term commitment by all member states to provide Ukraine with broad support for ten years, in various key areas including military, financial, humanitarian and political assistance. At the same time, the document set out long-term commitments to support Ukraine until it joins the EU, as well as the readiness of the European Union and its member states to support Ukraine on its path to full membership.[15]

Despite all of the above, it is hard to make an accurate assessment of how the negotiations on Ukraine's accession to the EU will develop and proceed. It seems clear, however, that the accession will be a merit-based process, one that ensures Ukraine is ready before joining. In such comprehensive and complex negotiations, both setbacks and quick wins can be expected. What seems clear, though, is that progress on the 'fundamentals' cluster will determine the overall pace of the negotiations. In an initital report on the enlargement process, dated 17 December 2024, the EU Council welcomed the fact that

> the screening process [of Ukrainian legislation for compliance with EU law] is progressing according to plan and [we look]

> forward to its conclusion and to the next steps in Ukraine's accession process by opening clusters, starting with the fundamentals cluster as soon as possible, when conditions are met.

'We expect that the European Commission's report on the results of the screening within Cluster 1 (fundamentals) will allow us to open this cluster as soon as possible in 2025,' declared Olha Stefanishyna, chief negotiator, Deputy Prime Minister and Minister of Justice of Ukraine.[16] In a statement from the European Council on 20 March 2025, twenty-six EU countries reiterated

> the inherent right of Ukraine to choose its own destiny, based on the UN Charter and international law. The European Union will intensify support for Ukraine's reform efforts on its path towards EU membership. The European Council underlines the importance of progress in the negotiating process in line with the merit-based approach, opening clusters when the conditions are met, starting with the fundamentals cluster as soon as possible.

In the latest assessment from November 2025 by the EU Commission on the enlargement and the ongoing negotiation process, it was stated,

> Ukraine has met the conditions required to open clusters: one (fundamentals), six (external relations), and two (internal market). The Commission expects Ukraine to meet the conditions to open the remaining three clusters and works to ensure that the Council is in a position to take forward the opening of all clusters before the end of the year. The Ukrainian government has signalled its objective to close accession negotiations by the end

> of 2028. The Commission is committed to support this ambitious objective but considers that to meet it an acceleration of the pace of reforms is required, notably with regards to the fundamentals, in particular rule of law.[17]

On the EU side, there seems to be both overwhelming political support for Ukraine and a simultaneous acknowledgement that the negotiations may take some time. The absorption capacity of the EU must be readapted, which implies changes to EU treaties and internal reforms, it has been claimed. 'We need an ambitious reform agenda to ensure the functioning of a larger Union and to increase democratic legitimacy. While reforms were necessary before, with enlargement they become indispensable,' Ursula von der Leyen stated in a speech to the European Parliament on 18 July 2024. In any case, the personality and role of the EU Enlargement Commissioner, Slovenia's Marta Kos, will be very important. 'Overall, 2025 was a year of significant progress for EU enlargement,' she pointed out. 'Montenegro, Albania, Ukraine and Moldova stand out. They advanced most on reforms in the past year. At the current pace and quality of reforms, we may be able to conclude accession negotiations in the coming years.'[18]

At the same time, a reference to Ukraine joining the EU in 2027 has been included in the drafts of the US-led twenty-point peace plan, which has triggered an urgent, internal discussion in Brussels that might dramatically alter the current accession rules, agreed back in 1993. One of the options that is being discussed is to offer Ukraine a 'special arrangement' or an 'enlargement-lite' option that will enable Ukraine to join the bloc very soon, but with far fewer decision-making powers. The country will gain incremental access to part of the European Union's single market, its agricultural subsidies and internal development funding, after meeting post-membership milestones. 'Extraordinary times call for extraordinary measures,' as a senior EU diplomat put it in an interview with the *Financial Times*, while explaining that 'we are enlarging the concept of enlargement, as the rules were written more than thirty years ago. And they need to be more flexible. This is a once-in-a-generation moment, and we have to meet it'. But it is important to note that some EU countries have a deep unease with this new concept, as they feel it could have a negative impact on the bloc's future stability, cheapening the value of membership and upsetting other candidate countries such as Montenegro and Albania.[19]

In another major development, the EU adopted a set of legislative proposals to secure continuous financial support to Ukraine for 2026 and 2027, by establishing a support loan for Ukraine for an amount of €90 billion.

Russia's war of aggression against Ukraine has no doubt prompted an overhaul of the entire enlargement policy of the European Union, ushering in a period of heightened engagement and outreach in Brussels, although not all twenty-seven EU countries see eye-to-eye on the enlargement process. Hungary has openly expressed a view that Ukraine's membership in the EU is not realistic for a long time and demanded, among other things, that Kyiv needs to do more to protect the rights of the ethnic Hungarians living in Ukraine. Regarding this, President Zelenskyy said in a speech to EU colleagues last year,

> It's simply anti-European when one person blocks decisions that are important for the entire continent or that have already been agreed upon. Ukraine fulfilled the requirements, but right now,

> there are serious difficulties in opening Ukraine's first [...] negotiation clusters for EU accession. European efforts that should be bringing more security and peace are also constantly being obstructed. And I believe this is wrong. Europe must have a way to prevent individual actors from blocking what's necessary for all.[20]

Despite diverging views inside the EU, both Ukraine and Moldova became candidate countries in June 2022, with Georgia becoming a candidate in December 2023, on the understanding that Tbilisi takes the relevant steps as set out in a Commission recommendation. In late 2024, however, Georgian Prime Minister Irakli Kobakhidze issued a statement explaining his party's decision not to pursue the opening of EU accession negotiations and rejecting EU financial support until 2028. In a joint statement by Kaja Kallas and Marta Kos, it was noted that Georgia's announcement 'marks a shift from the policies of all previous Georgian governments and the European aspirations of the vast majority of the Georgian people, as enshrined in the Constitution of Georgia'. At the end of the statement the EU leaders underlined that 'the EU stands with the Georgian people and their choice for a European future. The door to the EU remains open and the return of Georgia to European values and the EU accession path is in the hands of the Georgian leadership.'[21]

To complete our overview, it can be added here that Brussels has started talks with the six Western Balkan countries, after years of stalemate. To conclude, in the epilogue to his celebrated memoirs of the Second World War, Sir Winston Churchill offered some far-reaching observations regarding the European movement and European integration that remain relevant today:

> In large enterprises it is a mistake to try to settle everything at

> once. In matters of this kind, it was not possible to plan movements as in a military operation. We were not acting in the field of force, but in the domain of opinion. I several times stressed my views on this point. It was of importance that when the inevitable lulls, delays and obstacles occurred we should not be considered to have abandoned our ultimate goal. Moreover, I did not wish to compete with governments in the executive sphere. The task was to build up moral, cultural, sentimental and social unities and affinities throughout Europe.
>
> The European Movement gained greatly in vigour and strength and played a substantial part in governmental thinking. General Marshall [former US Secretary of State and Secretary of Defense under President Harry S. Truman] referred to the concept as one of the reasons which had led him to his plan for economic aid to Europe. The culmination of many discussions that took place came in the creation of the Council of Europe in 1949, with its seat in Strasbourg. With varying fortunes and shades of publicity much useful work was done in Strasbourg. There are those who are disappointed that the rapid creation of a federation of European States did not ensue, but there is every justification for a slow and empirical approach. Such weighty matters cannot be imposed on people from above, however brilliant the planning. They must grow gradually from genuine and widely held convictions.[22]

Perhaps this is exactly what we are seeing in Europe today, a necessity to act and strengthen the EU and incite further European integration – most importantly, the accession of Ukraine, Moldova and others, in light of the fundamental threat the continent is facing and at a time when the US is shifting its focus elsewhere. In addition, given the many challenges of multilateralism and the crumbling of the rules-based international order, a stronger European will to act – 'growing gradually from genuine and widely held convictions' – will help to create a continent capable of defending itself. It will help Europe to project its fundamental interests and once again contain and curtail an old ghost that is haunting us once more – namely the rise of violent and aggressive nationalism.

'We are living in the most momentous and dangerous of times,' concludes Ursula von der Leyen. 'Europe is ready to assume its responsibilities. ReArm Europe could mobilise close to €800 billion for a safe and resilient Europe. We will continue working closely with our partners in NATO. This is a moment for Europe. And we are ready to step up.'[23]

'EU admission is particularly crucial, as it would make Ukraine a full-fledged member of the West,' concludes Kuleba.

> To arm Ukraine without bringing it into the EU would mean preserving Putin's hope of one day dragging it back into his sphere of influence. Europe, of course, is mostly responsible for Kyiv's accession. But Washington is also essential to the process. President Trump may be the only person capable of swaying Hungarian Prime Minister Viktor Orban, who is friendly with Putin, to stop blocking the EU from advancing Ukraine's integration.[24]

STATEMENT BY DMYTRO KULEBA

18 JULY 2022, EU FOREIGN AFFAIRS COUNCIL, BRUSSELS

Dear High Representative, dear Commissioner, dear colleagues and friends,

I am grateful to the EU High Representative Josep Borrell for the invitation to exchange views. It is important to focus together on the prospects of Russian aggression against Ukraine and ways to jointly protect Europe from security and economic challenges posed by aggressive Russia. By acting in unity, we will overcome them.

We meet together for the first time since the historic decision to grant Ukraine EU candidate status. I am deeply grateful to each one of your countries, dear colleagues, for making this historic step. This was a moment of strength and unity for the EU, for Ukraine and for the whole of Europe. I commend the EU for living up to the scale of the challenges. What we face now is truly unprecedented in our lifetime.

We have seen horrific Russian missile terror in Ukraine over the past weeks. July 14th, a peaceful Ukrainian city of Vinnytsia, hundreds of kilometres from the front line. Morning, the city centre, a beautiful Ukrainian mother and her sweet four-year-old daughter. She posts an Instagram story talking and smiling to her kid. Less than an hour later a Russian cruise missile that has flown all the way from the Black Sea strikes the place. The child dies immediately and the mother is severely injured. Twenty-four people died; many dozens were wounded. The Russians knew exactly where they were striking and that no military objects were anywhere around. That was their goal. They want to spread fear and provoke reprisal; this is pure terror. Russia must be legally and politically recognised a terrorist state, while we all must realise what kind of evil we are dealing with.

It is wrong and naive to think that Russia's goals are limited to Ukraine. Putin's plan is not only to destroy my country, but to plunge the whole of Europe into crisis. You can already see how he uses Europe's every dependence on Russia to achieve his goals. This is why getting rid of such dependencies is the only way forward. Aggressive and revanchist Russia is the greatest threat to Europe and the major source of problems facing our continent today.

Putin wants to steal normal life and stability from every European family – be it by energy blackmail and rising prices, shortages of agricultural goods, by propaganda and lies or by attempting to destabilise governments.

Russia's true objective is the immiseration of Europe. He wants Europeans and Russians to live equally badly. He wants to turn public opinion against acting governments in the hope to replace them with radical forces that would be more favourable to Russia.

We have seen this movie before, in the years following Russia's invasion of Ukraine in 2014. One difference now is that Moscow is more aggressive; the other difference is that we have experience and know their playbook. Let's be smarter, faster and tougher than Putin this time so we can outsmart him and make his plan fail.

Backing down and bowing to his demands will not work; it has never worked. This is a trap. I am sure that in the following weeks there will be more Kremlin-leaning voices nudging the public opinion into giving Putin what he wants so that he leaves Europe alone. We should actively counter these narratives. Not only will he not leave Ukraine and Europe alone if we satisfy his ultimatums, but he will increase pressure and blackmail.

If Russia senses weakness now, the consequences will be far

worse than what we are seeing now. We must defeat Russia. Don't worry about cornering Putin. Russian propaganda will find a way to make any defeat look like a win.

There will be no return to business as usual with Russia in the foreseeable future. As the greatest source of threats to Europe, Russia must be fully isolated. And the best way to counter Russia and reduce its malicious influence in Europe is to support Ukraine and enable a Ukrainian victory.

With sufficient and timely assistance, Ukraine can and will prevail, while the EU needs to stay the course and remain unfaltering in the face of Russian bullying.

Russia keeps saying sanctions don't work. At the same time, they use every opportunity to try to lift them. Why? Because sanctions *do* work – they weaken Russia's ability to wage the war. We need to maintain and step up the pressure until Putin's war machine malfunctions. With higher pressure, he will have to back down.

The recent sanctions packages are an important breakthrough but in order to deter Russia we should keep moving further with restrictive measures like energy embargoes, including on oil, gas and coal imports.

I welcome announcements of new EU sanctions. I am grateful for including my proposals outlined in the letter to the High Representative and closing loopholes for sanctions circumvention. I also insist that all Russian television channels must be banned from European cable and satellite networks. This is not about freedom of speech, but about depriving Russia of tools to spread disinformation and state propaganda.

Energy is key, and I urge all of you to expedite decisions on a price cap for Russian oil. Our next target must be Russian maritime logistics.

Weapons assistance is essential. Ukraine is grateful for all the support provided so far but as the war rages on, we need more, in particular long-range artillery and air-defence systems. Strengthening Ukraine now is the best investment in long-term security and stability of Europe.

We welcome today's decision to allocate the fifth package of financial assistance worth €500 million under the European Peace Facility.

Let's also forget the narrative of war fatigue. No one has ever wanted this war except Russia, and we all want it to be over as soon as possible. But the only way to achieve lasting peace is for Ukraine to win. This includes overcoming fatigue and the attempts of Russia to amplify it.

Russian propaganda aims to increase war fatigue, discredit Ukraine and reduce its support. This includes groundless accusations of potential weapons smuggling to undermine military aid, as well as persuading that sanctions are inefficient. I am grateful to the EU for countering these claims, including the prompt response to disinformation on weapons.

Ukraine ensures that all procedures for obtaining, storing and using weapons are transparent. Our control system functions well.

Dear colleagues, while living through the horror of the ongoing aggression and terrorism, we need to think about the future. Because it is the future that we are protecting from Russia's attempts to drag us all into the worst times of the past.

As an EU candidate country, Ukraine is committed to proceeding on our path towards EU membership and we have already taken action.

We are determined to implement the steps defined by the European Commission in its conclusions, and we have elaborated a special road map and an action plan of legislative and executive steps towards the membership criteria.

We will further bring our legislation closer to EU legislation at an accelerated pace and in accordance with the list of priority European Integration bills for 2022.

We proceed with implementing crucial reforms, in particular to strengthen rule of law and anti-corruption institutions.

We keep working on integrating into the EU internal market and advancing sectoral integration. Our priorities are removing all barriers in the customs, industrial and transport areas, integrating into the energy, digital, roaming and payment areas of the EU, as well as implementing the Green Deal.

We have our homework and are determined to do it properly. We rely on the same approach of our partners.

Dear friends, in almost five months of the new wave of war, Russia has violated each and every basic human right. Forced deportation of Ukrainian citizens to Russia, filtration camps, mass murders, genocide, rapes: everything the world faced during the Second World War has once again become a reality for Europe.

Missile terror is just another stage of Russia's barbaric war on humanity.

Once again, I thank the EU High Representative Josep Borrell and Commissioner Lenarčič for their statement on Russian attacks against civilian targets released on July 14th.

We must spare no effort to ensure accountability for violations of human rights and international humanitarian law, as well as Russian terrorism and deliberate targeting of civilians. I welcome all relevant efforts. It is important to note that none of these crimes would be possible without the crime of aggression, as such. This is why Ukraine has initiated a special tribunal for the crime of aggression against Ukraine and I encourage all of you to look into this initiative and consider joining it.

Weapons, sanctions and accountability are the three ways to restore peace, enhance security and protect stability in Europe.

Every moment of doubt, every prolongation in taking the strict measures against Moscow cost hundreds of lives. Today, these are the lives of Ukrainians, but we do not know how far Russia is ready to go.

Russia's war costs Putin more in manpower and hardware than he anticipated and provokes unity that he did not expect. In order to counter the Russian threat, we should implement a long-term strategy of isolation, containment and defence.

The weaker Putin becomes in Ukraine, the weaker his grip on Europe will be.

I look forward to your discussion today and to listening to your views.

Thank you once again for your attention and the opportunity to join you today.

CHAPTER 10

NATO: PAST, PRESENT, FUTURE

Russia's economy is on a war footing.
Danger is moving towards us at full speed.

MARK RUTTE, SECRETARY-GENERAL OF NATO

When the North Atlantic Treaty was signed in 1949, President Harry S. Truman referred to the resultant creation of NATO as a 'neighbourly act'. 'We are like a group of householders,' he said, 'who express their community of interests by entering into an association for their mutual protection.' At the same time, Canadian Secretary of State Lester Pearson said, 'The North Atlantic community is part of the world community, and as we grow stronger to preserve the peace, all free men and women grow stronger with us.' Prime Minister Paul-Henri Spaak of Belgium added, 'The new NATO pact is purely defensive; it threatens no one. It should therefore disturb no one, except those who might foster the criminal idea of having recourse to war.'

'Though all the world has changed since these statements were made, the verities they express have not,' emphasised US Secretary of State Madeleine K. Albright in 1999, fifty years after the creation of NATO.

> Our alliance still is bound together by a community of interests. Our strength still is a source of strength to those everywhere who labour for freedom and peace. Our power still shields those who love the law and still threatens none, except those who would threaten others with aggression and harm. Our alliance endures because the principles it defends are timeless and because they reflect the deepest aspirations of the human spirit.[1]

The Czech Republic, Hungary and Poland became members in NATO's first post-Cold War round of enlargement in 1999. The Membership Action Plan (MAP) was launched that same year at the alliance's Washington summit in April, to help countries who aspired to NATO membership with their preparations. The second post-Cold War round of enlargement involved Bulgaria, Estonia, Latvia, Lithuania, Romania, Slovakia and Slovenia, which were invited to begin accession talks at NATO's Prague summit in 2002. On 29 March 2004, they all became members of the alliance, making this the largest wave of enlargement in NATO's history. All seven countries participated in the MAP before acceding to NATO. Importantly, the critical reform processes the MAP triggered in the new member states also proved fundamental to possible later membership in the EU. But participation in the MAP does not in any way prejudge any decision by the alliance on future NATO membership. Indeed, the MAP process can last several years (for the Republic of North Macedonia, the process took nearly twenty-one years, from 1999 to 2020).

As we have touched on in previous chapters, at the NATO Summit in Bucharest in 2008, important decisions were taken as regards both Georgia and Ukraine. In the final declaration, NATO welcomed the nation's aspirations for membership, while underlining that 'MAP is the next step for Ukraine and Georgia on their direct way to membership. Today we make clear that we support these countries' applications for MAP.'[2] As we have seen, this is a way for NATO leaders to indirectly promise future membership while suggesting preparation and patience in the meantime. Looking back, Dmytro Kuleba is far more candid and blunt in his assessment of the famous 'invitation' in Bucharest.

> At NATO's 2008 summit in Bucharest, members agreed to make Ukrainian membership an objective but spent more time signalling to Russia that this would not happen (at least at any point in the foreseeable future) than taking practical steps to make it a reality. The alliance expressed its will to keep the door to membership open, in other words, but only on the assumption that Ukraine will not darken NATO's doorstep any time soon. Three wars later – in Georgia in 2008, in Ukraine in 2014 and now again in Ukraine – it is clear that ambiguity is Putin's best ally.[3]

In other words, NATO left Ukraine and Georgia in a perilous limbo by declaring that those countries would join the alliance sometime in the future but providing no timetable and no military protection. Putin, all too predictably, exploited the ambiguity to dismember both countries in the six years that followed. Hal Brands, of Johns Hopkins University School of Advanced International Studies, stresses, 'But even after Russia invaded and illegally annexed Crimea in 2014 – the most egregious act of conquest in Europe since 1945 – it encountered only a half-hearted Western response.'[4]

Despite the categorical condemnation of the Russian invasion of Ukraine in 2022 and extraordinary efforts – including vital economic and military assistance offered to Ukraine by a large number of NATO countries – there remains a lingering reluctance among some NATO allies when it comes to full Ukrainian membership. Various arguments have been voiced, both formally and informally, in this regard. Let us go through some of the most critical ones.

First of all, it has been argued that the alliance cannot offer Ukraine security guarantees, nor full membership, given the country is currently at war, particularly as NATO's Article 5 guarantees that an attack against one member will be considered an attack against all.[5] The former US Ambassador to NATO, Ivo Daalder, warns, 'The problem confronting NATO countries is that as long as the conflict continues, bringing Ukraine into the Alliance is tantamount to joining the war.'[6]

Despite this, with the requisite political will discussions can take place and solutions can be found to identify appropriate transitional arrangements to help secure membership, while avoiding thirty-two NATO countries automatically becoming direct parties to the current war. As Kuleba pointed out in a key speech at the NATO Ukraine Commission in Brussels on 4 April 2023 (appended to this chapter),

> We are realistic people. We don't seek to drag you into the war. This is our war, and we are fighting it successfully with your generous support. We have never requested anyone's boots on the ground and we have no such intention. We don't seek a magic wand that will end the war instead of winning it on the battlefield. What we seek and what we ask you for is a simple thing: a clear signal to Russia that the game is over. Ukraine is part of the West;

it's at the doorstep of NATO, and it will walk in rather sooner than later.

There is certainly room for some pragmatism and ingenuity. During its 75-year history, NATO has not always imposed 'one-size-fits-all' membership requirements; some countries have been able to negotiate adjusted or modified terms. France, for example, remained an ally even after President Charles de Gaulle withdrew France from NATO's integrated military command in the mid-1960s. Two other examples are even more relevant – Norway and West Germany – both of which found ways of joining the alliance despite specific challenges.

As a matter of fact, the Norwegian government issued a unilateral declaration on 1 February 1949, two months before the formation of NATO, stating that it would not 'make available for the armed forces of foreign powers bases on Norwegian territory, as long as Norway is not attacked or subject to the threat of attack'. It later added similar restrictions on nuclear weapons on Norwegian territory.[7] This was a unilateral declaration with a necessary degree of flexibility or dynamism, and it was the prerogative of the Norwegian government to interpret the content of the declaration. The latest example of the flexible application of this unilateral declaration is the so-called SDCA (Supplementary Defence Cooperation Agreement) with the United States. This gives the US access to several bases/areas in Norway (Evenes, Ramsund, Rygge and Sola). Some observers have pointed out that this could be a source of possible tension in relation to the declaration and the traditional Norwegian 'base policy', but both the government and Parliament in Norway believe it is an appropriate arrangement and within the scope of the unilateral declaration (Sweden, Finland and Denmark have subsequently entered into similar agreements with the United States).

As for West Germany's path to NATO membership in 1955, this shows how a state can potentially become a NATO member despite being divided. M. E. Sarotte of Johns Hopkins School of Advanced International Studies stated in an article in *Foreign Affairs* in 2024,

> Given the lessons in these models, leaders of NATO member states should, in private, encourage Kyiv to do three things: first, define a provisional, militarily defensible border. Second, agree to self-limitations on infrastructure on unoccupied territory (such as the permanent stationing of foreign troops or nuclear weapons) with the important Norwegian disclaimer that these limits are valid only as long as Ukraine is not under attack or threat of attack. Third, and most painful, undertake not to use military force beyond that border except in self-defence, as the West Germans did, in order to assure NATO allies that they won't suddenly find themselves at war with Russia as soon as Ukraine becomes a member. The cost of this step would be acceptance of open-ended division, but the benefit would be to give most of Ukraine a safe haven in NATO. Once settled, Kyiv and the alliance would go public with these agreements. NATO could amplify Kyiv's unilateral statement with a similar declaration. The goal would be for independent Ukraine to join NATO as soon as feasible. While these announcements would, taken together, represent a fait accompli – that is, they would not be negotiated with Russia – there would still be an implicit negotiation: instead of a land-for-peace deal, the carrot would be no infrastructure for peace.

As a matter of fact, what Zelenskyy and the Ukrainian government have been requesting is not *immediate* membership in NATO but a concrete *timetable* for Ukraine's future accession to NATO. In this regard, Kuleba has said, 'To put an end to this story of lost opportunities, it is necessary to finally make a decision that is long overdue: to define specific plans and prospects for Ukraine's accession to NATO.'

In Kyiv, there is certainly an understanding that such a process will take some time, but what is needed now is a political commitment and appreciation among NATO allies that Ukraine is more than qualified to join. Ukraine can also be an asset and can contribute significantly to the overall military strength of the alliance, a point that Kuleba underlined in his speech at the NATO–Ukraine Commission in Brussels:

> We gratefully receive a lot of your vitally important assistance. At the same time, you benefit, as we are literally testing NATO principles in a real fight right now and we are already actively sharing our conclusions with specialists in NATO member states. The invaluable experience of Ukrainian defenders serves as a guide for further strengthening and reforming the alliance so that NATO member states are fully prepared to deter aggressors and conduct modern high-intensity warfare. This process of mutual learning is a two-way street, and I take this opportunity to thank allies who are actively training our defenders. The amount and quality of training are two of the crucial advantages we have over Russian forces in this war.

In addition to this defensive strength, Ukraine has unparalleled experience in countering hybrid threats, information warfare and counterpropaganda. The country has been highly successful in ensuring the cyber-resilience of its state institutions and critical infrastructure.

In an interesting report on what the armed forces in NATO should learn from Ukraine's homeland defence, prepared by Nico Lange of European think tank GLOBSEC, several valuable lessons are highlighted. These include the success Ukraine has achieved with small, highly mobile military units; the importance of operating with decentralised networks with much command-and-control responsibility at lower and intermediate levels; the ubiquitous use of drones en masse for many operational purposes; how the entirety of Ukrainian society is engaged in total defence through data-based means in the newest of ways; and how Ukraine is leading the renaissance of artillery but in an expanded, advanced form.[8]

'We started this as the first world war with drones,' explains Oleksandr Kamyshin, an adviser to the Ukrainian government. The trenches that used to define the front lines are disappearing, since they are too vulnerable to drone attacks. Instead, soldiers are scattered into foxholes in groups of two or three. By the same token, drones with bigger payloads have made tanks far too vulnerable to lead assaults or even to venture within ten kilometres of the front line. And then there are the naval drones that have neutralised the Russian Black Sea fleet.[9] In many ways, Ukraine's fight represents a watershed in modern warfare. Kyiv has shown that it is possible to hold a stronger adversary at bay with advanced, affordable and adaptable drones and other defence technologies.[10]

For the same reason, due to Ukraine's extensive war experience, there is already an agreement among allies that it is unnecessary for the country to be the subject of a MAP process outlining specific benchmarks for the country to meet. This has, of course, been a requirement in past NATO expansion processes, but for Finland

and Sweden, which most recently became members in the alliance, as well as Ukraine, it was decided it would not be necessary to go through a MAP process. A noteworthy new initiative adopted at the NATO Summit in Vilnius in 2023 was the establishment of the NATO–Ukraine Council, replacing the previous NATO–Ukraine Commission, the main benefit being that Ukraine and its allies now sit as equals, signifying the strengthening of political ties and Ukraine's increasing integration with NATO.

Nevertheless, if political leaders in NATO countries continue to make security guarantees and NATO membership dependent on the cessation of hostilities, this simply gives Putin an additional incentive to continue the war so as to prevent Ukrainian membership.

By extension, some NATO members have claimed that admitting new members sharing a border with Russia might provoke Moscow. However, NATO admitted Finland – a nation with the longest European border with the Russian Federation – as a new member on 4 April 2023, while Sweden joined NATO on 7 March 2024. This argument does not, therefore, seem to be consistent or relevant. It's worth noting that Finland is known to have a longstanding and in-depth knowledge of how to handle Russia. In one of his early statements, Finnish President Alexander Stubb encouraged other NATO leaders to be less belligerent in their rhetoric against Russia and instead prepare their armies for a potential conflict. 'What I call on all European states to do is to become more Finnish. In other words, more prepared. You have to prepare for the worst in order to avoid it,' he said.[11] If one analyses the Russian response to Finland joining NATO, Putin and the Russian leadership tried to downplay its significance, presumably to avoid highlighting its own failure to keep Finland (and Sweden) outside the alliance.

A related point, and one we've touched on earlier, is that certain analysts, not only in Moscow but also in the West, have argued that 'NATO expansion' was the main reason why Russia invaded Ukraine. Proponents of such a view include the controversial John Mearsheimer of the University of Chicago[12] and the former US Ambassador to Russia, Jack Matlock, who described NATO enlargement as a 'profound strategic blunder', as well as TV host Tucker Carlson, who broadcast an appalling TV interview with Putin. But, as we have shown, this is a fictitious justification ignoring key historical facts.[13]

NATO expansion has, of course, been a source of longstanding tension between Moscow and the West, dating back to the alliance's creation in 1949 and the subsequent Cold War period. But NATO enlargement was certainly not the main reason for Putin's decision to invade Ukraine in 2022, as there was no movement underway to offer Ukraine membership in NATO at that time. In practice, and as already referred to, there has not been any real movement on this issue since 2008. This is to the great frustration of Ukrainian leaders, as Kuleba has clearly reminded us.[14] In addition, when Russia occupied and illegally annexed Crimea in 2014, Ukraine was officially a non-aligned country with no ambition to join NATO.[15] It was not until December 2014, eight months after Russia invaded Crimea and Donbas, that the Ukrainian Parliament revoked its non-aligned policy.

'Back in 2014, Ukraine was a neutral country, both on paper and in reality,' underlines Kuleba.

> Four years earlier, in July 2010, it had formally put an end to its ambitions for NATO membership when it passed a law clearly stating that it was a non-aligned country that had no intention of joining any military alliance. There was no nationwide public

> discussion of NATO membership back then, either; the Euromaidan protests that began in 2013 centred not on the military alliance but on economic and political integration with the EU. If neutrality failed to stop Putin from launching the war in 2014, it is hard to see why it would stop him now.[16]

There are several examples of the indifference and/or pragmatism that can be seen in the Russian position on NATO, although these examples are duly neglected by the same observers that so readily blame NATO expansion for Russia's invasion. In a speech in London in March 2000, Putin even suggested that Russia might join NATO:

> I do not rule out such a possibility. In the case that Russia's interests will be reckoned with, if it will be an equal partner. Russia is part of European culture, and I do not consider my own country in isolation from Europe. [...] Therefore, it is with difficulty that I imagine NATO as an enemy.[17]

Putin expanded further on this topic during a visit to Washington DC. in November 2001, declaring in an interview that 'Russia acknowledges the role of NATO in the world today' and that 'Russia is prepared to expand its cooperation with this organisation'. Asked directly about the possible future NATO membership of the three Baltic States Lithuania, Latvia and Estonia, he responded, 'We of course are not in a position to tell people what to do. We cannot forbid people to make certain choices if they want to increase the security of their nations in a particular way.'[18] It therefore seems Putin's red line over Ukraine's possible NATO membership did not exist early in his rule. During a joint press conference with Ukrainian President Leonid Kuchma in May 2002, Putin even stated,

> I am absolutely convinced that Ukraine will not shy away from the process of expanding interaction with NATO and the Western allies as a whole. Ukraine has its own relations with NATO. There is the NATO–Ukraine Commission. At the end of the day, the decision is to be taken by NATO and Ukraine. It is a matter for those two partners.[19]

As Russia illegally annexed Crimea and started a civil war with proxies in eastern Ukraine in 2014, he certainly did not need to invade Ukraine again in 2022 with the excuse of preventing NATO expansion – because NATO expansion was not taking place. Therefore, the main reason behind Russia's invasion of Ukraine in February 2022 was that, according to Putin, Ukraine lacked the right to exist as a sovereign country and its independence threatened Russia's existence.[20] In addition, despite numerous efforts from 2014 onwards, Putin failed to destabilise and topple Kyiv's democratic government, even in the face of a Russian-manufactured and -funded civil war in the east of the country. To him, the threat of Ukrainian democracy to Russia remained. Growing impatient and encouraged by his sycophants, the Russian President probably felt he had only one option left to help solve his 'Ukraine problem' once and for all: a full-scale invasion to achieve regime change.[21]

Those who oppose Ukrainian accession to NATO have also argued that Ukraine itself is divided over whether to join the alliance. 'In the past this was true, but no longer,' explains Kuleba.

> Ukrainians have grown steadily more supportive of joining the alliance since 2014, when Russia illegally seized Crimea and ignited a war in the Donbas. In 2019, Ukraine formally amended its Constitution to enshrine its commitment to join NATO. The vast

majority of Ukrainians – 82 per cent, according to a February 2023 poll by the International Republican Institute – now support joining. And there is no longer a regional divide on the issue: a majority of Ukrainians are pro-NATO in all parts of the country.

What is also striking is that the populations of NATO countries increasingly see Ukraine as part of their broader community. According to an EU-wide survey conducted in February 2023, 68 per cent of EU citizens consider Russia's attack on Ukraine an attack on Europe as a whole. This is the view of 80 per cent of Poles and Spaniards, 70 per cent of Dutch people, and 65 per cent of Germans and French.

'Both the leaders of most NATO countries and their publics view Ukraine as an integral part of Western security architecture. It is time to act on these beliefs,' Kuleba has said.[22] Research conducted in Ukraine and fourteen other European countries by the ECFR (European Council on Foreign Relations) in 2024 revealed that Ukraine's determination to fight and European support for arming Ukraine have not been affected by Russian advances on the battlefield. Despite this, many feel that lurking beneath this appearance of unity is a major divide between Ukraine and Europe on how the war should end and what the allied support is destined to achieve. While Ukrainians want more weapons and ammunition to help them win the war, most Europeans want to give Ukraine weapons and ammunitions in order to put Kyiv in a better *negotiating* position to end the war. While Ukrainians think they should be granted membership of the EU and NATO to mark their victory, most Europeans see this as part of a settlement.[23]

It is important to note the major initiatives that NATO countries are taking in further enhancing their support of Ukraine during the war. Most significantly, at the summit in Washington, the allies decided that NATO would create a new structure to help plan, coordinate and arrange delivery of the overall military aid and assistance that Ukraine will receive from the West. Previously, military assistance to Ukraine had been coordinated under the leadership of the US through the Ukraine Defence Contact Group (UDCG, also known as the 'Ramstein group'), but now this has been institutionalised with the establishment of the NATO Security Assistance and Training for Ukraine (NSATU), headquartered in Wiesbaden, Germany. NSATU is comprised of approximately 700 personnel from NATO countries and selected partners. In concrete terms, it has the following three focus areas:

- To oversee training of Ukrainian armed forces at training facilities in allied countries.
- To provide support to the long-term development of Ukraine's Armed Forces.
- To support Ukraine through planning, coordination of donations with allies and partners, transfer of security assistance material and repair of equipment.

In addition, NATO allies have sought to identify and apply lessons from Russia's war against Ukraine, as well as to increase Ukraine's interoperability with NATO. Last but not least, they announced a pledge of long-term security assistance for Ukraine, with the intention of providing minimum funding of €40 billion. 'We will review this level at forthcoming summits to ensure that our support continues to meet Ukraine's needs,' NATO Secretary-General Jens Stoltenberg underlined in 2024 in Washington DC, while pointing out that 'Europeans are more than matching the overall US support for Ukraine. This pledge will ensure greater burden sharing of military support [and will] also provide Ukraine with the reliable support it needs to deter and defend against future Russian aggression now and in the future.'[24] At the Washington summit, NATO allies also made announcements of immediate military aid, including critical air defence, and several NATO countries signed bilateral security agreements with Ukraine, bringing the total number of countries with such agreements to more than twenty.

However, the Trump administration has made things more challenging for the NATO allies. Matthias Matthijs and Nathalie Tocci at Johns Hopkins University School of Advanced International Studies explain,

> The catastrophic Oval Office meeting between Trump and Ukrainian President Volodymyr Zelenskyy in February 2025, in which the latter was berated and humiliated, was an ominous sign that the United States could abandon Ukraine entirely, immediately threatening the security of Europe's eastern flank. As a result, at the NATO summit in June 2025, European allies acknowledged Washington's concerns about burden sharing in Ukraine and in general promised to drastically increase their defense spending to five percent of GDP while also buying a lot more American-made weapons in support of Kyiv's war effort.
>
> Then, after Trump rolled out the red carpet for Russian President Vladimir Putin in Anchorage, Alaska, in mid-August, a group of European leaders, including Zelenskyy, flocked to Washington in a collective effort to sweet-talk Trump. They managed to box in the US President by backing his mediation ambitions and by developing plans for a European 'reassurance force' to be deployed to Ukraine in the event that Trump succeeded in brokering a ceasefire. These careful placation efforts, one can argue,

> have worked: Trump today appears to have much higher regard for European leaders; he seems to have settled on allowing Europeans to buy weapons for Ukraine; he has extended sanctions to the Russian oil companies Lukoil and Rosneft; and he has not actually pulled out of NATO.[25]

It is clear that Ukraine will need enhanced security cooperation and relevant guarantees until it – hopefully – becomes a full member of NATO. A working group on 'international security guarantees' for Ukraine, under the leadership of Anders Fogh Rasmussen, former Secretary-General of NATO, and Andrii Yermak, previous Head of the Office of the President of Ukraine, have worked on a special security concept: the Kyiv Security Compact.[26] In this concept paper, introduced in Kyiv in September 2022, four key recommendations are elaborated.

- First of all, that 'the strongest security guarantee for Ukraine lies in its capacity to defend itself against an aggressor under the UN Charter's Article 51 [on self-defence]. To do so, Ukraine needs the resources to maintain a significant defensive force capable of withstanding the Russian Federation's armed forces and paramilitaries.'
- Second, 'this requires a multi-decade effort of sustained investment in Ukraine's industrial base, scalable weapons transfers and intelligence support from allies, intensive training missions and joint exercises under the European Union and NATO flags'.
- Third, 'the security guarantees will be positive, and lay out a range of commitments made by a group of guarantors, together with Ukraine. They need to be binding, based on bilateral agreements but brought together under a joint strategic partnership document – the Kyiv Security Compact.'

- Finally, 'the Compact will bring a core group of allied countries together with Ukraine. This could include the US, UK, Canada, Poland, Italy, Germany, France, Australia, Turkey and Nordic, Baltic, Central and Eastern European countries.'

Since the Kyiv Security Compact was introduced in 2022, discussions took place among the G7 countries – France, the US, the UK, Germany, Japan, Italy and Canada – which led to the adoption of a strong joint appeal on 12 July 2023, in the margins of the NATO Summit in Vilnius, where it was affirmed 'that the security of Ukraine is integral to the security of the Euro-Atlantic region.'[27] Russia's invasion was also deemed to be 'a threat to international peace and security, a flagrant violation of international law, including the UN Charter, and incompatible with our security interests.' The G7 countries invited other countries wishing to contribute to join this Joint Declaration at any time.

The G7 leaders instructed their teams to begin these discussions immediately, working with Ukraine on 'specific, bilateral, long-term security commitments and arrangements' with the task of:

- Ensuring a sustainable force capable of defending Ukraine now and deterring Russian aggression in the future, through the continued provision of security assistance and modern military equipment, across land, air, and sea domains; prioritising air defence, artillery and long-range fires, armoured vehicles and other key capabilities, such as combat air, and by promoting increased interoperability with Euro-Atlantic partners; support to further develop Ukraine's defence industrial base; training and training exercises for Ukrainian forces; intelligence sharing and cooperation; support for cyber defence, security, and resilience initiatives, including to address hybrid threats.

- Strengthening Ukraine's economic stability and resilience, including through reconstruction and recovery efforts, to create the conditions conducive to promoting Ukraine's economic prosperity, including its energy security.
- Providing technical and financial support for Ukraine's immediate needs stemming from Russia's war, as well as to enable Ukraine to continue implementing the effective reform agenda that will support the good governance necessary to advance towards its Euro-Atlantic aspirations.

So far, thirty-two countries have signed on to this G7 declaration and are holding consultations to conclude bilateral agreements with Ukraine. Over twenty countries, as mentioned, have also signed bilateral security cooperation agreements with Ukraine.[28] 'These bilateral agreements will ensure that Ukrainian forces have the weapons they need to defeat Russia on the battlefield,' emphasised Fogh Rasmussen and Andrii Yermak in a joint article in *Foreign Affairs* in January 2024, while underlining that 'commitments to protect Ukraine over the long term refute Putin's narrative that Western support for Ukraine is weakening'.[29] Finally, at the NATO Summit in Washington DC, NATO allies welcomed the 'bilateral long-term security commitments allies and partners have agreed with Ukraine, based on the G7 Joint Declaration of Support for Ukraine launched in Vilnius'.[30]

It is the long-term commitment to support Ukraine that is essential; the bilateral agreements on security cooperation with validity for ten years will, in this regard, be most helpful. In the event that Ukraine becomes a NATO member before the end of a security agreement, the participants can collectively decide on the agreement's future status. It is also important to note here that the security cooperation agreement with France (as with others) also covers highly important non-military issues, such as Ukraine's recovery and reconstruction, compensation for losses, injuries and damages caused by Russian aggression, as well as sanctions and accountability.[31]

President Zelenskyy has touted these agreements as the 'new pillars for the rules-based international order'. In the security agreements, Ukraine's partners/participants commit themselves, at a minimum, to maintaining the type and scale of military and other support they have provided since the start of Russia's full-scale invasion in 2022. That alone is a significant development for Kyiv, which had no such commitments on paper in the past. The partners/participants also pledge to enable Ukraine to deter and, if necessary, defend itself after current hostilities end from future Russian armed attacks. To do so, they pledge to build Ukraine's future military force and to consult with Kyiv and take further measures, in the event the country comes under armed attack again.[32] The bilateral security cooperation agreements are starkly different to the ambiguous Budapest Memorandum in 1994 (discussed above), in which the US, the UK and Russia provided Ukraine with non-functional 'security assurances', in exchange for its denuclearisation. While the new agreements fall short of mutual defence obligations – as they do not oblige the signatories to send their armed forces to Ukraine's defence – they do contain firm, meaningful and robust commitments on a range of important issues.

The efforts by President Trump and his administration to secure a ceasefire and/or a peace agreement have taken their turbulent twists and turns. The original US-led 28-point peace plan was seen by Kyiv and its European allies as heavily influenced by Moscow. This triggered weeks of intense high-level diplomacy. Kuleba underlined,

> Every new initiative from Washington unfolds according to the same pattern: a diplomatic cavalry charge against Ukraine, which Kyiv, with other European capitals, manages to fend off. They stabilise the situation, but never actually win the battle. This pattern will, no doubt, persist.

And in December 2025, Kyiv sent the US administration an updated twenty-point plan, as well as a separate document outlining potential security guarantees and provisions for Ukraine's reconstruction.

A 'Coalition of the Willing', led by France, has had intense discussions on how to secure that the Ukrainians are offered very strong security guarantees, and that such guarantees must be a precondition for supporting a ceasefire or a peace agreement. 'I can tell you today that we're ready,' said President Emmanuel Macron in Paris in September 2025.

> This Coalition of the Willing, which was established right here in Paris on 17 February this year, building on what we began in our work right here in February 2024 – this Coalition of the Willing, which is a coalition of peace, has actually put on the table, and clarified through a military and political commitment, the thirty-five members' contribution to provide Ukraine with those very guarantees of peace and security. Their aim is firstly to ensure that, in the negotiation, there's no limitation on format or on capabilities for the Ukrainian army. That's what we're upholding, what we'll uphold to the end. So, we put ourselves in a position to provide the means to regenerate the Ukrainian army so that it cannot only resist any fresh attack but also deter Russia from any further aggression. It's the first pillar of the security guarantees,

the most important one, the most essential one, and so we've brought together every country's contribution.

The second element of these peace and security guarantees is what's called 'reassurance force'. Today we actually have twenty-six countries which have formally pledged – with several others yet to strengthen their position – but twenty-six countries have pledged to deploy troops in Ukraine as reassurance forces or to be present on the ground, at sea or in the air, to provide this reassurance to Ukrainian territory and to Ukraine the day after the ceasefire or peace. The desire or goal of this force isn't to wage some sort of war against Russia, but it's a force that must guarantee peace and very clearly send a strategic signal. It will be deployed in the framework of a ceasefire, not on the front line but in geographical areas currently being defined, but it aims to prevent any further major aggression and involve the twenty-six states very clearly in Ukraine's long-term security.[33]

Early in January 2026, members of the Coalition of the Willing, Ukraine and the United States met in Paris, stressing their commitment to a just and lasting peace in Ukraine, and expressed their readiness to commit to a system of politically and legally binding security guarantees that will be activated once a ceasefire enters into force. These guarantees included five key components:[34]

1. *Participation in a proposed US-led ceasefire monitoring and verification mechanism.* There will be a continuous, reliable ceasefire monitoring system, including contributions from members of the Coalition of the Willing. The Coalition of the Willing will also be represented in the Special Commission that will be established

to address any breaches, attribute responsibility and determine remedies.

2. *Support for the Armed Forces of Ukraine.* The Coalition agreed to continue critical long-term military assistance and armament to the Armed Forces of Ukraine to ensure their sustained capability, as they will remain the first line of defence and deterrence. This will include but not be limited to long-term defence packages; support for financing the purchase of weapons; continued cooperation with Ukraine on its national budget to finance the armed forces; access to defence depots which can deliver rapid additional support in the case of a future armed attack; provision of practical and technical support to Ukraine in building defensive fortifications.
3. *A Multinational Force for Ukraine* made up from contributions from willing nations within the framework of the Coalition, to support the rebuilding of Ukraine's armed forces and support deterrence. Coordinated military planning has been conducted to prepare for reassurance measures in the air, at sea and on land and for the regeneration of the armed forces of Ukraine. It was confirmed that these reassurance measures should be strictly implemented at Ukraine's request once a credible cessation of hostilities has taken place. These elements will be European-led, with the involvement also of non-European members of the Coalition and the proposed support of the US.
4. *Binding commitments to support Ukraine in the case of a future armed attack by Russia in order to restore peace.* It was agreed to finalise binding commitments setting out an approach to support Ukraine and to restore peace and security in the case of a future armed attack by Russia. These commitments may include the use

of military capabilities, intelligence and logistical support, diplomatic initiatives, adoption of additional sanctions.

5. *Commitment to deepen long-term defence cooperation with Ukraine.* This included training, defence industrial joint production, including with the use of European relevant instruments, and intelligence cooperation.

There is no doubt that these long-term commitments to assist Ukraine and ensure the country's security, self-defence and deterrence capacity will provide a vital bridge until Ukraine can finally accede to NATO as a full member. Moving Ukraine along its path to EU membership will also be indispensable, as it will provide the political and financial framework for Ukraine to recover and rebuild, while also bringing an added layer of security through the 'mutual defence clause' – Article 42(7) – of the Treaty on European Union.[35]

• • •

NATO must remain a cornerstone in preserving peace in the Euro-Atlantic area, as it has been for over seventy-five years. And as Madeleine K. Albright reminded us more than twenty-five years ago, 'Our alliance endures because the principles it defends are timeless and because they reflect the deepest aspirations of the human spirit.' It remains vital in upholding and respecting the territorial integrity and sovereignty of nations, as well as respecting decisions taken by their leaders and governments – duly elected through democratic elections – as regards their preferred security arrangements. To subscribe to so-called 'spheres of influence,' however, and to attribute special rights or privileges to certain countries, as some observers have argued should be granted the Russian Federation, is extremely dangerous. The moment the community of nations gives unique or special rights and privileges to larger countries, we are subjugated to the 'law of the jungle', thereby grossly undermining the rules-based international order and the timeless principles of the United Nations Charter.

But as we look to the future, there is no reason to anguish or despair, as Foreign Minister Dmytro Kuleba so movingly stated in his speech in Brussels at the NATO–Ukraine Commission:

> Together, we have no other choice but to prevail. Not only for the sake of my children but also yours. Ukraine did not choose this battle. You did not choose it either. Russia was the one that questioned the basic rules of coexistence, the security order in Europe, and our freedom as a whole. But it is we who must end it with a just victory that will guarantee peace and stability for generations to come.

STATEMENT BY DMYTRO KULEBA: 'VILNIUS 2023 MUST NOT BECOME BUCHAREST 2008'

NATO-UKRAINE COMMISSION, BRUSSELS, 4 APRIL 2023

Dear Secretary-General, dear allies,

I would like to begin by thanking you. We in Ukraine are deeply grateful for every piece of your support. It enables us to defend our homes, our families and our children. Likewise, it enables you to stay out of the war while standing by Ukraine.

However, this war is not only about Russians killing Ukrainians and trying to steal Ukrainian land. Putin is trying to destroy the very foundations of the security order formed after 1945. This is why the stakes are so high, not only for Ukraine but for the entire Euro-Atlantic community. Russia will not stop until it is *stopped*.

Like other decisive confrontations of the past, this war is not a sprint but a marathon. Everything relies on strategic endurance and the resolve to keep moving forward in moments of great exhaustion and despair. The truth of the matter is that none of us present in the room can allow ourselves to get tired.

Together, we have no other choice but to prevail. Not only for the sake of my children but also yours. Ukraine did not choose this battle. You did not choose it either. Russia was the one that questioned the basic rules of coexistence, the security order in Europe, and our freedom as a whole. But it is we who must end it with a just victory that will guarantee peace and stability for generations to come.

Dear colleagues, war demands from us that we be sober and frank with each other in our strategic assessments. Throughout the decades, NATO has been a reliable guarantor of peace for hundreds of millions of people. Over decades, NATO remained politically sexy. More members are joining, and I sincerely congratulate Finland on this historic day. Finland's accession proves two things. First, what felt like a decades-long policy needs to be changed now, given the extraordinary challenges of Russian aggression. Second, the argument about not irritating Moscow by not inviting new members who have a shared border with Russia simply does not hold water.

No other collective security alliance in history has been as successful as NATO. This result required a lot of will and determination. Paradoxically enough, the very same will and determination have worked quite the opposite when it comes to Ukraine's accession to NATO. Since 2008, there has been a will to maintain determination in keeping the door for Ukraine open. However, the will and determination to ensure that Ukraine would not darken the doorstep of NATO soon have been equally strong.

Instead of the fifth article, we were advised to follow our sixth sense. Instead of a mutually beneficial integration, we were kept at arm's length by a friendly handshake. Fear-driven caution replaced strategy.

Don't get me wrong here: I am not questioning your help. I am questioning the strategy this alliance is pursuing when it comes to Ukraine and its own security.

This flawed strategy led to fatal consequences for all of us. You, dear colleagues, were not the ones who made these misguided decisions. Strategic mistakes accumulated over the years. But now it is you who can break the vicious cycle.

To put an end to this story of lost opportunities, it is necessary to finally make a decision that is long overdue: to define specific plans and prospects for Ukraine's accession to NATO. I therefore call on you to take the necessary steps in the near future so that Vilnius 2023 does not become another Bucharest 2008.

Of course, we as a nation seek the protection of Article 5. Who wouldn't, in our place? But we are realistic people. We don't seek to drag you into the war. This is our war, and we are fighting it successfully with your generous support. We have never requested anyone's boots on the ground and we have no such intention. We don't seek a magic wand that will end the war instead of winning it on the battlefield. What we seek and what we ask you for is a simple thing: a clear signal to Russia that the game is over. Ukraine is part of the West; it's at the doorstep of NATO, and it will walk in rather sooner than later.

We are aware of the argument that Ukraine's membership divides the alliance. I will dare to offer two thoughts in this regard.

First, we have heard this argument before on our path towards EU membership. One year ago, we were told that the issue of granting Ukraine EU candidate status divided the bloc. However, when the decision was made and Ukraine received its status, this became the day of the greatest EU unity and strength. The EU has reinstated itself as a strong and determined global leader, which has boosted its confidence. This is exactly what is going to happen to the alliance on the day when determined decisions are taken on Ukraine's path towards NATO.

My second thought on this is much shorter: keeping Ukraine stalled on the path towards membership is nothing but the devil in disguise.

NATO should be at the forefront of change; should think big and act historically. The alliance must seize the strategic initiative and fully participate in the development of the continent's new security architecture. And it is the accession of Ukraine that will allow us to realise this ambitious but entirely realistic vision. Other ways of thinking will not allow the Euro-Atlantic coalition to strengthen its leadership and influence.

The NATO summit in Vilnius offers all of us a unique opportunity to make a leap for the door. Ukraine therefore proposes that, among other things, in the Vilnius Declaration, allies will instruct NATO Foreign Ministers to prepare, until the end of 2023, a Ukraine–NATO Action Plan that will focus on specific steps to expedite Ukraine's Euro-Atlantic integration. In particular, it will define a foreseeable timeline for when Ukraine will be invited to open accession talks.

We also propose that, by the same declaration, the allies will establish a mechanism for crisis consultations with Ukraine based on Article 4 of the Washington Treaty, which will enable consultations in the event of a threat to the territorial integrity, political independence or security of Ukraine or any other NATO member state.

One more proposal is to transform the NATO–Ukraine Commission into a NATO–Ukraine Council. This will allow us to address strategic NATO–Ukraine issues and advance Ukraine's path towards NATO through the political process.

Ministers, I appreciate in advance all calls to focus on practical support for Ukraine for now. But who said that practical support today and membership tomorrow contradict each other?

On the practical side of preparations for Vilnius, we highly value your support within the Comprehensive Assistance Package as well as the recent steps to strengthen it. Currently, the CAP Trust Fund is not yet sufficiently funded. We need to increase voluntary contributions to it. I encourage your capitals to consider additional pledges and establish relevant mechanisms.

We are interested in launching a number of priority projects within CAP, including mine clearance, medical treatment and rehabilitation, the transition of Ukraine's Armed Forces to Western-type weapons, the recovery of our defence facilities through CAP funds and training and education for our servicemen, including through the Polish initiative to establish a Joint Analysis, Education and Training Centre.

We gratefully receive a lot of your vitally important assistance. At the same time, you benefit, as we are literally testing NATO principles in a real fight right now and we are already actively sharing our conclusions with specialists in NATO member states.

The invaluable experience of Ukrainian defenders serves as a guide for further strengthening and reforming the alliance so that NATO member states are fully prepared to deter aggressors and conduct modern high-intensity warfare.

This process of mutual learning is a two-way street, and I take this opportunity to thank allies who are actively training our defenders. The amount and quality of training are two of the crucial advantages we have over Russian forces in this war.

In addition, Ukrainians have unprecedented experience in countering hybrid threats, information warfare and counterpropaganda, ensuring the cyber-resilience of state institutions and critical infrastructure. In our cooperation with the alliance and with NATO member states, we always implement the principle of added value, building mutually beneficial pragmatic partnerships that strengthen all sides.

Today, millions of Ukrainians are gaining experience in Europe's most bloody war of the twenty-first century. Tomorrow, they will contribute this experience to strengthening NATO's collective security. This is the experience of fighting a war where the enemy knows no rules. We are already gladly sharing this experience. You are teaching us, but we are also teaching you.

These are very practical things. However, there is no better strategic way to ensure Euro-Atlantic security than to take Ukraine on board. The Ukrainian people demonstrated unprecedented courage. By joining NATO, Ukraine will protect the bloc from Russia and other potential aggressors for decades to come. Furthermore, Russia's failure will serve as a warning to all potential aggressors.

While your military aid to Ukraine is an investment in your security, Ukraine's membership in NATO is an added value that will not depreciate. Our strength has been hardened on the battlefield, in the fierce fight for survival, in hellish battles and at a very high price.

Colleagues, as we are discussing the 'don't divide the alliance' argument, I cannot help but recall another long-standing rock-solid obstacle on the path of Ukraine's integration: the 'don't divide Ukraine' argument. This one is gone once and for all. If a referendum on joining NATO were held today, 82 per cent of Ukrainians would support it. But not only Ukrainians share this view. People in NATO countries do so, too.

Sixty-eight per cent of EU citizens believe Russia's attack on Ukraine is an attack on Europe as a whole. This is the view of 80 per cent of Poles and Spaniards, 70 per cent of the Dutch and 65 per cent of Germans and French. This means that both Euro-Atlantic leaders and the public view Ukraine as an integral part of the Western security architecture.

This people's reality demands political decisions. I have no doubts that neither you nor we need another war for these decisions to become reality.

I thank you again for all your support, and I thank you for your attention.

CHAPTER 11

SEVEN PATRIOTS CAN CHANGE THE WHOLE GAME

Helping Ukraine is not only a good deed. It's also a good deal.

Radosław Sikorski, Foreign Minister of Poland

In war, extraordinary things happen. In war, both the human factor and innovative weapon systems can be decisive. In war, a few words at the right moment can make a huge difference.

'We in Ukraine are genuinely grateful for all the support we have received from you since the beginning of the full-scale war. This gratitude is unconditional and unlimited,' explained Dmytro Kuleba to his colleagues at the NATO headquarters in Brussels on 4 April 2024 (the whole speech can be found at the end of the chapter).

> Thank you for the military aid packages. Thank you for finding a way to buy ammunition in third countries. Thank you for all the strong decisions that destroy the myth of 'fatigue'. I know how much effort many of you personally invest in supporting Ukraine. And I will never forget it.

Kuleba raised his head, giving the ministers and the ambassadors in the meeting room a quick, confident smile. Some of them were new, while some he had met so many times since the war started that he considered them to be close friends.

He felt that this was the moment. He must tell them as clearly and convincingly as possible. To try to make them finally realise and understand what is needed and what is at stake. One thing was clear: this was not going to be the sort of speech they had heard many times before.

And it was not ingratitude but rather the horrific reality prompting him to be this direct, honest and frank.

> With the current scale of Russian terror, Ukraine's air defence is not even close to being sufficient. Today, the course of European history really boils down to very practical things, like bringing seven Patriot batteries to Ukraine – that would change the whole situation.

Kuleba knew that the majority of those around the table – his NATO partners – were expecting him to talk about preparations for the important NATO summit in Washington in July: the anticipated outcomes, the need for additional funding, reform of support mechanisms and many other key issues. But this morning he had one, very different objective. This task was given to him by President Zelenskyy himself. Ukraine desperately need more Patriot air missile defence systems. End of story. Therefore, Kuleba and his speechwriter had to shift the whole narrative, both publicly and behind closed doors.

He continued giving them the cold hard facts.

> 778 Russian missiles and drones were fired at Ukraine in March alone. Ninety-four of them were ballistic missiles. This accounts for three ballistic missiles per day on average. This is an unseen scale of air terror by one state against another. We shoot a lot of Russian missiles and drones down, but a portion of them still reach targets.

He could see they were listening carefully to him, but he also recognised that unless you experience it yourself it is very hard for others to fully understand the horror and terror of war. The massive death and destruction. The constant uncertainty. The nagging worry about whether your family and friends are still safe and sound. But today, he wants to go beyond that.

> Our energy system is damaged to the extent that its functioning right now is a miracle. Our professionals say that after two more attacks like the two we suffered in March, we will have to switch from electricity to candles.

As a matter of fact, since mid-March 2024, Russian forces have been attacking Ukrainian thermal and hydropower stations as well as main power transmission networks on an almost daily basis, leading to blackouts in many regions. These devastating drone and missile attacks on the Ukrainian energy system have caused more than $1 billion worth of damage to the sector, according to the Ukrainian Ministry of Energy.[1] Before the invasion, Ukraine's generating capacity was thirty-six gigawatts of electricity. Russia started targeting Ukraine's electricity infrastructure in late 2022, and over half of that capacity has now been lost – either occupied, destroyed or damaged. Ukraine has managed to restore some capacity, with many Ukrainians just about managing to keep the lights on. But recent attacks have destroyed an additional nine gigawatts of capacity. All that is left now comes more or less from nuclear power stations, which the Russians so far have refrained from attacking. Meanwhile, local municipalities, desperate to be able to provide the critical services of heating and water-pumping during winter, are decentralising power generation, installing mini power plants in the form of modern, efficient gas turbines that have a capacity of anything from five to seventy megawatts.[2]

On the front lines and border areas, Ukrainians 'suffer from relentless Russian bombardment with guided aerial bombs weighing between 500 and 1,500 kilograms', Kuleba informed his audience.

The mass use of glide bombs by Russia is a relatively recent development, one that has proven devastating for Ukrainian forces. Russian glide bombs are built by adding fold-out wings and satellite navigation to old Soviet bombs, such as 1.5-ton FAB-1500 and the new 3.4-ton FAB-3000. They are cheap but destructive. Lobbed from high altitudes by Russian aircrafts beyond the range of most Ukrainian anti-aircraft missiles, the devices are near-impossible to intercept. A recent report by CEPA (Centre for European Policy Analysis) laims that they were decisive in the February 2024 capture of the once heavily fortified eastern Ukrainian town of Avdiivka. It is estimated that Russia dropped more than 3,500 glide bombs in 2024 with that deluge of explosives likely to continue and even expand.[3]

The moment came for Kuleba to convey to NATO ministers his main message, the real reason he had travelled the long and complicated journey from Kyiv by train and car, and why he wanted to sit in front of them.

> There is currently only one type of air defence system in the world that has proven capable of intercepting Russian ballistic missiles. And it has a beautiful name: Patriots. Russia boasted that its Kinzhals and Cyrcons are impossible to intercept. But we shoot them down. And I want to thank every country that has provided Patriots to us.

The Patriot air missile defence system, which stands for Phased Array Tracking Radar for Intercept on Target, is manufactured by RTX Corporation in the US. Its surface-to-air missile and anti-ballistic system is thought to be one of the most sophisticated in the world. What makes the Patriot one of the most sought-after air defence systems is its ability to stop cruise missiles and short-range ballistic missiles before they reach their intended target, as well as target aircraft. The system is mounted on trucks, making them mobile, and each system has a battery capable of holding up to four missiles with a total of eight launchers, with a range between twenty to 100 miles. Raytheon has built several hundred Patriot systems, which are currently used by more than nineteen countries, including Ukraine.

Ukraine urgently needed only seven of them, but Kuleba knew there were hundreds of them spread around the world. He saw that some around the table were looking baffled and surprised. It's my job to make them understand, he thought to himself, as he continued:

> Yesterday, I was asked in an interview how many Patriot air defence systems are there. I publicly said that there are over a hundred around the world. The true number is much, much higher.

> There are at least eight hundred of them. And perhaps even more. Eight hundred!
>
> We have three Patriot systems in Ukraine.
>
> Three.
>
> Against ninety-four ballistic missiles per month.

He stared at them for a second. This was the moment.

> Friends, with all my respect, I cannot believe that the entire Western coalition does not have available Patriot systems that it can deliver to Ukraine – at the most critical moment in Western post-Second World War history. Ukraine is currently the only country in the world facing almost daily ballistic missile strikes. Most of those 800 systems are stationed in places where the missile threat is zero. Just seven Patriot systems would have changed the situation completely.

Their significance would be nothing less than decisive. Then the final appeal, and the end to an exceptional speech: 'Dear colleagues, please find a way to send additional air defence systems to Ukraine as soon as possible, particularly Patriots. Thank you for your attention.'

Silent, solemn appreciation was felt around the meeting room; all had witnessed a truly exceptional and effective appeal by an assiduous and articulate Ukrainian leader.

The Polish Foreign Minister, Radek Sikorski, who took the floor right after Kuleba had finished his statement, later said that this was the most dramatic address by a Foreign Minister that he had ever heard in the NATO chamber. Several other ministers and ambassadors were also touched by Kuleba's strong and convincing appeal.

'I remember that right after the speech I leaned over to my Turkish colleague, Ambassador Zeki Levent Gümrükçü, and I said, "This is just a very heartfelt plea for support to survive, to be able to withstand"', recalls the Swedish Ambassador to NATO, Axel Wernhoff.

> That was certainly the general impression of the speech among those present. We also had a bilateral meeting with Ukraine that very same morning and I remember when the Ukrainian delegation came to the office, both Foreign Minister Dmytro Kuleba and his NATO Ambassador, Ms Nataliia Galibarenko, had a very sombre and serious expression on their faces. As we sat down and had our meeting, they were focused on one thing alone: Ukraine urgently needs more air defence. This was back in April 2024 and the situation on the ground was indeed very serious and grave. There were even fears that there could be a major military breakthrough from the Russian side, which would be a disaster by itself. And there was also speculation that maybe the Ukrainians would have to evacuate Kharkiv – and if that happened, the whole NATO summit in Washington DC would be in jeopardy. It would be extremely embarrassing for all NATO allies and for the West to celebrate NATO's seventy-fifth anniversary while Russian troops were approaching Kyiv. But back to the speech: I am convinced it was a hugely important speech that made a strong impression on all of us and had a great impact.[4]

Around a week later, on 14 April 2024, President Zelenskyy announced, 'Today we have a very good result of our international work: Germany will provide us with an additional Patriot system – Chancellor Scholz and I agreed on this today.'[5] And early in June, the US declared that it too would deliver a Patriot system and that it had pledged to prioritise missile deliveries to Ukraine and halt deliveries to other allies. At the end of June, Ukrainian Prime Minister Denys Shmyhal announced, 'Italy will provide us with a second SAMP/T system. Romania will offer one Patriot system, and the Netherlands is currently assembling another Patriot system for us.' And in early July it was reported that

> the United States is involved in discussions about the possibility of transferring up to eight Patriot air defence batteries from Israel to Ukraine, in what would be a major boost for the latter in its fight against Russia. While no agreement has been reached yet, a deal would likely involve transferring the batteries from Israel to the US, and then on to Ukraine.[6]

The NATO Secretary-General's visit to Kyiv in late April 2024 can also be seen as a direct consequence of Kuleba's NATO speech a few weeks earlier; Secretary-General Stoltenberg publicly admitted that serious delays in military support had translated into serious consequences for Ukraine on the battlefield. 'Ukraine has been outgunned for months; fewer Russian missiles and drones have been shot down, and Russia has been able to push forward on the front line', he underlined during the visit.

In sum, since the Russian invasion of Ukraine, urgent and persistent calls for missiles, drones and other vital military support from the US, the EU and other countries have been one of the most essential tasks for Foreign Minister Kuleba. A rather unusual set of objectives and a most extraordinary agenda for a Foreign Minister, it must be said. These efforts have consumed a lot of his time but have led to concrete results.

STATEMENT BY DMYTRO KULEBA

4 APRIL 2024, NATO-UKRAINE COUNCIL, BRUSSELS

Dear Jens, dear allies,

First of all, happy seventy-fifth anniversary to NATO! Seventy-five is a lot. At the same time, you know, we often discuss NATO troubles, but we should not miss the big picture. No other security alliance in world history has lasted for that long. Hence, long live NATO!

It is also true that at no point in these three quarters of a century has the Euro-Atlantic area been so dangerously close to a new big war. I have no doubt that Putin will expand his aggression to other European nations if he prevails in Ukraine. Moldova, the Baltics, Poland, the Suwalki Gap and Gotland Island, drawing other allies into war.

Or even before that, if Putin's militarised economy allows him to gather resources. The more he denies it, the scarier it looks. I would like to remind everyone that he denied plans to attack Ukraine in exactly the same manner.

Two days ago, Hanke [Dutch Foreign Minister Hanke Bruins Slot] and I co-hosted a big diplomatic event in The Hague. An old colleague of mine approached me in the corridor – we worked together in the Council of Europe six years ago. He said, 'Dmytro, I must admit, you were right back then when you warned us of Russia's threat, and we didn't listen. But today, I have no problem recognising I was wrong.' To which I replied, 'It's great you recognise it, but we had to pay with tens of thousands of lives and the destruction of our economy for you to realise that we were right.'

I am not trying to scare anyone. This is the reality. One can deny it, ignore it, or play it down. But this will not change reality itself.

We in Ukraine are genuinely grateful for all the support we have received from you since the beginning of the full-scale war. This gratitude is unconditional and unlimited. Thank you for the military aid packages. Thank you for finding a way to buy ammunition in third countries. Thank you for all the strong decisions that destroy the myth of 'fatigue'. I know how much effort many of you personally invest in supporting Ukraine. And I will never forget it. But with this scale of war and the magnitude of the challenge, we need to further step up our efforts.

It is not ungratefulness, but the horrific reality that prompts me to be frank. And the honest assessment is that, with the current scale of Russian terror, Ukraine's air defence is not even close to being sufficient. Today, the course of European history really boils down to very practical things, like bringing seven Patriot batteries to Ukraine – that would change the whole situation.

I came from a country where I couldn't answer the questions I was being asked. Such as, what stands in your way to find seven Patriot systems, to save lives in Ukraine, to save its economy and increase the chances of your country not facing war a few years later? It's impossible to explain to people what I hear in response. Please don't say there are no available Patriot batteries around the world that can be delivered. People don't believe it.

Dear friends, 778 Russian missiles and drones were fired at Ukraine in March alone. Ninety-four of them were ballistic missiles. This accounts for three ballistic missiles per day on average. Ten days ago, I walked out of my office to go to the Kyiv botanical gardens [the M. M. Hryshko National Botanical Garden] in order to record a video address devoted to the Hindu festival of Diwali and the announcement of my upcoming visit to India. The moment I stepped out, an air raid siren went off and around a minute later, two powerful blasts rocked the sky over the capital. These were the two most recent Russian Zircon missiles that Patriots successfully intercepted over my head.

This is an unseen scale of air terror by one state against another. We shoot a lot of Russian missiles and drones down, but a portion of them still reach targets. And their targets are ordinary residential buildings, energy facilities and critical infrastructure. Three days ago, a Russian missile struck Dnipro, the second-most protected city, damaging a kindergarten, a college and nine residential buildings. Five children were injured. Imagine what happens in other cities: Kharkiv, Odesa and others. What happens on the front lines is a different story, too.

Front line and border areas suffer from relentless Russian bombardment with guided aerial bombs weighing between 500 and 1,500 kilograms. Our energy system is damaged to the extent that its functioning right now is a miracle. Our professionals say that after two more attacks like the two we suffered in March, we will have to switch from electricity to candles.

We are also running out of interceptors. We have a few Western systems and I am grateful to all the partners who have provided them. But the backbone of our air defence system is still Soviet-era S-300 systems. We have almost no missiles left for them. I am not exaggerating. It's painful to see all the destruction while spending weeks and months convincing partners to share their S-300 interceptors with us.

There is currently only one type of air defence system in the world that has proven capable of intercepting Russian ballistic missiles. And it has a beautiful name: Patriots. Russia boasted that its Kinzhals and Cyrcons are impossible to intercept. But we shoot them down. And I want to thank every country that has provided Patriots to us.

Yesterday, I was asked in an interview how many Patriot air defence systems there are. I publicly said that there are over a hundred around the world. The true number is much, much higher. There are at least 800 of them. And perhaps even more. Eight hundred. We have three Patriot systems in Ukraine. Three. Against ninety-four ballistic missiles per month.

Friends, with all my respect, I cannot believe that the entire Western coalition does not have available Patriot systems that it can deliver to Ukraine, at the most critical moment in Western post-Second World War history. Ukraine is currently the only country in the world facing almost daily ballistic missile strikes. Most of those 800 systems are stationed in places where the missile threat is zero.

Just seven Patriot systems would have changed the situation completely. They would allow us to reliably protect seven big Ukrainian cities. This would not only save thousands of lives for Ukrainian men, women, children and the elderly but also save Ukraine's economy and make us far less dependent on imports.

Seven Patriots could be game changers and defeat Russian air terror. Why can't we do this? What are the obstacles? You think that this Patriot battery stands in your territory now and does nothing but somehow gives you a feeling of protection. But each day of it standing idly instead of helping Ukraine survive is a day when a big war in Europe comes closer to you.

By the way, there are also Patriot batteries right across the Ukrainian border in the neighbouring states. The only threat to them is the same one that threatens Ukraine. Why can't we simply move those batteries to the Ukrainian side of the border and let us protect both our skies and yours from drones and missiles? This makes perfect sense. When Russia is attacking Ukrainian energy facilities, they shoot three to five ballistic missiles into one spot – first and foremost, the machinery halls of the facilities – making it impossible to protect them with insufficient air defence and extremely difficult to restore those facilities later.

Dear colleagues, please find a way to send additional air defence systems to Ukraine as soon as possible, particularly Patriots.

Thank you for your attention.

CHAPTER 12

NO PEACE WITHOUT JUSTICE

Japan will never waver in its consistent
position of standing with Ukraine.

Sanae Takaichi, Prime Minister of Japan

Eight days after the Russian invasion of Ukraine, a group of lawyers, politicians and international experts came together to discuss the broader legal and political consequences of Russia's actions. More specifically, they sought to establish a new international criminal tribunal for the crime of aggression. An impromptu on-the-record meeting at Chatham House in London was quickly organised online, with a number of prominent international legal experts and other high-profile figures, including Dmytro Kuleba. They viewed the Russian aggression against Ukraine as a manifest violation of the prohibition of the use of force under the United Nations Charter. The United Nations General Assembly (UNGA) had unequivocally announced on 2 March 2022 that it 'deplores in the strongest terms the aggression by the Russian Federation against Ukraine in violation of Article 2(4) of the Charter'.[1] The

Secretary-General of the United Nations, António Guterres, was also unambiguously critical in his statement after the invasion.

But it was an article in the *Financial Times* four days earlier, on 28 February 2022, written by Philippe Sands, that triggered the Chatham House event. Sands's message was that Putin's invasion of Ukraine posed a 'grave challenge', one that sanctions and financial measures alone could not address, so 'why not create a dedicated international criminal tribunal to investigate Putin and his acolytes for this crime?'[2]

Sands recalls,

> A few days after the Russian invasion of Ukraine, the *Financial Times* invited me to write an opinion piece on the subject. After a little reflection, I settled on an idea of proposing the creation of a special tribunal for the crime of aggression, something that had not happened since the establishment of the Nuremberg and Tokyo tribunals, nearly eighty years earlier. I had been approached because of my work in Ukraine and the city of Lviv, researching the book that became *East West Street: On the Origins of Genocide and Crimes against Humanity*. I chose the theme for two main reasons: the ICC [International Criminal Court] has no jurisdiction over the crime of aggression in relation to Ukraine, so there is a significant gap in the legal architecture of accountability; and the crime of aggression is *primus inter pares*, as the war crimes and crimes against humanity that appear to have followed would not have occurred but for the unlawful use of force. [...] Aggression is a leadership crime, and I considered it important to put the accent of accountability on those most responsible for the horrors that have occurred.[3]

To many political leaders, including Ukraine's Foreign Minister, as well as several legal experts, it seemed evident that the Russian leaders who planned, prepared and initiated or executed the unprovoked military invasion of Ukraine should be identified and prosecuted. Without their decision to wage this war of aggression against Ukraine, war crimes, crimes against humanity and possible genocide would not have occurred, nor would the destruction, death and damage resulting from the war, including from lawful acts of war.[4]

There was no doubt that the International Criminal Court – a child of the International Military Tribunal (IMT) in Nuremberg, set up after the Second World War to investigate and sanction Nazi Germany's 'crimes against peace' (as crimes of aggression were called at the time) – was highly relevant as regards the most serious international crimes, and it was fully operational and had a relatively strong and important mandate. So why did international legal experts and political leaders around the world call for the creation of a new special tribunal on the crime of aggression?

The short answer is that the ICC has powers to investigate any act of genocide, war crimes and crimes against humanity. It cannot however exercise any jurisdiction in relation to the crime of aggression, if the aggression is committed by a state that is not a party to the ICC – which is generally the case for the Russian Federation, unless the United Nations Security Council (UNSC) refers the matter to it (Art. 15ter, ICC Statute). The latter is exceedingly unlikely, as long as Russia, as a permanent member of the UNSC, has veto rights on all decisions of the Security Council related to international peace and security. Claus Kreß, an authority in international law and Director of the Institute for International Peace and Security Law at the University of Cologne, explains it in this way:

While having been the central crime at Nuremberg and Tokyo,

> in 1998, the crime of aggression barely made it into the Statute for the International Criminal Court. And when the jurisdiction of the ICC was belatedly activated as from 17 July 2018, this occurred under debilitating restraints governing the Court's exercise of jurisdiction. As a result, when Russia began its aggression against Ukraine in 2014, the crime of aggression, while belonging to it, was hanging by a thread in the firmament of international offences.[5]

Looking back, given the seriousness and momentous consequences of the crime of aggression, it is quite astonishing that the world community has been unable to address the issue in an adequate manner. A clear warning was given in the brilliant opening speech by Robert Jackson, the US Chief Prosecutor at the Nuremberg Tribunal, nearly eighty years ago:

> The ultimate step in avoiding periodic wars, which are inevitable in a system of international lawlessness, is to make statesmen responsible to law. And let me make clear that while this is first applied against German aggressors, the law includes, and if it is to serve a useful purpose it must condemn, aggression by other nations, including those which sit here now in judgment.[6]

Nevertheless, since 1945 and at least up until the Russian invasion of Ukraine in 2022, there has been little progress closing the gap in international law and criminal prosecution as regards the mother of all crimes: the crimes of aggression.

The reasons for this are certainly varied and complex, ranging from the stand-off and stalemate of the Cold War to disagreements on the definition of the crime itself. In spite of these disagreements, in 1950 the International Law Commission was able to formulate the so-called Nuremberg Principles, containing the definition of the crimes against peace. While the UN General Assembly did not follow up on these principles, in 1974 it managed to adopt the landmark resolution No. 3314 – on the definition of aggression – which is now considered customary international law (a set of unwritten legal obligations that arise from the established, consistent practices of nations, rather than from formal written treaties). After the fall of the Berlin Wall, substantial work was initiated by the creation of the criminal tribunals for the former Yugoslavia (1993) and Rwanda (1995) and finally the establishment of the ICC by the adoption of the Rome Statute in 1998, which formally came into force on 1 July 2002. But on the crime of aggression itself, the progress was limited to the inclusion of this crime in the Rome Statute, without providing a definition. Such a definition only came in 2010 at the Review Conference of the Rome Statute in Kampala.

At the historic meeting at Chatham House in London on 4 March 2022, the participants clearly voiced their support for the creation of a new international special tribunal on the crime of aggression. Kuleba himself said,

> Eighty years ago, representatives of nine countries met in London to set up a legal framework for the persecution of war criminals during the Second World War. And we all know that led to the establishment of a precedent in international law that's basically defined the future development of international criminal law. Now, eight years ago, Russia launched an aggression against Ukraine by occupying Crimea and some parts of our territory in eastern Ukraine. And eight days ago, Russia, in a rather barbarian way, launched another wave of aggression against Ukraine. And

> the question is now how the international community will handle it. We welcome the initiative of the International Criminal Court to investigate crimes which fall under its jurisdiction, namely war crimes and crimes against humanity. [...] The prosecutor of the ICC has also demonstrated leadership in this effort and Ukraine will cooperate fully with the ICC, while not being a full party to the Rome Statute, but we recognise ICC's jurisdiction on war crimes and crimes against humanity since 2014. And so, the moment I learned about the initiative to set up an international tribunal to investigate the crime of aggression against Ukraine, I immediately said yes, and this yes comes from me, not only as a person, but also as a representative of the government of Ukraine.[7]

At the online meeting in London, former UK Prime Minister Gordon Brown, who immediately reached out to Dr Sands after reading the article in the *Financial Times*, argued for the establishment of the new special tribunal on the crime of aggression, although he understood and acknowledged that it was not going to be a quick and easy process.

One of the issues that was discussed in some detail at the meeting regarded what would happen to all other cases of violations of international law and Article 2(4) of the UN Charter if a tribunal for this instance of aggression against Ukraine was created. In short, this was a question of the selectivity of international law. Dapo Akande, a law professor at the University of Oxford, responded that one could also have questioned setting up criminal tribunals for the former Yugoslavia and Rwanda. 'Are those the only places where international crimes have been committed?' he asked, before answering his own question. 'But now we look thirty years on. Not only have we seen international criminal tribunals for other countries. We now have the International Criminal Court, so just because we can't do everything, it does not mean that we shouldn't do anything.'

Another pertinent question raised during the Chatham House event was whether Putin, as an acting head of state, was immune to any such jurisdiction and to any such tribunal. Again Akande responded, confirming that serving heads of state do have immunity in general international law, certainly from national criminal jurisdiction. But then there are relevant questions about whether they have immunity if they are to be prosecuted by an international tribunal. Akande said,

> There has been a range of views on that question, on whether or not they have immunity before international tribunals. The ICC gave a decision a couple of years ago with respect to the Sudanese president – the then Sudanese President Omar al-Bashir – who was facing a charge of genocide at the ICC. And the ICC held that though he was then a serving head of state, he was not immune under customary international law, because these were proceedings before an international tribunal. Now, that ruling by the ICC was controversial, but that's what they held; they relied on an earlier judgment, which had been given in a case involving Charles Taylor, who was then the head of state of Liberia, who was sought by the Special Court for Sierra Leone, which is also an international tribunal. So that's one view. [...] Not everyone accepts that view, but actually in this case there's another issue which arises, which is that this is not just a case of an international criminal tribunal; this is a case where the government of Ukraine would be delegating the national jurisdiction that it has to prosecute the crime of aggression, that occurs on its territory and against it, to this international tribunal.[8]

Finally, yet another issue that merited a discussion at the meeting was the possible next steps towards the creation of a new special tribunal on the crime of aggression, including how many governments would need to sign up. Here, Philippe Sands argued that 'it really all depends on political will'. He also said,

> It may be there can be an agreement between Ukraine and the United Nations and that is sufficient to get it up and running, or it maybe you do it in a different way. [...] My hope is that there will be five or six countries that will now say 'let's run with this', and it may or may not include some of the bigger countries like the UK and France. My own hope is that they are on board. They've been playing a leadership role. They've been playing a very positive role. They both have commitments to the rule of law internationally, and they can provide important input and support.[9]

At the end of the meeting – which was moderated by Elizabeth Wilmshurst, a distinguished fellow of the international law programme at Chatham House – a statement and declaration[10] calling for the creation of a special criminal tribunal to try those responsible for aggression in Ukraine were adopted and thereafter signed by thirty-eight international legal experts and other high-profile personalities, including the former President of the European Court of Human Rights, Sir Nicolas Bratza.

The statement highlighted that there were three main ways under international law that Putin's action could be subject to the scrutiny of the world. First, by the fact that Ukraine had already started proceedings before the International Court of Justice (ICJ) in The Hague, specifically stating that Russia is subjecting Ukraine to a false claim of genocide.[11] Second, the European Court of Human

Rights (ECHR) in Strasbourg could also decide on Russia's actions (even though the Russian Federation had been suspended the day after the invasion of Ukraine from its rights of representation in the Committee of Ministers and the Parliamentary Assembly in the Council of Europe, although Russia still remained a member of the organisation when the Chatham House event took place).[12] Third, following the referral by thirty-nine states of the situation in Ukraine to the ICC, the prosecutor had now opened an investigation into current events in Ukraine. However, as already noted, the ICC cannot exercise its jurisdiction with regard to the specific crime of aggression. The participants at Chatham House reiterated their expectation that to complement the initiatives now underway before the ICC, ICJ and ECHR, they would propose the creation of a special tribunal on the crime of aggression. They also conveyed a hope that such a tribunal could be set up with speed and determination; as Philippe Sands phrased it, 'Could one ever imagine Mr Putin in the Court? Who knows, when Charles de Gaulle and others met in London in January 1942, it must have been unimaginable that ever Nazi leaders like Hitler and Göring and others would find themselves in the Court, and yet three years later, that is what happened.'

None of the legal experts expected proceedings to be a walk in the park. Mykola Gnatovskyy, former adviser to Foreign Minister Kuleba, international law professor and participant at the Chatham House event, said,

> It is true that it was obvious to us, even back then in March 2022, that the project was extremely ambitious and that it was not going to be easy to come quickly to a concrete result. However, it was also clear that it was no longer possible to continue the so-called 'business as usual' and to tolerate the most dangerous

> and fundamental attack on international legal order, simply for the lack of an international tribunal vested with the appropriate scope of jurisdiction. Several paths for creating the tribunal were open and were being discussed since then.[13]

After taking the time in the midst of war to participate in the Chatham House event, Dmytro Kuleba published an official statement on 7 March 2022. In the statement, he expressed his gratitude to leading experts in international law who called for the creation of the tribunal. At the same time, Kuleba highlighted that 'this effort is not meant to replace but rather complement the existing international proceedings on various war crimes and crimes against humanity committed in the course of Russian aggression against Ukraine'. Both the timing of the statement, appended to this chapter, and its content were no doubt important in mobilising international support for the initiative.

Subsequently, and rather rapidly, more than 150 leading international lawyers and political leaders voiced their support to the initiative.[14] In late November 2022, Ursula von der Leyen announced the support of the European Union for the special tribunal, stressing that

> Russia must pay for its horrific crimes, including for its crime of aggression against a sovereign state. This is why, while continuing to support the International Criminal Court, we are proposing to set up a specialised court, backed by the United Nations, to investigate and prosecute Russia's crime of aggression. We are ready to start working with the international community to get the broadest international support possible for this specialised court.[15]

Large and influential countries such as France, previously reluctant to commit to such a tribunal, confirmed that same week that they were working with European partners on the proposal. And on 12 December 2022, the Dutch Foreign Minister, Wopke Hoekstra, announced that the Netherlands would be willing to host the tribunal in The Hague.

The impromptu event at Chatham House in London, with a huge and distinguished online participation and audience (along with the official Ukrainian statement on the initiative), signalled the start of in-depth informal discussion among international legal experts, primarily in the so-called Core Group but also at G7 level.

Starting in Prague on 26 January 2023, over fifteen Core Group meetings have taken place on the establishment of a tribunal. These meetings allowed for in-depth, informal and sometimes diverging and intense discussions among international legal experts from forty-one countries, as well as the European Union and the Council of Europe.

At this juncture, one of the most viable options seemed to be the establishment of a new special tribunal through a bilateral treaty between the Council of Europe – the leading human rights institution in Europe – and Ukraine. 'It would not, in fact, be the first treaty that provides for the possibility of prosecuting the crime of aggression through a tribunal established by a regional organisation,' said Dapo Akande.

> The African Union, in the Malabo Protocol which amended the Protocol on the Statute of the African Court of Justice and Human Rights (although not yet in force), already included the crime of aggression within the statute of a tribunal that may come to exist on a regional basis.[16]

It is also important to note that justice is one of the ten points in President Zelenskyy's initial peace plan; there can certainly not be any sustainable peace without justice. Moreover, there is also a need to register the damage caused by Russian aggression and for an international mechanism to make Russia compensate for the damages caused by the war. As a consequence, in early 2024, the Council of Europe established a Register of Damage for Ukraine caused by the Russian aggression, through an enlarged partial agreement. Iulian Bulai, a Romanian parliamentarian and leader of the Liberals (ALDE) group in the Parliamentary Assembly of the Council of Europe, explains,

> As the war continued, it became more and more clear to all of us that we needed an institution that could do the complex work of collecting and registering all the evidence. This is how we, parliamentarians from all over Europe, pushed for the creation of the Register of Damage caused by the aggression of the Russian Federation against Ukraine.[17]

The Register seeks a truly global membership and any state that voted in favour of the United Nations General Assembly Resolution on the 'Furtherance of remedy and reparation for aggression against Ukraine' may become a participant or an associate member. Today, it is fully operational and a key component of securing the victims of Russia's onslaught in Ukraine justice and future compensation.

Reparation for victims of an act of aggression is not merely permitted under international law – it is required. This principle – also reflected in the mentioned United Nations General Assembly resolution from November 2022 – stands as the foundation for international efforts to secure reparations for Ukraine and its people. Justice for Ukraine demands not only accountability for those who planned and executed the act of aggression but also meaningful redress for the victims whose lives, homes and futures have been shattered, as well as tools for meaningful recovery and reconstruction of Ukraine, its infrastructure and economy.

'The Register of Damage for Ukraine stands as the first operational pillar of a compensation mechanism,' explains Markiyan Kliuchkovskyi, the executive director of the Register of Damage in The Hague. Since its launch, the Register has received over 100,000 claims for compensation from individuals, each one representing a story of loss and resilience. It is expected that many, many more claims will be submitted in the months ahead, as the full scale of harm caused by Russia's aggression continues to unfold. The Register transforms these individual losses into practical claims, creating a robust evidentiary foundation for fair and transparent compensation.

'Let me also point out that the establishment and rapid operationalisation of the Register would not have been possible without the swift and principled leadership of the Council of Europe,' Kliuchkovskyi highlights.

> The Council's commitment to justice and its ability to respond to the call for accountability and offer its robust organisational framework enabled us to move from concept to reality in record time. The Register is now fully functional, providing a secure and accessible platform for victims to submit their claims, and ensuring that the process is governed by the highest standards of integrity and accountability, and employing cutting-edge innovative tools to ensure efficiency. This achievement is a testament to what can be accomplished when international institutions act decisively and in concert towards a common goal.

Looking to the future, it is important to note that the Register is, in the words of Kliuchkovskyi,

> now on the threshold of the next critical step: the establishment of the claims commission for Ukraine, which will serve as the second essential component of the reparations and compensation framework and which will assess claims recorded by the Register and determine what compensation is due to every person and entity that has suffered from the war. We are now closer than ever to delivering comprehensive justice – justice that is not only punitive, but also restorative. Together, the Register and the forthcoming claims commission embody the international community's commitment to justice, accountability and the restoration of rights for all those affected by Russia's aggression. They send a clear message: the world will not turn away from the victims, and peace will only be meaningful if it is built on the foundations of truth, accountability and repair.[18]

Another important step towards Russia's accountability for its war of aggression on Ukraine was the landmark judgment of the European Court of Human Rights on 9 July 2025. The top human rights court in Europe unanimously found the Russian Federation accountable for a series of widespread and flagrant abuses of human rights, including in relation to the downing of Malaysian Airlines flight MH17. It concluded that those violations were committed in flagrant disregard for the foundations of the international legal order established after the Second World War.

At the same time, the discussions on the complex issue of establishing a new tribunal have made significant progress in the Core Group under the able leadership of Anton Korynevych, ambassador-at-large in the Ministry of Foreign Affairs of Ukraine. It is helpful to highlight here some of the main elements and key features that have been subject to discussion, which were also largely spelled out in the important Resolution 2482 by the Parliamentary Assembly of the Council of Europe on 26 January 2023.

The tribunal's jurisdiction would be limited to the crime of aggression committed against Ukraine and would extend *ratione temporis* to the aggression started by the Russian Federation in February 2014. Its jurisdiction would include the role and complicity of the leaders of Belarus in the war of aggression against Ukraine.

Its statute should contain a definition of the crime of aggression in line with Article 8 *bis* of the ICC Statute,[19] which builds upon UN General Assembly Resolution 3314, adopted on 14 December 1974. 'This is the consensual definition of the crime of aggression,' explains Judge Gnatovskyy. 'It is already part of general international law. [...] It has this very important precision about the manifest nature of the violation that should also help reassure the partners from G7 countries.'[20]

In principle, its statute should clearly state that personal immunities would not apply to incumbent state officials, in line with the practice of other international criminal tribunals, and that functional immunities would in any event not be applicable to the crime of aggression. On the other hand, this is one of the more complex and difficult issues that have been discussed both within the Core Group and the International Law Commission, with diverging views among international legal experts. 'The main underlying reason is that without responsibility, without answering the question, or at least raising the question of individual responsibility for the crime of aggression, it is impossible to return to international rule of law,' explains Judge Gnatovskyy, before he proposes a very interesting compromise on the controversial issue of immunities:

> The most complicated legal issue is of course the personal immunities of the Troika (head of State, head of government and Foreign Minister). The complexity lies in the fact that there is no consensus on the question in the international community in general, as such. And the ongoing discussion at the UN International Law Commission has shown that the question is far from being solved. There are conflicting views. They don't appear to be able to be reconciled. So one of the good solutions, in my view, would be simply not to answer this question at this stage, but to leave it rather to the judges of the tribunal when the time comes.[21]

Finally on this point, there are indeed precedents in international law that allow the question of immunities to be solved by the judges of a tribunal, such as the Special Court for Sierra Leone, where the question was solved with respect to Liberia's President Charles Taylor.

The issue of legitimacy will be essential. When the tribunal is established by a treaty between Ukraine and the Council of Europe, there will be some clear challenges to such a regional solution that will need to be addressed. One is the need for broad legitimacy, which such a European solution will not necessarily bring, as it is often only by involving the United Nations (and particularly the General Assembly) that this kind of legitimacy can be achieved. A UN link could be perfectly possible as a matter of international law, as several member states of the Council of Europe have also voiced their preference for it. Yet it seems as if the political situation is far from conducive to implementing such an option, according to Claus Kreß, director of the Institute for International Peace and Security Law at the University of Cologne, Germany. 'In this situation, the Council of Europe could, while falling short of the UN path, provide an avenue for a compromise solution, which is not only workable, but also meets essential demands of legitimacy,' he concludes.[22]

However, additional steps could be taken to increase such a solution's legitimacy and its global outreach, such as to adopt the international consensus definition of the crime of aggression, as referred to in a previous point above, as well as to elect non-European judges to the bench of a new tribunal. Moreover, collecting statements of support from countries outside Europe will be important. It's clear that the war in Gaza is having an impact on perceptions and attitudes. The situation in Gaza is lamentable and tragic, but it provides some reassurance that the ICC is currently investigating possible war crimes and crimes against humanity. Furthermore, the crime of aggression is about attacking another state in order to deny its right to exist or in order to conquer a part of the territory. This is not what we have seen in Gaza – so far, at least. Kreß summarises,

> In a nutshell, the less introvert a European contribution through the Council of Europe would be, the better it would meet the historic challenge before us which consists of giving an international criminal law response that duly reflects the fundamental assault by the Russian leadership both on Ukraine and its incredibly brave people and on the global legal order.

The tribunal's statute would contain a list of fair trial rights of the accused, as well as a reference to the principles of legality and *non bis in idem* (literally 'not twice for the same'; as in modern legal systems, it is the foundational principle that a person should not be tried or punished twice for the same crime), in line with international human rights law and the European Convention on Human Rights.

Its role would be complementary to the ICC's jurisdiction and in no way limit or affect the latter's exercise of jurisdiction over war crimes, crimes against humanity and possible genocide committed in the context of the ongoing aggression and its jurisdiction in general. Both the ICC and the special tribunal should agree on practical and legal issues such as sharing of evidence, custody of suspects, developing common witness protection schemes and sequencing of trials of individuals prosecuted by both courts.

Its seat should be established in The Hague, with a view to ensuring complementarity and cooperation with the ICC and other international courts and institutions.

States and international organisations supporting the special tribunal should provide to it sufficient human and financial resources, ensuring its full independence and effective operational functioning. During the informal discussions on the creation of a tribunal, the legal adviser of the Council of Europe and director of the Directorate of Legal Advice and Public International Law (DLAPIL), Jörg Polakiewicz, proposed the establishment of such a tribunal through a bilateral agreement between the Council of Europe and Ukraine, accompanied by an enlarged partial agreement (EPA) governing the modalities of support to such a tribunal (the EPA was also used when the Council of Europe set up the Register of Damage for Ukraine). The EPA will at the same time create a 'Management Committee' for the tribunal. Its purpose will be to provide the funding of the tribunal and to assist in other administrative aspects of its operation. In addition, there is no reason to believe that establishing such a tribunal should necessarily involve a large number of staff and huge costs for the parties. 'It's enough to have, let's say, maximum three judges for any procedural decisions that have to be taken, and perhaps one could envisage establishing a list of people on a non-permanent basis, to whom you can apply, and you don't have to have them as full-time employees,' emphasises Judge Gnatovskyy.[23]

The first formal step towards agreeing on the legal model – based on a bilateral treaty between Ukraine and the Council of Europe – was made by the Council of Europe's forty-six member states on 30 April 2024, when it adopted a decision to authorise the Secretary-General

> to prepare any necessary documents to contribute to consultations within the Core Group on a possible draft Agreement between the Council of Europe and the Government of Ukraine on the Establishment of a Special Tribunal for the Crime of Aggression of the Russian Federation against Ukraine, including its Statute, and on a possible draft enlarged partial agreement governing the modalities of support to such a Tribunal, its financing and other administrative matters.

This unprecedented decision, proposed and negotiated by Petr Válek, the Czech Ambassador, gave the Secretary-General the necessary mandate to start working on the creation of a special tribunal.

'The Council of Europe has stood alongside Ukraine since the very first day of the war,' said Alain Berset, the Secretary-General of the Council of Europe.

> Last April, we opened a Register of Damage for those affected by Russia's aggression and work on a compensation mechanism is now well under way. Furthermore, the European Court of Human Rights is still dealing with over 4,000 cases against Russia related to events in Crimea, Donbas and the wider war

> in Ukraine. Alongside this ongoing work, establishing the Special Tribunal for the Crime of Aggression within the Council of Europe framework will enable our international partners – notably including Ukraine and the European Union – to make full use of our experience and expertise in upholding human rights and the rule of law across the continent. Today we have seen important progress which will have a major impact on the people of Ukraine for generations to come. However, the hard work is only just beginning. We will not stop until Russia is held fully accountable and justice is done.[24]

'At the Brussels meeting [in 2025], we identified the elements of a package deal – a compromise on the main outstanding issues, which are related to immunity, trials in absentia, jurisdiction and the definition of aggression,' explains legal adviser Jörg Polakiewicz.[25] Later in February 2025, the United States decided to withdraw from the Core Group, but as the current EU High Representative on Foreign Affairs and Security Policy, Kaja Kallas, has previously underlined, 'This is the European hour, and we need to rise to the challenge. It's on us.' Later on, the EU also provided substantial financial support to the initial phase of the set-up of the tribunal.

Moreover, in late February 2025, an impressive ninety-three countries voted in favour of a UN General Assembly resolution in New York that underlined

> the need to ensure accountability for the most serious crimes under international law committed in the territory of Ukraine, through appropriate, fair and independent investigations and prosecutions at the national or international level, and ensure justice for all victims and the prevention of future crimes.

This is why you'll likely see the special tribunal created through a treaty between Ukraine and the Council of Europe, with strong support from the EU and numerous countries in Europe and even beyond. At the annual Foreign Ministers meeting of the Council of Europe in Luxembourg in May 2025, a letter from President Zelenskyy was handed over to Secretary-General Berset, asking him to set up a new special tribunal on the crime of aggression under the auspices of the Council of Europe. Later in June that year, during a historic visit by President Zelenskyy to the Council of Europe, the Ukrainian Head of State and the Secretary-General of the Council of Europe, Alain Berset, signed the treaty, paving the way for the work to commence.

'Every war criminal must know: there will be justice, and that includes Russia,' underlined President Zelenskyy during the visit to Strasbourg.

> Politically, we have already made big progress, and I am grateful to the Council of Europe and to everyone showing leadership. Justice takes time, but it must happen, I am sure. And today's agreement and this tribunal give us a real chance to bring justice for the crime of aggression. Other institutions don't have the tools to do this. And we need to show clearly: aggression leads to punishment, and we must make it happen together.

Ian Borg, the Chair of the Council of Europe's Committee of Ministers and Foreign Minister of Malta, stated,

> Today's agreement is living proof that genuine international cooperation, grounded in legal clarity and political courage, can achieve what once might have seemed improbable. The Council

> of Europe's swift, principled and unwavering response has reaffirmed its enduring relevance and moral authority, in Europe and well beyond.[26]

Looking back on his seminal article, Philippe Sands reflects,

> To be honest, I did not imagine that the article in the *Financial Times* would generate such interest, and the actual negotiation of an instrument. The fact that it did, and that it has, is a source of satisfaction, not as to my own role, but to the notion that in these challenging times ideas and words can make a difference. In this I pay tribute to Hersch Lauterpacht and Raphael Lemkin, whose ideas and words gave the world the new legal terms of genocide and crimes against humanity. I am not starry-eyed about international law, but it is basically the best we have in forging decency, accountability and reconciliation. I express my deep appreciation for all those individuals, organisations, countries and institutions who have made a special tribunal on the crime of aggression in Ukraine a real possibility. It offers hope at a time of lawlessness, impunity and other challenges.[27]

In January 2026, the Council of Europe and the European Union signed an agreement on the financing of an advance team to establish the Special Tribunal for the Crime of Aggression against Ukraine, within the framework of the Council. 'The European Union's release of the first €10 million to help set up a Special Tribunal for the Crime of Aggression against Ukraine is a concrete step towards justice,' said the European Union's High Representative for Foreign Affairs and the Security Policy and European Commission Vice President, Kaja Kallas.[28]

There is still a way to go, but a breakthrough has no doubt been made.

• • •

Given the current context, Claus Kreß warns,

> Under these dire circumstances, a failure even now to act, resulting in a negative precedent regarding the crime of aggression, would entail a serious risk to embolden President Putin and future leaders of other most powerful states to move forward toward a fundamentally different international order. This order would be one where the world got divided into a couple of vast spaces, each under the domination of an imperial power. In such an order, the prohibition of the use of force would cease to provide all states – including, most importantly, the weaker ones – with protection. Posthumously, the infamous German theorist Carl Schmitt would then have prevailed with his vision of a world structured along 'Großräume' – to use his German word (which literally translates to 'large-scale places' or 'great spaces', which carries a heavy historical and political weight due to its association with Nazi-era legal theory and expansionist ideologies). This is why Russia's war of aggression against Ukraine, which continues unabated, marks a critical moment in history.[29]

Indeed, Putin has not bothered to hide his imperial intentions and the need for a new world order. He has repeatedly argued that the collapse of the Soviet Union was 'the biggest geopolitical catastrophe of the century' and he is determined to rebuild this empire.

'If Russia is allowed to win in Ukraine, this kind of imperialism will make a comeback all over the world,' explains Yuval Noah Harari. 'What will then restrain Venezuela, for example, from conquering Guyana, or Iran from conquering the United Arab Emirates? What will restrain Russia itself from conquering Estonia or Kazakhstan? No border and no state could find safety in anything except armaments and alliances.'[30] Or only in nuclear weapons, as already underlined by some European political leaders. The German Chancellor, Friedrich Merz, has stated that, 'Germany would thus need to talk to Europe's two nuclear powers, France and the UK, about extending their deterrence umbrella to Germany.'[31] It seems that both the UK Prime Minister and the French President could be open to discussing such an idea. Today, there are also those in Kyiv who bitterly regret that Ukraine had to abandon its nuclear arsenal in 1994, while acknowledging that the most efficient way for Ukraine to counter or halt Russian aggression and revanchism could have been to maintain its nuclear capability.

It was the American political scientist Kenneth Waltz who famously argued that when it came to the spread of nuclear weapons 'more may be better', because all international rivalries would be durably stabilised by the prospect of mutually assured destruction. 'The world may be about to test his hypothesis,' explains Gideon Rose, an Axel Springer fellow at the American Academy in Berlin and a senior fellow at the Council on Foreign Relations, in an article in *Foreign Affairs*. He continues, 'Everyone should understand that if the liberal order falls, the non-proliferation regime would fall with it. And the powers rushing for nukes then would be newly orphaned friends of the United States who are no longer convinced they can rely on American security guarantees, and might even have to fear American coercion.'[32]

The danger of the collapse of the current liberal world order is not lost on observers in former imperial colonies. In a speech in February 2022, the Kenyan Ambassador to the United Nations, Martin Kimani, explained that after the collapse of the European empires newly liberated people in Africa and elsewhere treated international borders as sacrosanct, understanding the alternative was waging endless wars.[33] One good example was the Biafran Civil War in the late 1960s, when the oil-rich Christian Igbos in the south-east of Nigeria sought to gain full independence from the rest of the country. A long and bloody civil war followed. In the end, Biafra had no other choice than to surrender. Despite the sympathy that many in Europe, the United States and elsewhere felt for the Biafrans, very few countries and their leaders could envisage the break-up of Africa's most populous country. The precedent and potential consequences seemed too alarming, not only to Nigeria but to the whole of Africa and to the world community.

With the Russian invasion of Ukraine, the global community is again facing a fundamental challenge to the existing world order, founded on the principles of the UN Charter and international law. Nothing other than military might seems to deter Putin, but the creation of a tribunal on the crime of aggression could have a subduing effect. It could also send a very important signal to other leaders around the world with similar ambitions as Putin: we will not tolerate it. You will be prosecuted one day, rest assured. As Ursula von der Leyen has clearly pointed out, 'When Russia chose to roll its tanks over Ukraine's borders, breaking the UN Charter, it committed one of the gravest violations: the crime of aggression. Now, justice is coming. Justice for Ukraine. We have laid down the legal foundations for a special tribunal.'[34]

STATEMENT BY DMYTRO KULEBA ON THE INITIATIVE TO CREATE A TRIBUNAL FOR BRINGING THE LEADERSHIP OF THE RUSSIAN FEDERATION TO JUSTICE FOR THE CRIME OF AGGRESSION AGAINST UKRAINE

7 MARCH 2022

In February 2014, the Russian Federation committed an act of armed aggression against Ukraine. Russia's occupation of Crimea and the launch of the war in Donetsk and Luhansk oblasts of Ukraine blatantly violated the fundamental principles of international peace and security, namely the prohibition of the use of force against the sovereignty, political independence and territorial integrity of another state and the right of states to freely determine their own path of development.

On 24 February 2022, the Russian Federation launched a new stage of aggression, a full-scale aggressive war against Ukraine. In his speeches before and during the invasion, the Russian President outlined his motives in detail. He publicly denied Ukraine and the people of Ukraine their right to exist, which points at the inhuman ideology in which the crime of aggression of the Russian Federation is rooted.

In the course of aggression, the Russian Armed Forces have committed and continue to commit multiple war crimes against the civilian population, as well as crimes against humanity. These include indiscriminate artillery shelling, air bombardment and missile strikes on residential areas of Ukrainian cities, kindergartens, orphanages, nuclear power plants and critical infrastructure objects. All of those and other crimes are being thoroughly documented, laying the groundwork for further probes by international and Ukrainian justice.

Together with partners, Ukraine has initiated a number of legal international proceedings aimed at bringing perpetrators of those crimes to justice. In particular, such proceedings are unfolding in the International Court of Justice, the International Criminal Court and the European Court of Human Rights.

These cases focus on particular violations and crimes committed in the course of aggression. At the same time, none of them would be possible without the principal crime: the armed aggression of the Russian Federation against Ukraine.

Taking into account the fact that such unprovoked aggression is unprecedented in over eighty years and the fact that there are no relevant international legal mechanisms to hold the Russian Federation accountable for such a grave crime, I supported the initiative by the international scholar community to create a special tribunal aimed at delivering justice for the crime of Russia's aggression against Ukraine. A coalition of states will take part in its creation. Meanwhile, Ukraine is working on collecting all the necessary evidence related to the crime of aggression, and we are grateful to our partners for their readiness to support our efforts.

The last century has seen the creation of a similar mechanism for international justice. In January 1942, in London, representatives of nine states signed a declaration that later laid the foundation for the Nuremberg tribunal.

I am grateful to leading experts in international law who developed the draft declaration and statement calling to create such a special tribunal to hold the Russian leadership accountable for the crime of aggression against Ukraine. Ukraine fully supports this initiative, and the Ministry of Foreign Affairs of Ukraine has already begun working on its implementation.

Let me underline that this effort is not meant to replace but rather complement the existing international proceedings on various war crimes and crimes against humanity committed in the course of Russian aggression against Ukraine, which are underway in the International Court of Justice, the International Criminal Court and the European Court of Human Rights.

I am confident that with joint efforts, we will be successful in holding the Russian Federation and its leadership accountable for the crime of aggression against Ukraine.

CHAPTER 13

THE PATH TO PEACE

Russia is and will remain, for the long term, the greatest threat to freedom, peace and stability in Europe.

Friedrich Merz, Chancellor of Germany

'Making peace is harder than waging war,' the French Prime Minister George Clemenceau declared in 1919 at the Paris Peace Conference after the First World War. And it seems the longer and more costly the war, the harder the task is of making a durable peace.

'When powers come together to end wars, the stakes are of life and death,' explains the renowned historian Margaret MacMillan.

> Incompatible national goals and the high emotions raised by a punishing and costly conflict make establishing peace a hard and painful process. We may dream of better and fairer international orders, of making war an aberration and, worse, a crime, but in the aftermath of conflicts, the accumulated hatreds and the desire for revenge and retribution make it hard to take the high road.[1]

Richard Overy recognises the difficulty of moving beyond global conflict, writing, 'There are scant grounds for thinking that a war-less world is about to emerge from the current or future international order. The causes of war have been persistent for millennia. If war has a very long human history, it also has a future.'[2] There is, however, a widespread desire to see an end to our war-torn age, as Timothy Garton Ash has noted: 'Our publics are desperate to believe we can quickly revert to our old post-1989 peacetime ways. It is now the duty of European leaders not just to rekindle the fighting spirit of Churchill and De Gaulle but also to explain honestly to voters that we face another long struggle.'

• • •

> We the peoples of the United Nations, determined to save succeeding generations from the scourge of war, which twice in our lifetime has brought untold sorrow to mankind, and to reaffirm faith in fundamental human rights, in the dignity and worth of the human person, in the equal rights of men and women and of nations large and small, and to establish conditions under which justice and respect for the obligations arising from treaties and other sources of international law can be maintained.[3]

These are the first solemn words of the UN Charter – the world's constitution – adopted in 1948 by all the participating states of the United Nations. Written at the end of the Second World War, they capture the essence of President Zelenskyy's peace formula that was presented at a G7 meeting in October 2022. Thereafter, a ten-point peace plan was introduced at the G20 leaders' summit in Indonesia in November 2022.

Politically and tactically, this was a wise and cunning move, as it managed to bring together up to ninety countries, as well as observers from the United Nations, the European Union and the Council of Europe, for an informal and honest discussion based on a notion of peace as elaborated by Ukraine. Some have argued that the main antagonist – the Russian Federation – should have been present at these talks, but for Ukraine it was a way of building a strong global coalition around a set of clear positions ahead of any negotiations with the Russians, and to collect worldwide support, particularly in the Global South. 'There is a place for everyone in the formula,' Dmytro Kuleba highlighted. 'It is a pragmatic document bringing the principles of the UN Charter to life.'[4]

President Zelenskyy's peace formula included the following ten points, as presented on the official website of Ukraine:[5]

1) *Radiation and nuclear safety.* No one has the right to blackmail the world with a radioactive disaster. Despite its constant attempts to rattle its nuclear arsenal, Russia is not an exemption. This nuclear blackmail must stop. Russia is also constantly endangering Ukrainian nuclear power plants, temporarily occupying the Zaporizhzhia (NPP) in particular. Russia must instantly withdraw all its military forces from the plant. The plant must be transferred to the control of the IAEA (International Atomic Energy Agency) and Ukrainian personnel. The connection of the plant to the normal power grid must be restored immediately so that nothing threatens the stability of the reactors.

2) *Food security.* Once again, people's lives and wellbeing should not be a part of Russia's blackmail or famine games. Thanks to the 'Black Sea Grain Initiative', Ukraine was able to export 32.8 million

tons of food to countries in Asia, Africa and Europe. Now, with Russia's withdrawal from the agreement, people will suffer the consequences. The grain initiative and Ukrainian agricultural exports must be restored for the sake of millions of people around the world.

3) *Energy security*. Attacks on critical civilian infrastructure are unacceptable. Russia is trying to turn the winter and cold into a weapon against civilians. Ukrainian power plants, power lines and other energy infrastructure must be properly protected. Moreover, steps must be taken, such as price restrictions on Russian energy resources (including oil and gas), so as to further restrict the income generated by Russian sales.

4) *Release of all prisoners and deportees*. Today, thousands of Ukrainian people, both military and civilians, are in Russian captivity. Many have been forcefully deported, including at least 20,000 children. Many are subjected to brutal torture and abuse right now. Ukraine proposes the release of prisoners – 'all for all', including the release of all children and adults who were illegally deported to Russia.

5) *Implementation of the UN Charter and restoration of Ukraine's territorial integrity and the world order*. In Article 2 of the UN Charter, it is clearly stated that 'all members shall refrain in their international relations from the threat or use of force against the territorial integrity or political independence of any state'. By invading Ukraine, Russia has violated numerous international agreements, laws and principles. Those cannot be applied partially, if we want to build a future where sovereignty and international borders are respected. That order, brutally attacked by Russia, must be

restored. Furthermore, Ukraine's territorial integrity is not up for negotiation.

6) Withdrawal of Russian troops and cessation of hostilities. To cease the hostilities, Russia must withdraw all its troops and armed formations from the territory of Ukraine. As long as Russian soldiers remain on Ukrainian land, Ukrainians have to fight and die to protect their homes and to shield the world from the long-lasting consequences of this aggression.

7) Restoration of justice. No crime should be left unpunished – and as of August 2023, Ukraine had registered more than 100,000 war crimes committed by the Russian military in this war. Hardly a day has passed in the years of Russian aggression without civilians being killed or injured by Russia's drones, missiles and shelling. With every part of the country Ukraine liberated, the world witnessed new mass graves, torture chambers and many other horrors as a result of the Russian occupation. That is why the special tribunal on the crime of aggression must be established. There is also a need for an international mechanism to make Russia compensate for all the damages caused by this war.

8) Immediate protection of the environment. There has been huge damage to the environment and wildlife caused by the Russian invasion, such as numerous minefields, burned forests, polluted waters and injured and killed animals. The environmental damage caused by the Russians' blowing up of the Kakhovka Dam alone has been estimated at $1.5 billion, but it is hard to assess the exact environmental damage of the Russian destruction as it has changed the ecosystem for decades to come.

9) Prevention of escalation Ukraine is not a member of any military alliance and the so-called 'Budapest Memorandum' has not been able to ensure the country's safety. Therefore, when the current Russian invasion is repelled, it is essential to prevent any chance of its repetition or any further aggression. This can only be achieved with proper and effective security guarantees for Ukraine, as well as a renewed post-war security architecture in the Euro-Atlantic space that will include Ukraine.

10) Confirmation of the end of the war. After the hostilities are ceased and security and justice are restored, the parties should sign an official document confirming the end of the war.

• • •

After the launch of the ten-point peace plan, four separate meetings were organised, hosted by Denmark, Saudi Arabia, Malta and Switzerland, respectively in Copenhagen, Jedda, Valetta and Davos, with the participation of international advisers and security experts from many of the 193 member states of the United Nations. During the deliberations, dedicated working groups were set up around each of the ten points in the peace formula and specific countries helped co-chair the groups – France, Sweden and the Czech Republic took the lead on radiation and nuclear safety, Turkey on food security, Canada on the release of prisoners and deported persons, the Netherlands on the restoration of justice, Germany on ecological safety (environment and demining), and Denmark and Poland on energy security.

Finally, a summit of world leaders based on the Ukrainian peace formula was held in Bürgenstock, Switzerland (15–16 June 2024), with 101 countries and international organisations taking part. 'Today is the day when the world begins to bring a just peace closer,' President Zelenskyy stated at the opening, before he outlined the main objective of the meeting.

> Now we will focus on three points – on what is useful to everyone in the world – without exception. The first point is radiation and nuclear safety. The second is food security. The third is release of prisoners and deportees, adults and children, military and civilians whose lives have been broken by war. We will focus on these initial points of the Peace Formula, and in the process of working on them we can reach an agreement and create an action plan for each point of the formula.[6]

At the end of the summit, a joint communiqué was adopted, highlighting that 'a fruitful, comprehensive and constructive exchange of various views on pathways towards a framework for a comprehensive, just and lasting peace, based on international law, including the United Nations Charter' had taken place, while participants repeated their 'commitment to refraining from the threat or use of force against the territorial integrity or political independence of any state, the principles of sovereignty, independence, and territorial integrity of all states, including Ukraine, within their internationally recognised borders'.[7] Later the Turkish Foreign Minister, Hakan Fidan, told journalists that 'this summit could have been more result oriented if the other party to the conflict – Russia – was present in the room'. In an instructive response to the absence of Russia from the summit, President Zelenskyy told reporters, 'There is no Russia here. Why? Because if Russia was interested in peace, there would be no war.'[8] As a matter of fact, 'the Russians have blocked all our initiatives from the very beginning, and they continue to do so', Zelenskyy underlined in an interview with the *New Yorker* in September 2024.[9]

The People's Republic of China, the country widely seen as having the most influence on the Russian Federation, decided not to participate at the summit, and Brazil did not send a high-level delegation. According to the French Institute for International and Strategic Affairs (IRIS), none of the BRICS (Brazil, Russia, India, China, South Africa, Egypt, Ethiopia, Iran, Indonesia and the United Arab Emirates) countries wanted to play along, so they either boycotted the meeting or refused to endorse the final communiqué, which had been stylised to a certain degree to attract their approval. At the same time, China and Brazil backed their own peace proposal, insisting that Russia and Ukraine needed to negotiate directly.[10] At the first meeting of the 'Friends of Peace' group in New York – set up by China and Brazil in 2024 – where representatives from seventeen countries from the Global South also took part, the Chinese Foreign Minister, Wang Yi, stated the importance of 'observing three principles for de-escalating the conflict, namely no expansion of the battlefield, no escalation of fighting, and no fanning up of the flames by any party, in particular no use of weapons of mass destruction or no attack on nuclear power plants and other peaceful nuclear facilities'.[11]

There have been some claims that in the first days and weeks of the Russian invasion of Ukraine in February 2022, bilateral talks between Ukraine and Russia took place that could have ended the war. It has been asserted that 'the Russians and Ukrainians almost finalised an agreement that would have ended the war and provided Ukraine with multilateral security guarantees, paving the way to its permanent neutrality and, down the road, its membership in the

EU'.[12] The Russians and the Ukrainians were, however, never even close to any sort of a final compromise text. Kuleba explains,

> There was no peace settlement to be had in 2022. I've heard this argument everywhere, in Africa, in Asia and even in America. They say, 'But you were close to peace and the bloody West did not allow you to do it, because the West wants you to fight until the last Ukrainian.' This commonly held view is a complete inversion of reality. Knowing our Western partners, who I cherish and appreciate very much, if there was the slightest chance in 2022 to end the war, they would have pushed down on our shoulders and said, 'Do it.'

The reality was that the so-called 'Russian peace proposals' were more of an ultimatum and completely unacceptable, if not unserious. Kuleba concludes, 'They even had one provision that all Ukrainian heavy armour had to be placed in warehouses and these warehouses should remain under the control of the Russian forces. So, the plan was clear: neutralise Ukraine, stay where they are in Ukraine, demilitarise Ukraine. And then make the final shot.'[13]

Based on the discussions in Switzerland, President Zelenskyy later reviewed and elaborated on several of the ten points in the peace formula; in October 2024, he issued the 'Victory Plan' for Ukraine. Zelenskyy likely saw that the ten-point peace plan was heading into a deadlock, and as a reaction to the US Presidential elections he was most likely looking for a way to capture the attention of both candidates – Donald Trump and Kamala Harris – by proposing his own, revised and updated peace plan. 'Ukraine's Victory Plan is a plan to strengthen our state and strengthen our positions – to be strong enough to end the war,' Zelenskyy said in an interview.[14] In his speech to the Ukrainian Parliament unveiling the plan, he claimed his focus was a strategy based on 'peace through strength', while criticising how often Kyiv's partners mentioned 'negotiations' without using the word 'justice'.[15]

In his address to the parliamentarians, Zelenskyy explained his five key aims:

1) Securing an invitation to Ukraine to join NATO. He emphasised that

> determination on the NATO issue for Ukraine also means the inevitability of European integration for Ukraine and the fact that there is no alternative to democracy in Ukraine. That is why this is the initial point of the Victory Plan. The first and very important point. The sign of determination.[16]

NATO Secretary-General Mark Rutte replied at a press conference in Brussels on the very same day that the Ukrainian President presented his victory plan in Kyiv:

> It is my firm belief that one day, Ukraine will be a member of NATO, and I will applaud when that day comes. It's also very clear that Putin or Russia has no say in this. And then obviously it is up to the allies to discuss among themselves how to take this forward. But the fact that we are doing all this work on improving the interoperability of Ukraine with NATO, not only the money, but also the training and the other programmes we are running currently with Ukraine as allies, but also, of course, the individual commitments allies made in terms of their security agreements with Ukraine. This all is about making sure that Ukraine stands

> ready when the day comes when NATO membership is possible. But I cannot today now exactly sketch out what that path will be, but I am absolutely confident that in the future, Ukraine will join us.[17]

2) Strengthening the Ukrainian defence against Russian aggression, including the use of foreign supplied weapons for strikes deep inside Russian territory, where some of Ukraine's allies had been reluctant to give their permission in fear of Russian retaliation. President Zelenskyy said, 'The defense point of the Plan has a secret annex – and it is accessible only to those partners who have the appropriate military assistance capabilities.'[18] In addition, under this point, the Ukrainian President underlined the continuation of Ukraine's military operations on Russian territory to avoid creation of '*buffer zones*' within Ukraine's borders.

3) Ukraine could accept the deployment of a comprehensive non-nuclear strategic deterrence package on its territory, sufficient to protect the country from any military threat posed by Russia. 'The deterrence package is the fact that Russia is either going into diplomacy or going to lose its war machine. Peace through strength,' Zelenskyy emphasised.

4) Ukraine would offer its strategic partners a special agreement for the joint protection of the country's critical resources, as well as joint investment and use of its huge economic potential. This involved natural resources and critical metals worth trillions of US dollars, including uranium, titanium, lithium, graphite, as well as other strategically valuable resources. 'The deposits of critical resources in Ukraine, along with Ukraine's globally important energy

and food production potential, are among the key predatory objectives of the Russian Federation in this war. And this is our opportunity for growth,' the Ukrainian President said.[19]

5) The last point included security-related issues designed for a post-war period, involving, if partners agreed, the replacement of certain US military contingents stationed in Europe with Ukrainian units that had gained real experience in modern warfare; the use of Western weapons; and cooperation with NATO troops. 'This Ukrainian experience should be used to strengthen the defence of the entire Alliance and ensure security in Europe. This is a worthy mission for our heroes,' Zelenskyy concluded.[20]

Not everyone in the Ukrainian Parliament that morning was passionate about President Zelenskyy's plan. Some opposition lawmakers even called the proposal unrealistic, stressing how dependent on other countries it would make Ukraine. 'According to the plan, it seems that someone else has to do everything for us,' stated Oleksiy Goncharenko, a member of Ukraine's European Solidarity group.[21]

'The Victory Plan is a bridge,' explained Zelenskyy.

> After the first peace summit, our partners saw that Russia was not prepared for any talks at all – which confirmed my message to them and my insistence that without making Ukraine strong, they will never force Putin to negotiate fairly and on equal terms. No one believed me. They said, 'We will invite them to the second summit, and they will come running.'[22]

However, there would not be a second peace summit, as the election of President Donald Trump initiated a process of frequent bilateral diplomatic contacts between the US, the Russian Federation and Ukraine, leading to a concern in many European capitals that the intention of the US was to seek a ceasefire and/or peace agreement without sufficiently taking into account Ukrainian positions.

The sidelining of Trump's Special Envoy on Russia and Ukraine, General Keith Kellogg, whom Putin had refused to meet, also raised concerns. This was largely because Kellogg was seen as pragmatic; he acknowledged the need to give Ukraine more leverage in potential peace talks with Russia. Kellogg explained the sudden change at a Ukrainian lunch at the Munich Security Conference in mid-February 2025: 'We've got an envoy for the Middle East, Witkoff, involved. He's got the Russian lane. And I work in the American/Ukrainian allied lane as well. We're doing that for speed because all we want to do is say "When is this going to end?" I'm on Trump time. And Trump time means to do a job today and he wants to know tomorrow why is it not solved.'[23]

Already in April 2024, in a highly interesting report co-authored with Fred Fleitz, Kellogg outlined what it will require for a strong America First leadership to deliver a peace deal for Ukraine. In the report, Kellogg recognised that

> although some US critics of military aid to Volodymyr Zelenskyy's government might indeed be isolationist, the vast majority are Americans worried about whether America's vital strategic interests are at stake in the Ukraine war, the potential of the involvement of US military forces and whether America is engaged in a proxy war with Russia that could escalate into a nuclear conflict. They also see the need to establish a plan to end this war and not simply provide weapons for a conflict that appears to have become a long-term stalemate.[24] [...] On Ukraine, the [first]

> Trump Administration promoted a strong deterrent approach by authorising the first-ever lethal military aid package to Ukraine, equipping its armed forces with advanced Javelin anti-armour missiles, naval vessels, and Mark VI patrol boats. [...] At the same time, Trump was open to co-operation with Russia and dialogue with Putin. Trump expressed respect for Putin as a world leader and did not demonise him in public statements. This was a transactional approach to US-Russia relations in which Trump used his experience as a dealmaker to find ways to coexist and lower tensions with Putin while standing firm on American security interests.[24]

Kellogg also indirectly criticised President Zelenskyy's ten-point peace plan, claiming that although 'the plan's call for restoring Ukraine's territorial integrity and a Russian affirmation in accord with the UN Charter, withdrawal of Russian troops, and a special tribunal to prosecute Russian war crimes were ambitious and just', it was 'no way to force Russia to agree to such terms'. In his words, 'Zelenskyy's plan went nowhere'.

On the contrary, what was needed, Kellogg argued, was a new approach and a comprehensive strategy for the Ukraine war, while he underlined rhetorically that

> America First is not isolationist, nor is it a call to retreat America from engagement in the world. An America First approach to national security is, however, characteristically distinct from a foreign policy establishment that often keeps the United States mired in endless wars to the detriment of the country by putting idealistic principles ahead of the interests of the American people.[25]

The only way forward was to 'start with a formal US policy to bring the war to a conclusion'. More specifically, this would

> mean a formal US policy to seek a ceasefire and negotiated settlement of the Ukraine conflict. The United States would continue to arm Ukraine and strengthen its defences to ensure Russia will make no further advances and will not attack again after a ceasefire or peace agreement. Future American military aid, however, will require Ukraine to participate in peace talks with Russia.

To convince Putin to join the peace talks, the US President and other NATO leaders 'should offer to put off NATO membership for Ukraine for an extended period in exchange for a comprehensive and verifiable peace deal with security guarantees'. On this point, Kellogg also made a reference to an op-ed article in *Foreign Affairs* in April 2023 by Richard Haas and Charles Kupchan[26] that proposed,

> In exchange for abiding by a ceasefire, a demilitarised zone and participating in peace talks, Russia could be offered some limited sanctions relief. Ukraine would not be asked to relinquish the goal of regaining all its territory, but it would agree to use diplomacy, not force, with the understanding that this would require a future diplomatic breakthrough which probably will not occur before Putin leaves office. Until that happens, the United States and its allies would pledge to only fully lift sanctions against Russia and normalise relations after it signs a peace agreement acceptable to Ukraine.

Kellogg's third recommendation stated,

> By enabling Ukraine to negotiate from a position of strength while also communicating to Russia the consequences if it fails to abide by future peace talk conditions, the United States could implement a negotiated end-state with terms aligned with US and Ukrainian interests. Part of this negotiated end-state should include provisions in which we establish a long-term security architecture for Ukraine's defence that focuses on bilateral security defence. Including this in a Russia-Ukraine peace deal offers a path toward long-term peace in the region and a means of preventing future hostilities between the two nations.

Kellogg's report was seemingly endorsed to a considerable extent by Donald Trump both during his election campaign and after becoming President; it no doubt also triggered the appointment of Kellogg as Trump's Special Envoy to Russia and Ukraine. It was, however, the US Special Envoy to the Middle East, the real-estate mogul Steve Witkoff, and later joined by President Trump's son-in-law Jared Kushner, who had an expanding role in the Trump administration's foreign policy and who became the crucial American interlocutor for Moscow. Finally, late in November 2025, reports emerged that General Kellogg was going to leave his post, early in 2026.

What Kellogg had presented was only 'a few creative ideas for an America First approach to end the war'. As President Trump's strategy – or 'hand of cards' – is becoming more and more apparent as time passes by, several European and other foreign leaders have expressed deep concern. Most notably, of course, there was shock and disbelief at the treatment of President Zelenskyy in the infamous meeting in the Oval Office at the end of February 2025. Many also found the allegations that Ukraine started the war and that

President Zelenskyy was a 'dictator' groundless and unwarranted. 'That was a train wreck by design,' said Sam Greene, a professor of Russian politics at King's College London. 'The quiet conversation since Munich has been about setting Ukraine up for a fall.'[27]

'Now is the moment to stay calm, but not carry on,' wrote Camille Grand, a distinguished policy fellow at the European Council on Foreign Relations and former Assistant Secretary-General for Defence Investment at NATO. 'The US ally has now officially decided to take a stance inconsistent with our traditionally shared interests and values. This might be temporary or lasting, but this will have profound and enduring consequences.'[28]

Yuval Noah Harari, meanwhile, has compellingly argued,

> When Trump blamed Ukraine for the Russian invasion, many people couldn't understand how he could hold such a preposterous view. Some assumed he'd been hoodwinked by Russian propaganda. But there is a simpler explanation. According to the Trumpian worldview, considerations of justice, morality and international law are irrelevant, and the only thing that matters in international relations is power. Since Ukraine is weaker than Russia, it should have surrendered. In the Trumpian vision, peace means surrender, and since Ukraine refused to surrender, the war is its fault. The Trumpian vision is not a novelty. It has been the predominant vision for thousands of years prior to the rise of the liberal world order. The Trumpian formula has been tried and tested so many times before that we know where it usually leads – to a never-ending cycle of empire-building and war.[29]

Finally, the undue pressure on Ukrainian leaders to accept a highly advantageous deal for the United States on Ukrainian rare earth minerals raised many questions about the real intentions behind Washington's engagement with finding an end to the war in Ukraine.[30] However, after months of complex and tense negotiations, Ukraine and the United States signed a minerals deal that, according to Scott Bessent, the US Treasury Secretary, 'signals clearly to Russia that the Trump administration is committed to a peace process centered on a free, sovereign and prosperous Ukraine over the long term'. Moreover, the Ukrainian Prime Minister, Denys Shmyhal, described the deal as 'truly a good, equal and beneficial international agreement on joint investments in the development and recovery of Ukraine'.[31]

Furthermore, and according to some observers, the new administration in Washington DC sadly ignored what is surely fundamental to any negotiation: refusing to concede at the start of any process to the maximalist demands of the other side. Trump and his Secretary of War, Pete Hegseth, seemed to assure Putin, even before any real negotiations had commenced, that Putin was likely to be able to keep territory Russia had occupied and seized – and that Ukraine will not be admitted to NATO.[32]

The UK Foreign Secretary, David Lammy, speaking at the Munich Security Conference in February 2025, voiced a clear and sombre warning on the danger of being too accommodating towards Putin and the Russians:

> It was the American diplomat, George Kennan, who wrote a long telegram back to the United States that began the foreign policy of containment of Russia. And in crafting that policy, which was a shared policy, we understood two things. We understood that – and sadly Putin is indicative of this – that there is a Tsarist tradition that he is leaning into. And there is a Soviet tradition. Let us

> remember that he is a KGB agent. He is a man of deception, and in negotiating with him we have to understand that and relate to that. And of course, what we know is it is usually war that stops that ambition. To the south, the Crimean War; to the east, the Russian war with Japan; and to the West, the Cold War. And we should be deadly serious about those imperial ambitions.[33]

Yes indeed. What we see on the continent today is not only utopian dreams of re-establishing a long-lost empire but the return of violent, aggressive nationalism. At the same time, Russia has rapidly developed into a full-fledged war-economy, which certainly does not bode well for the future. A recent report by the Center for European Policy Analysis concludes, 'Russia's economic growth is heavily tied to military spending, with investments tilted toward war-related industries, import substitution, and infrastructure projects to facilitate trade with China. In the absence of defense spending, Russia's economy would likely stagnate.'[34] For most Russians, the war has been good economically, with overall increases in Russia's GDP.

At the same time, we should always keep in mind the relative strength of the economy of Russia and its allies compared to that of the Ukrainians and their respective supporters.

'Well, if you do a simple math exercise,' explained Dmytro Kuleba in an interview with *Foreign Affairs* in January 2024,

> I take a list of countries who militarily support Ukraine, and I take a list of countries who militarily support Russia, and then I combine GDPs of the countries on both lists, and I find out that the combined GDP from the Ukraine list is twenty-one times higher than the combined GDP of countries on Russia's list. Therefore,

> the conclusion is, 'I have the resources available not only to win in the war, but also to win the war of attrition.'

But what is deeply worrying is that we see the rise of political forces today that seriously question the validity of indispensable principles of international law and the UN Charter: respect for the sovereignty and territorial integrity of nations, the settlement of international disputes in a peaceful manner and the need to preserve a rules-based international order. These are the core 'building blocks' of an international system that we have carefully constructed on the promise of 'never again' since the end of the Second World War.

'The norm against territorial conquest is a pillar of the post-1945 international order, but that pillar is now crumbling,' explains Tanisha M. Fazal, Arleen C. Carlson professor of political science at the University of Minnesota.

> Russia's invasion of Ukraine in 2022 is certainly the most egregious recent violation of this prohibition – an outlier, as an attempt to capture an entire sovereign country. Yet if Moscow gets to walk away with pieces of Ukrainian territory, and particularly if that transfer wins international recognition, other powers may be more tempted to wage wars of conquest.[35]

Putin seems determined to end the existing world order once and for all. In several speeches he has pointed out that 'international relations have entered an era of global, fundamental changes' and that 'a new world order is being formed that reflects the diversity of the entire planet', concluding that 'this natural process is irreversible'.[36] On top of this, Putin has made antagonism against the West and its so-called 'material decadence and moral depravity' a long-term policy priority. 'No ceasefire, not even brokered by a US President fond of his Russian counterpart, can reverse the degree to which Putin has made confrontation with the West the organising principle of Russian life,' explains Alexander Gabuev, director of the Carnegie Russia Eurasia Center in Berlin. 'And no cessation of hostilities in Ukraine can roll back the extent to which he has deepened his country's relationship with China.'[37]

Regrettably, also Trump and his administration seem resolute in their determination to change the global liberal order, by expressing a certain sympathy for Russia's claims for Ukrainian territory, dramatically reducing the US contribution to international organisations and by unleashing financial chaos and turmoil with his tariff announcements. And as Secretary of State Marco Rubio stated during his Senate confirmation hearing in January 2025, 'The postwar global order is not just obsolete, it is now a weapon being used against us.'[38]

Consequently, we can safely say that the world we are living in is entering deeply troubling and treacherous waters, where it seems that it will be 'the law of the jungle' and not the fundamental principles of the UN Charter and international law that will guide us and prevail. This leaves the big and the mighty to do exactly what they want. What is truly astonishing is the speed at which these changes have happened.

This is why it is more important than ever to fight back and stand firm against the unacceptable policies of Putin and other authoritarian political leaders. If the Russians should get their way with Ukraine, it will no doubt send signals which may only encourage other political leaders around the world to do similar. Put simply, Putin's willingness to invade a neighbour, assault democratic societies and generally violate accepted norms – and his seeming ability to get away with it – paves the way for others to do the same.[39] Just reflect for a minute on the haphazard and accidental way the borders of countries in Africa were determined by arrogant colonial powers during the nineteenth century. Think about the wisdom of African leaders through generations who have preserved the status quo – despite all its deficiencies – for fear of the chaos and suffering a major reshuffle would bring to the continent. This would be a development that would no doubt bring the worst of nightmares to the people and their leaders throughout the African continent.

But today, nothing is sacrosanct, and we may see a shift towards a post-liberal world disorder. 'The liberal, rules-based order that arose after the end of the Second World War is now dying,' claims the President of Finland, Alexander Stubb. 'Multilateral cooperation is giving way to multipolar competition. Opportunistic transactions seem to matter more than defending international rules. Great-power competition is back, as the rivalry between China and the United States sets the frame of geopolitics,' he concludes.[40]

In any case, Europe and the United States, despite their differences, need to find a way to secure a comprehensive, just and lasting peace in Ukraine, based on the principles of the UN Charter and international law. This is unavoidable. At the same time, there should not be negotiations on Ukraine without Ukraine, and there should be no negotiations that affect European security without Europe's involvement in some way or another. Moreover, any truce or ceasefire should take place as part of a process leading to a comprehensive peace agreement, while such an agreement needs to be accompanied by robust and credible security guarantees for Ukraine that efficiently deter any future Russian aggression. Finally, such a peace must also respect Ukraine's independence, sovereignty and territorial integrity. These are the fundamental principles that twenty-six European leaders agreed to in early March 2025.

Furthermore, there is a need for the United States and its active involvement in order to hammer out a just and lasting peace in Ukraine, even if the current administration views its national interest through the narrow prism of 'America First' and may find little value in reinforcing NATO. The United States seems, however, to have a clear self-interest in taking into account the following four considerations:

1. Since the war began, Russia has significantly deepened its cooperation with China, North Korea and Iran; this cooperation is enduring, and no doubt poses a real threat to US interests. And if Russia for some reason prevails in Ukraine, it will be a victory as well for each of the three mentioned partners – without whom Moscow would already have lost the war.
2. The survival of a free and independent Ukraine will be good for the United States, given the Ukrainian military will emerge from the war as Europe's third largest, after Russia and Turkey, and Ukraine has pioneered cutting-edge technological developments, especially in drone warfare and the application of artificial intelligence in warfare.
3. A Russian victory in Ukraine will significantly increase the threat to several European states that are staunchly pro-American and spend a high percentage of their GDP on defence – such as Poland, Lithuania, Estonia and Latvia.
4. The United States has an interest in a stable and peaceful Europe, as the continent is the US's largest source of foreign investment and its largest export market.[41]

Among the American people there is a great deal of sympathy with the Ukrainians; on the Republican side in both the Senate and the Congress there are prominent politicians who are firmly on Ukraine's side in this war. The former Chairman of the Foreign Affairs Committee in Congress, the Texas Republican Michael T. McCaul, has on several occasions underlined the need to stand by Ukraine and has stated that 'Russia's war against Ukraine has become a bellwether to see if the United States and the rest of the free world can stand up to unprovoked aggression.'

'The United States also knows well the dangers of leaving Europe to deal with Russia,' explains Wolfgang Ischinger, the President of the Munich Security Conference Foundation Council and former German Ambassador to the United States.

> After Russia's annexation of Crimea and its invasion of eastern Ukraine in 2014, Washington decided to largely leave the confrontation with Moscow to the Europeans. The key vehicle for this was the so-called Minsk process – the talks aimed at a settlement for eastern Ukraine – and the so-called Normandy Four, the contact group of France, Germany, Russia and Ukraine that met between 2014 and 2022. Unfortunately, the Minsk and Normandy process failed, and an American leadership vacuum only encouraged the Russian side to escalate further, culminating with the invasion in February 2022.[42]

We should not underestimate that Moscow also has an interest in bringing an end to the on-going war. In the words of Antony J. Blinken, 'Russia has suffered more than 700,000 dead and injured since Putin began his war. Now he increasingly faces a painful dilemma: either endure high casualties for minimal gains, perhaps order a mobilisation that triggers domestic instability or negotiate seriously with Ukraine to end his war.'[43]

• • •

Irrespective of whatever view one may hold on this sad and tragic war, the Ukrainians have defied all odds and shown great determination, courage and bravery. The military, political, financial and humanitarian support from the United States, the EU and many European countries, as well as many others, has at the same time been of utmost importance.

The war has been a tragedy for Ukraine, but at the same time it has also helped nurture and create a strong national identity. Today, there is an unprecedented level of purpose, unity and identity, stronger than ever before in Ukraine's history.

'This long and awful war has taught Ukrainians to love and value their country – and its beauty – even more,' the Ukrainian novelist and author Andrey Kurkov points out.

> I am free, and I am alive, but more than 100 writers, poets, publishers and translators have died since February 2022. Remember this and do not allow yourselves to fall into a cosy stupor – not now or even after the end of the war – because freedom does not tolerate being forgotten. When people assume that it will not go anywhere – that freedom is a given – that is the most dangerous moment.[44]

Today, we cannot take anything for granted. On the contrary, we must be ready to fight for our freedom, our fundamental rights and we must strengthen and revitalise our democracies. At the same time, we must do what we can to secure a comprehensive, just and lasting peace for Ukraine, which is not only vital for Ukraine, but for all of Europe and the entire world community. Accordingly, it is not only Ukraine's freedom, sovereignty and independence that are on the line, but Europe's own fundamental security interests. Russia's war of aggression must not at any point end with handing over a nicely wrapped gift to the aggressor.

It is ultimately the Ukrainians themselves that will have to decide and take the necessary decisions on how to end the war, no matter how difficult and painful that may be.

'I hold the position that no one can send Ukraine down the drain except the Ukrainians themselves,' explains Dmytro Kuleba.

> No decision can be imposed on us. When we look at Ukraine from the perspective of today's headlines in the news and social media, we seem weak, bleeding and exhausted. But when we zoom out, we inevitably come to a conclusion that today, Ukraine is in the strongest position ever in its history.
>
> For the first time in hundreds of years, we have the state, the army and the leadership. With all discussions taking place in the media and on the streets, we have national unity and clear national and political identity. For the first time, we are united in our attitude towards Russia.
>
> And finally, we have partners. We can complain a hundred times about what they've done wrong, but they've done a lot for us. And this is the first time in history that we have partners who actually stand by us, despite all of their shortcomings.
>
> So, in this generation, we have no right to lose this struggle, because we are today in the strongest position possible compared to all the preceding generations of Ukrainians who had fought and lost, unfortunately.
>
> We should not repeat their mistakes. And we have all the conditions for this. We don't have the right not to succeed.[45]

EPILOGUE

THE 'COME BACK ALIVE' FOUNDATION

The book you are now holding in your hand is a unique solidarity project. A substantial part of the income, meaning my royalties as an author, generated by the sales of this book in English-speaking countries will be donated to the largest non-governmental charitable organisation in Ukraine, the 'Come Back Alive' Foundation.

The 'Come Back Alive' Foundation has been operational since 2014, and its primary objective is to save the lives of Ukrainian servicemen and -women and help enhance the effectiveness of the Ukrainian Defence Forces. To achieve this, the Foundation regularly procures equipment, including thermal optics, drones, more than 2,200 new vehicles, surveillance and reconnaissance systems, communication tools, demining equipment and other essential gear.

'Come Back Alive' became the first charitable foundation in Ukraine to receive official permission to import military and dual-use goods.

Among the procurements it has financed are the Bayraktar TB2 UAV defence systems, more than 4,800 units of collective infantry weapons – including machine guns, mortars and grenade launchers – a hundred sniper rifles, twelve armoured vehicles and hundreds of specialised vehicles which were developed with the military, such as mobile command posts, integrated communication complexes and UAV command and control centres.

In addition, the Foundation's instructors have trained over 10,000 highly skilled military specialists, including explosive ordnance disposal professionals, drone operators, artillery personnel, infantry weaponry experts, snipers and divers. It has also provided first aid training and set up medical training complexes within the Ukrainian Armed Forces. 'Come Back Alive' also organises multifunctional courses for service members, including the 'Captains' Training' programme, where unit commanders study best practices from NATO member states.

Over the last eleven years, the Foundation has raised over €335 million for the needs of the Defence Forces of Ukraine, while maintaining transparent financial reporting, allowing for easy tracking of every donation and purchase.

The 'CBA Initiatives Centre', founded in 2018, implements systemic solutions in the fields of national security, defence analytics and the reintegration of Ukrainian defenders.

The Centre's work takes place in a public environment that complements the activities of the charitable foundation. Currently, the Centre has two main areas of activity: analytical work, including conducting research and assessing military threats that serve as the basis for decisions made at the state level; and veteran support, including the physical and psychological recovery of veterans and service personnel after injuries, traumas and/or illnesses, particularly through adaptive sports. These programmes help service members transition to civilian life or continue their military service.

ACKNOWLEDGEMENTS

This book arose out of the shock and anger caused by the start of the full-scale Russian invasion of Ukraine on 24 February 2022. But more precisely, the tsunami of Russian lies, disinformation and propaganda that followed in its aftermath.

I have devoted a lot of time to laborious research, primarily by reading numerous articles, interviews and other relevant literature. I also started to dip into the very persuasive speeches of Ukrainian Foreign Minister Dmytro Kuleba and their impact, as well as the key role he played in helping President Zelenskyy to assemble massive international political, financial, humanitarian and military support, so vital to Ukraine's survival and success.

Reaching out to Foreign Minister Kuleba in the autumn of 2022, I suggested we work together on this project. Dmytro agreed immediately, as we had already become friends during his very successful tenure as Ukraine's Ambassador to the Council of Europe (2016–19). I have profited greatly from his deep understanding of Ukrainian history, his profound political experience and his willingness to share insights and analysis of the war and Ukraine's relations to key allies. I am also hugely indebted to Kuleba's truly exceptional speechwriter, Heorhii 'Gosha' Tykhyi. Both Dmytro and Gosha share a deep passion for the art of speechwriting and recognise its exceptional political significance, especially in times of crisis and war.

My deep thanks go to the former US Secretary of State, Antony J. Blinken, for writing a foreword to this book and to Philippe Sands, KC, for his outstanding preface.

I am also fortunate to have Biteback as my publisher and the excellent Alex Pathe as my editor.

The publication of this book would not have been possible without the financial support from the Norwegian foundation *Fritt Ord*.

In no particular order, my deep gratitude also goes to Polish Foreign Minister Radek Sikorski; Latvia's President Edgars Rinkēvičs; Moldova's Foreign Minister Mihai Popșoi; former Greek Foreign Minister, Dora Bakoyannis; former Foreign Minister of Lithuania, Gabrielius Landsbergis; former Foreign Minister of Iceland, Thórdís Kolbrún Rejkfjord Gylfadóttir; prominent Dutch politician, Pieter Omtzigt; Chair of the Foreign Affairs Committee of the Norwegian Parliament, Peter Frølich; the Romanian politician and Chair of the Liberal group (ALDE) in the Parliamentary Assembly of the Council of Europe, Iulian Bulai; director for advocacy, strategic litigation and assistance of Reporters Without Borders, Antoine Bernard; the Ukrainian judge at the European Court of Human Rights, Mykola Gnatovskyy; executive director of the Register of Damage Caused by the Aggression of the Russian Federation against Ukraine, Markiyan Kliuchkovskyi; the legal adviser of the Council of Europe, Jörg Polakiewicz; founder of the European Speechwriter Network, Brian Jenner; head of the Council of Europe's office in Brussels, Andriy Zayats; Ambassador Ion Junga, Romania; Ambassador Albana Dautllari, Albania; Ambassador Sandy Moss,

United Kingdom; Ambassador Michael Aastrup Jensen, Denmark; former UN Ambassador and current Permanent State Secretary in the Ministry of Foreign Affairs in Finland, Jukka Salovaara; former NATO Ambassador Axel Wernhoff, Sweden; former Ambassador to the Council of Europe, Petr Válek, the Czech Republic; former Polish Ambassador to the OSCE, Adam Hałaciński; former Ambassador to the Council of Europe, Jerzy Baurski, Poland; Dr Andrew Forde, Dublin City University; Knut Olav Åmås, Director of *Fritt Ord*; and Thomas Van-Dijck at the Parliamentary Assembly of the Council of Europe.

Several friends kindly read the manuscript in whole or part and provided indispensable feedback and spotted errors of fact and judgement. These include, in particular, Ambassador Keith McBean and Dr Jim A. Railey.

Finally, my gratitude goes to my good friends and colleagues in the Council of Europe for their outstanding work to promote human rights, democracy and the rule of law on our continent.

And most importantly, none of this would have been possible without the support of my dear wife Hanne and my lovely family.

This book is dedicated to the brave Ukrainian people, the nation's leaders and all those who have sacrificed their lives defending not only their own country and its freedom, but the democratic future of Europe.

Bjorn Berge
Strasbourg, 7 March 2026

NOTES

INTRODUCTION

1 The All-Russian Academy of Foreign Trade of the Ministry of Economic Development of the Russian Federation (RFTA) is a highly respected and elite university. Established in 1931 as the Soviet Academy of Foreign Trade, it has for more than ninety years trained professionals who have become specialists in the field of international trade, international finance and international economic law.

2 The Soviet Diplomatic Academy was established in 1934 and is among the oldest diplomatic institutes in the world. Today, the Diplomatic Academy of the Ministry of Foreign Affairs of the Russian Federation provides high-level education in the field of international relations, international economic relations and international law.

3 The entire text is based on the author's interview with Dmytro Kuleba on 14 July 2025.

CHAPTER 1

1 See the book *War in Ukraine – Conflict, Strategy, and the Return of a Fractured World*, edited by Hal Brands, Johns Hopkins University Press, Baltimore, 2024

2 Excerpts from the author's interview with Dmytro Kuleba and his former speechwriter, Heorhii 'Gosha' Tykhyi, Kyiv, 11 September 2024

3 Excerpts from the author's interview with the former Albanian Ambassador to the United Nations, Albana Dautllari, New York, 6 December 2023

4 Excerpts from the author's interview with the former Romanian Ambassador to the United Nations, Ion Jinga, Strasbourg, 15 August 2024

5 GA/12403, UN report on UNGA 23 February 2022

6 Statement by the UN Secretary-General, António Guterres, 24 February 2022

7 GA/12403, UN report on UNGA 23 February 2022

8 Ibid.

9 Ibid.

10 Ibid.

11 Ibid.

12 Address by the President of the Russian Federation, 24 February 2022

13 Excerpts from the author's interview with the former Romanian Ambassador to the United Nations, Ion Jinga, Strasbourg, 15 August 2024

CHAPTER 2

1 'Planning for the worst: the Russia-Ukraine "Tiger Team"', Alexander Bick in *War in Ukraine*, edited by Hal Brands, Johns Hopkins University Press, Baltimore, 2024
2 *The Showman: The Inside Story of the Invasion that Shook the World and Made a Leader of Volodymyr Zelensky*, Simon Shuster, William Morrow, New York, 2024
3 *The Russo-Ukrainian War: The Return of History*, Serhii Plokhy, W.W. Norton & Company, New York, 2023
4 'Russia facing setbacks in Ukraine, US intelligence officials say', *Al Jazeera*, 8 March 2022
5 *The Russo-Ukrainian War: The Return of History*, Serhii Plokhy, W.W. Norton & Company, New York, 2023
6 *On Freedom*, Timothy Snyder, Penguin Random House, London, 2024
7 *The Russo-Ukrainian War: The Return of History*, Serhii Plokhy, W.W. Norton & Company, New York, 2023
8 Excerpts from the author's interview with Dmytro Kuleba, 11 September 2024
9 Foreign Affairs Council: Press remarks by High Representative Josep Borrell, Brussels, 25 February 2022
10 Ibid.
11 Excerpts from the author's interview with Gabrielius Landsbergis, former Foreign Minister of Lithuania, 6 February 2025

CHAPTER 3

1 'On the Historical Unity of Russians and Ukrainians', Vladimir Putin, 12 July 2021. See http://en.kremlin.ru/events/president/news/66181
2 'Don't Sell Out Ukraine', Dmytro Kuleba, *Foreign Affairs*, 10 December 2021
3 *War in Ukraine: Conflict, Strategy, and the Return of a Fractured World*, edited by Hal Brands, Johns Hopkins University Press, Baltimore, 2024
4 'Casus Belli: Did Lenin Create Modern Ukraine?', Serhii Plokhy, Ukrainian Research Institute, Harvard University, 27 February 2022
5 'Don't Sell Out Ukraine,' Dmytro Kuleba, *Foreign Affairs*, 10 December 2021
6 Statement by Vladimir Putin at the 'ceremony for signing the treaties on the accession of the Donetsk People's Republic, the Lugansk People's Republic, the Zaporozhye Region and the Kherson Region to the Russian Federation', Grand Kremlin Palace's St George Hall, Moscow, 30 September 2022. See http://en.kremlin.ru/events/president/news/69465
7 Address by Vladimir Putin, Moscow, 21 February 2022. See http://en.kremlin.ru/events/president/news/67828
8 'How Ukraine Will Win', Dmytro Kuleba, *Foreign Affairs*, 17 June 2022
9 'What Makes Ukrainian History Interesting to the World', *Ukraine World*, 8 March 2022
10 'The War Over Ukrainian Identity', Georgiy Kasianov, Maria Curie-Sklodowska University in Lublin, Poland, *Foreign Affairs*, 4 May 2022
11 Ibid.
12 *The Russo-Ukrainian War: The Return of History*, Serhii Plokhy, W.W. Norton & Company, New York, 2023
13 'The War Over Ukrainian Identity', Georgiy Kasianov, *Foreign Affairs*, 4 May 2022
14 Ibid.
15 '*Ukraine: the Forging of a Nation* review', Luke Harding, *The Guardian*, 26 November 2023
16 'The War Over Ukrainian Identity', Georgiy Kasianov, *Foreign Affairs*, 4 May 2022
17 'Don't Sell Out Ukraine', Dmytro Kuleba, *Foreign Affairs*, 10 December 2021
18 'Ukraine is Part of the West', Dmytro Kuleba, *Foreign Affairs*, 2 August 2021
19 'The War Over Ukrainian Identity', Georgiy Kasianov, *Foreign Affairs*, 4 May 2022
20 'Tim Snyder will lead 90 scholars in rethinking Ukrainian history', Yurii Stasiuk and Nataliia Shuliakova, *Yale Daily News*, 8 December 2023

21 See https://uhgi.org
22 See https://www.kmu.gov.ua/en/news/statement-ministry-foreign-affairs-ukraine-russian-federations-decision-recognise-independence-so-called-dpr-and-lpr
23 Address by Vladimir Putin, The Kremlin, Moscow, 24 February 2022
24 *The Russo-Ukrainian War: The Return of History*, Serhii Plokhy, W.W. Norton & Company, New York, 2023

CHAPTER 4

1 'Disinformation is a Threat to Our Democracy,' Barack Obama at Stanford University, 22 April 2022
2 Excerpt from Vladimir Putin's speech to the Russian people on 21 February 2022
3 Ibid.
4 Briefing by Foreign Ministry Spokeswoman Maria Zakharova, Moscow, 12 July 2024
5 'Ukraine violated Chemical Weapons Convention – Russian MOD', *Russia Today*, 9 July 2024
6 'Provocation according to the White Helmets method: Ukraine is preparing a chemical disaster in the Donbass', *News Front*, 16 February 2022
7 'Military expert warns threat of crushing US strike on the Zaporozhye nuclear power plant', *News Front*, 16 February 2022
8 Address by Vladimir Putin, Moscow, 21 February 2022
9 See https://www.hrw.org/news/2022/04/03/ukraine-apparent-war-crimes-russia-controlled-areas and https://press.un.org/en/2022/sc15023.doc.htm
10 See https://www.state.gov/wp-content/uploads/2024/03/528267-UKRAINE-2023-HUMAN-RIGHTS-REPORT.pdf
11 Report 14 March 2023 (A/HRC/52/62); Report 15 March 2024 (A/HRC/55/66)
12 Report 25 October 2024 (A/79/549)
13 As described in the article 'Ukrainians hope for a New Year prisoner exchange with Russia', Will Vernon, BBC News, 28 December 2024
14 See https://www.unesco.org/en/articles/damaged-cultural-sites-ukraine-verified-unesco
15 'Ukrainian cultural landmarks suffer fresh blows as another museum is hit', CNN, 10 May 2022
16 'The all-out Russification of Ukraine's occupied territories', Faustine Vincent and Thomas d'Istria, *Le Monde*, 20 January 2024
17 'Ukrainian children abducted by Russia left with psychological scars, campaigners say,' *Reuters*, 15 June 2024
18 On 24 June 2024 the ICC judges issued arrest warrants against Sergei Kuzhugetovich Shoigu, the Russian Minister of Defence, and Valery Vasilyevich Gerasimov, Chief of the General Staff of the Armed Forces of the Russian Federation and First Deputy Minister of Defence of the Russian Federation
19 See https://www.icc-cpi.int/news/situation-ukraine-icc-judges-issue-arrest-warrants-against-vladimir-vladimirovich-putin-and
20 'Countries Participating in the Montreal Conference Commit to Returning All Captured and Deported Ukrainians', Official website of the President of Ukraine, 31 October 2024
21 See https://www.coe.int/en/web/portal/-/special-envoy-of-the-secretary-general-of-the-council-of-europe-on-the-situation-of-children-of-ukraine-appointed?p_l_back_url=%2Fen%2Fweb%2Fportal%2Fnewsroom%3Fdelta%3D20%26start%3D4
22 See https://ysph.yale.edu/news-article/ukraines-stolen-children-inside-russias-network-of-re-education-and-militarization/
23 Foreign Minister Sergey Lavrov's remarks and answers to media questions at the news conference on the performance of Russian diplomacy in 2022, Moscow, 18 January 2023
24 *On Freedom*, Timothy Snyder, Penguin Random House, London, 2024
25 Vladimir Putin's Address to the Federal Assembly, Moscow, 21 February 2023

26 'Ukraine war: President Putin speech fact-checked', Reality Check team, BBC News, 21 February 2023
27 See https://www.lemonde.fr/en/international/article/2024/07/07/russian-mps-at-war-with-satanism_6676911_4.html
28 '"God of war": Russian Orthodox Church stands by Putin, but at what cost?', Mansur Mirovalev, *Al Jazeera*, 9 February 2024
29 'Why Ukraine is dangerous for its inhabitants,' Dmitry Medvedev, Telegram, 17 January 2024
30 'Disinformation Is a Threat to Our Democracy,' Barack Obama at Stanford University, 22 April 2022
31 'White House condemns Tucker Carlson's "Nazi propaganda" interview as "disgusting and sadistic insult"', CNN, 5 September 2024

CHAPTER 5

1 'Global Risks 2024: Disinformation Tops Global Risks 2024 as Environmental Threats Intensify', report by the World Economic Forum
2 'How disinformation defined the 2024 election narrative', Darrell M. West, The Brookings Foundation, 7 November 2024
3 'Disinformation: sources, spread and impact', Eva Surawy Stepney and Clare Lally, UK Parliament POSTnote 719, 25 April 2024
4 'Social media manipulation by political actors an industrial scale problem', Oxford Internet Institute (2021), University of Oxford
5 'Mail-In Voter Fraud: Anatomy of a Disinformation Campaign', Berkman Klein Center (2020)
6 'Disinformation: sources, spread and impact', Eva Surawy Stepney and Clare Lally, UK Parliament POSTnote 719, 25 April 2024
7 See https://freedomhouse.org/article/new-report-election-meddling-and-growing-assault-free-expression-online-led-14th
8 'What the "year of democracy" taught us', John Burn Murdoch, *Financial Times*, 30 December 2024
9 See https://www.eeas.europa.eu/eeas/disinformation-opening-speech-high-representativevice-president-josep-borrell-eeas-conference_en
10 'Bad News', *The Economist*, 4 May 2024
11 Ibid.
12 'The Russian "Firehose of Falsehood" Propaganda Model – Why It Might Work and Options to Counter It', Christopher Paul and Miriam Matthews, The Rand Corporation, 11 July 2016
13 'Bad News', *The Economist*, 4 May 2024
14 'A Bugatti car, a first lady and the fake stories aimed at Americans', Paul Myers, Olga Robinson, Shayan Sardaizadeh and Mike Wendling, BBC Verify, BBC News, 3 July 2024
15 'Frequently asked questions: Disinformation related to the Russian war of aggression against Ukraine', Federal Ministry of the Interior and Community, Berlin, Germany, 2024
16 Excerpts from the author's interview with Dmytro Kuleba, 11 September 2024
17 As described in the op-ed 'Moment of truth' by Eliot Higgins, the founder of Bellingcat, in *Financial Times*, 16 December 2023
18 'How to beat Russia. What armed forces in NATO should learn from Ukraine's homeland defense', Nico Lange, GLOBSEC, February 2023
19 'Disinformation: sources, spread and impact', Eva Surawy Stepney and Clare Lally, UK Parliament POSTnote 719, 25 April 2024
20 'Moment of Truth', Eliot Higgins, founder of Bellingcat, *Financial Times*, 16 December 2023
21 Ibid.
22 'Guidance note on countering the spread of online mis- and disinformation through fact-checking and platform design solutions in a human rights compliant manner', adopted by the Steering Committee for Media and Information Society (CDMSI), The Council of Europe, 2023

23 Ibid.
24 'How disinformation defined the 2024 election narrative', Darrell M. West, The Brookings Foundation, 7 November 2024
25 'Meta is ushering in a "world without facts", says Nobel peace prize winner', Dan Milmo, *The Guardian*, 8 January 2025
26 'Meta to End Fact-Checking Program in Shift Ahead of Trump Term', Mike Isaac and Theodore Schleifer, *The New York Times*, 7 January 2025
27 Excerpt from the author's interview with Antoine Bernard, Director, RSF (Reporters Without Borders), 26 June 2025
28 'Disinformation and freedom of opinion and expression', a report of the Special Rapporteur on the promotion and protection of the right to freedom of opinion and expression, Office of the United Nations High Commissioner for Human Rights, 13 April 2021
29 'Meta exempted to advisers from standard content moderation process', Hannah Murphy and Madhumita Murgia, *Financial Times*, 9 January 2025
30 'How disinformation defined the 2024 election narrative', Darrell M. West, The Brookings Foundation, 7 November 2024
31 'Is this the end of soft power?', Joseph Nye, *Financial Times*, 8 March 2025
32 'A steep, steep hill', *The Economist*, 4 May 2024
33 'Disinformation: sources, spread and impact', Eva Surawy Stepney and Clare Lally, UK Parliament POSTnote 719, 25 April 2024
34 Excerpts from the author's interview with Dmytro Kuleba, 11 September 2024
35 'How Disinformation Corrodes Democracy', Nina Jankowicz, *Foreign Affairs*, 30 November 2021

CHAPTER 6

1 'The Dangers of Defeatism for Ukraine: A conversation with Dmytro Kuleba', Dan Kurtz-Phelan, *Foreign Affairs*, 25 January 2024
2 'Ukraine's Dmytro Kuleba: "If it continues like this, we will lose the war"', Gideon Rachman, *Financial Times*, 29 November 2024
3 Excerpt from the author's interview with Mihai Popşoi, Foreign Minister of the Republic of Moldova, 3 March 2025
4 Based on a video interview Dmytro Kuleba gave to *Kyiv Independent*, and later published under the title '"Ukraine today is in the strongest position ever", ex-Foreign Minister Kuleba says', Natalia Yermak, 2 January 2025
5 Excerpts from the author's interview with Heorhii Tykhyi, 11 September 2024
6 'Ukraine tells critics of slow counteroffensive to "shut up"', Tom Balmforth, Reuters, 31 August 2023, and 'Counteroffensive critics are "spitting into the face" of our soldiers, Ukraine says', Jacopo Barigazzi, *Politico*, 31 August 2023
7 'Attorney General's 2024 Bingham Lecture on the rule of law', Lord Hermer KC, 14 October 2024
8 'War of words – how Ukraine uses strategic communication to beat Russia on the information front', a report by Ivar Ekman and Per-Erik Nilsson, FOI Totalförsvarets forskningsinstitut, Stockholm, 21 April 2023
9 *White House Ghosts: Presidents and Their Speechwriters*, Robert Schlesinger, Simon & Schuster, New York, 2008
10 Excerpts from the author's interview with Heorhii Tykhyi, 11 September 2024
11 Excerpts from the author's interview with Dmytro Kuleba and Heorhii Tykhyi, 11 September 2024
12 Excerpts from the author's interview with Brian Jenner, founder of the European Speechwriter Network, 21 August 2024
13 Excerpts from the Foreword to the Second Edition of *The War For Reality: How to Win in the World of Fakes, Truths and Communities*, Dmytro Kuleba, Knigolav, Kyiv, 2023

CHAPTER 7

1 'Witness to the Fall', George F. Kennan, *New York Review of Books*, 16 November 1995
2 *The Russo-Ukrainian War: The Return of History*, Serhii Plokhy, W.W. Norton & Company, New York, 2023
3 See https://www.americanrhetoric.com/speeches/georgehwbushkyivspeech.htm
4 Ibid.
5 'Putin's "Chicken Kyiv"', William Safire, *The New York Times*, 6 December 2004
6 'Bush says Ukraine should accept loose union with USSR', Michael Kranish, *The Boston Globe*, 2 August 1991
7 'American dream, Soviet reality collide; After Cold War, gulf still divides superpowers', Michael Dobbs, *Chicago Sun-Times*, 4 August 1991
8 *A World Transformed*, George Bush and Brent Scowcroft, Knopf, New York, 1998
9 'Bush Sr clarifies "Chicken Kyiv" speech', *The Washington Times*, 23 May 2004
10 Excerpts from the author's interview with Dmytro Kuleba, 9 February 2025
11 Armenia, Azerbaijan, Belorussia (now Belarus), Estonia, Georgia, Kazakhstan, Kirgiziya (now Kyrgyzstan), Latvia, Lithuania, Moldavia (now Moldova), Russia, Tajikistan, Turkmenistan, Ukraine and Uzbekistan
12 'The December 1 1991 Referendum/Presidential Election in Ukraine', by the Commission on Security and Cooperation in Europe
13 *The New York Times*, 9 December 1991
14 *The New York Times*, 22 December 1991
15 *The New York Times*, 23 December 1991
16 See Appendix to the UN Doc 1991/RUSSIA as of 24 December 1991
17 See UN/DOC S/PV 3046 as of 31 January 1992
18 'Russia Took Over the Soviet Union's Seat at the United Nations', Yehuda Z. Blum, *European Journal of International Law*, 1992
19 'The Politics of Nuclear Renunciation: The Cases of Belarus, Kazakhstan and Ukraine', Occasional Paper, William Potter, Henry L. Stimson Centre, Washington DC, 1995
20 Official transcript from 'The Budapest Memorandum at 20: The US, Ukraine and Security Assurances,' The Brookings Institution, Washington DC, 9 December 2014
21 *Eco-Nationalism: Anti-Nuclear Activism and National Identity in Russia, Lithuania, and Ukraine*, Jane Dawson, Duke University Press, Durham, 1996 and 'Looking Back: Ukraine's Nuclear Predicament and the Non-proliferation Regime,' Mariana Budjeryn, Arms Control Association, 2024
22 *The Russo-Ukrainian War: The Return of History*, Serhii Plokhy, W.W. Norton & Company, New York, 2023
23 'The Breach: Ukraine's Territorial Integrity and the Budapest Memorandum', Mariana Budjeryn, Issue Brief #3, The Wilson Centre, Washington DC, 2014
24 'Noting Soviet Eclipse, Baker Sees Arms Risks', Keith Bradsher, *The New York Times*, 9 December 1991
25 'The Shoals of Ukraine', Serhii Plokhy and M. E. Sarotte, *Foreign Affairs*, January/February 2020
26 'On the nuclear status of Ukraine', Verkhovna Rada, 24 October 1991
27 Official transcript from 'The Budapest Memorandum at 20: The US, Ukraine and Security Assurances,' The Brookings Institution, Washington DC, 9 December 2014
28 A/49/765* S/1994/1399* 'Letter dated 7 December 1994 from the Permanent Representatives of the Russian Federation, Ukraine, the United Kingdom of Great Britain and Northern Ireland, and the United States of America to the UN addressed to the UN Secretary-General', UN General Assembly Security Council, 49th Session, Agenda items 62 and 70, 19 December 1994
29 'The Breach: Ukraine's Territorial Integrity and the Budapest Memorandum', Mariana Budjeryn, Issue Brief #3, The Wilson Centre, Washington DC, 2014

30 'The Shoals of Ukraine', Serhii Plokhy and M. E. Sarotte, *Foreign Affairs*, January/February 2020
31 Official transcript from 'The Budapest Memorandum at 20: The US, Ukraine and Security Assurances,' The Brookings Institution, Washington DC, 9 December 2014
32 Point 23, Bucharest Summit Declaration, issued by the Heads of State and Government participating in the meeting of the North Atlantic Council in Bucharest on 3 April 2008
33 *The Zelensky Effect*, Olga Onuch and Henry E. Hale, Hurst & Company, London, 2022
34 'Identity and Political Preferences in Ukraine: Before and after the Euromaidan', Grigore Pop-Eleches and Graeme B. Robertson, *Post-Soviet Affairs*, 2018
35 *The Russo-Ukrainian War: The Return of History*, Serhii Plokhy, W.W. Norton & Company, New York, 2023
36 Ibid.
37 *The Last Empire: The Final Days of the Soviet Union*, Serhii Plokhy, Basic Books, New York, 2014
38 *A History of Ukraine: The Land and Its People*, Paul Robert Magocsi, Toronto, 2010

CHAPTER 8

1 Excerpts from the author's interview with Heorhii Tykhyi, 17 September 2023
2 Ibid.
3 Ibid.
4 'Ukraine's Dmytro Kuleba: "If it continues like this, we will lose the war"', Gideon Rachman, *Financial Times*, 30 November 2024
5 Excerpts from interview with Dmytro Kuleba, *HARDTalk*, BBC, 21 June 2024
6 Excerpts from the author's interview with Heorhii Tykhyi, 17 September 2023
7 Annex to the Venice Declaration of the G7 Justice Ministers, Venice, 2024
8 Excerpts from the author's interview with Dmytro Kuleba, 11 September 2024
9 Excerpt from the author's interview with Thórdís Kolbrún Reykfjord Gylfadóttir, former Foreign Minister of Iceland, 4 March 2025

CHAPTER 9

1 'The need for the EU's continued support for Ukraine', European Parliament resolution of 17 July 2024
2 The EU leaders at their summit in Brussels on 20 March 2025 decided to speed up efforts to strengthen the Union's defence readiness. Building on the special European Council on 6 March 2025 and the Commission's white paper on the future of defence, leaders called for an acceleration of all work strands to ramp up Europe's defence readiness within the next five years.
3 Excerpt from President Emmanuel Macron's 'Europe Speech', Sorbonne University, 25 April 2024
4 'Ukraine 2023 Report', Commission Staff Working Document, Brussels, 8 November 2023
5 Foreign Affairs Council: Press remarks by High Representative Joseph Borrell after the meeting, EEAS Press, Brussels, 18 July 2022
6 'EU and UK lower price cap on Russian oil in bid to curb Kremlin's war on Ukraine', Jennifer Rankin, *The Guardian*, 18 July 2025
7 Excerpts from the author's interview with Andriy Zayats, 26 March 2025
8 'Lose-Lose – The Economic Sanctions of the Russo-Ukrainian War', Daniel W. Drezner, in *War in Ukraine: Conflict, Strategy, and the Return of a Fractured World*, edited by Hal Brands, Johns Hopkins University Press, Baltimore, 2024
9 1.3 Assessment of the implementation of the seven steps of the Commission's opinion, Ukraine 2023 Report, Commission Staff Working Document, Brussels, 8 November 2023
10 Address by President von der Leyen to Members of Verkhovna Rada, Kyiv, 4 November 2023
11 First Accession Conference with Ukraine, 25 June 2024
12 Point 12 of the Accession Document – General EU Position, Conference on accession to the European Union – Brussels, 21 June 2024

13 Point 37 of the Accession Document – General EU Position, Conference on accession to the European Union – Brussels, 21 June 2024
14 Points 38, 39 and 40 of the Accession Document – General EU Position, Conference on accession to the European Union – Brussels, 21 June 2024
15 'Ukraine and the EU Signed the Joint Security Commitments', President of Ukraine, 27 June 2024
16 'Ukraine has completed the legislation assessment for the first block of negotiations on EU accession', *Ukraine Business News*, 15 November 2024
17 '2025 Enlargement Package shows progress towards EU membership for key enlargement partners', European Commission, 2025
18 Ibid.
19 'EU eyes two-tier accession for Kyiv', Henry Foy, *Financial Times*, 17 January 2026
20 'Europe Needs Speed in Making Decisions and Clear Tools to Protect Itself from Unnecessary Blockages – Speech by the President at the Meeting of the European Council', President of Ukraine, 2025
21 'Statement by the High Representative/Vice President of the Commission Kaja Kallas and Commissioner for Enlargement Marta Kos on Georgia', Brussels, 1 December 2024
22 *Memoirs of the Second World War*, Winston S. Churchill, Houghton Mifflin Company, Boston, 1959
23 Press statement by President von der Leyen on the defence package, Brussels, 4 March 2025
24 'Ukraine will not be a pawn,' Dmytro Kuleba, *Foreign Affairs*, 22 August 2025

CHAPTER 10

1 Excerpts from a speech given by Secretary of State Madeleine K. Albright (and the Foreign Ministers of the Czech Republic, Hungary and Poland), Remarks on Accession to the North Atlantic Treaty Organization, Truman Presidential Library, Independence, Missouri, 12 March 1999
2 Point 23 in the Bucharest NATO Summit Declaration, issued by the Heads of State and Government participating in the meeting of the North Atlantic Council in Bucharest, 3 April 2008
3 'Why NATO Must Admit Ukraine', Dmytro Kuleba, *Foreign Affairs*, 25 April 2023
4 *A Little War That Shook the World*, Ronald Asmus, St. Martin's Press, New York, 2010
5 Article 5 of the North Atlantic Treaty, Washington DC, 4 April 1949: 'The Parties agree that an armed attack against one or more of them in Europe or North America shall be considered an attack against them all and consequently they agree that, if such an armed attack occurs, each of them, in exercise of the right of individual or collective self-defence recognised by Article 51 of the Charter of the United Nations, will assist the Party or Parties so attacked by taking forthwith, individually and in concert with the other Parties, such action as it deems necessary, including the use of armed force, to restore and maintain the security of the North Atlantic area. Any such armed attack and all measures taken as a result thereof shall immediately be reported to the Security Council. Such measures shall be terminated when the Security Council has taken the measures necessary to restore and maintain international peace and security.'
6 'How to ensure a strong, independent Ukraine', Ivo Daalder, *Politico*, 5 July 2023
7 NATO has no nuclear weapons of its own. They belong to the US (primarily) and the UK (the French are not part of NATO's nuclear weapons policy), and it is the countries with nuclear weapons that control them. There is thus no NATO obligation as such for member states to have nuclear weapons on its territory, and the Norwegian nuclear weapons policy is thus not a 'reservation' but an expression of a national nuclear weapons policy. However, like all the other NATO countries (except France), Norway participates in the HLG (High Level Group) and NPG (Nuclear Planning Group) at all levels.
8 'How to beat Russia. What armed forces in NATO should learn from Ukraine's homeland defence', Nico Lange, GLOBSEC, February 2023

9 'Complex post-industrial military', *The Economist*, 28 June 2025
10 'Ukraine's Drone Revolution', Jon Finer and David Shimer, *Foreign Affairs*, 7 July 2025
11 'Europe urged to help Kyiv and prepare against Kremlin threat', Richard Milne and Henry Foy, *Financial Times*, 11 April 2024
12 'Why the Ukraine crisis is the West's fault', John J. Mearsheimer, *Foreign Affairs*, September/October 2014
13 'I was there: NATO and the Origins of the Ukraine Crisis', Jack F. Matlock, Jr, *Responsible Statecraft*, 15 February 2022
14 An excellent overview of some of the key aspects of Russia's relationship with NATO and the real reasons why Putin decided to invade Ukraine can be found in the book *War in Ukraine: Conflict, Strategy, and the Return of a Fractured World*, edited by Hal Brands, Johns Hopkins University Press, Baltimore, 2024
15 As also referred to in the article 'Why NATO must admit Ukraine', Dmytro Kuleba, *Foreign Affairs*, 25 April 2023
16 'Don't Sell Out Ukraine', Dmytro Kuleba, *Foreign Affairs*, 10 December 2021
17 'Putin says "Why Not?" to Russia joining NATO', David Hoffman, *Washington Post*, 6 March 2000
18 Transcript of Robert Siegel's interview with Vladimir Putin, NPR, 15 November 2001
19 *War in Ukraine: Conflict, Strategy, and the Return of a Fractured World*, edited by Hal Brands, Johns Hopkins University Press, Baltimore, 2024 and 'Press Statement and 'Answers to Questions at a Joint News Conference with Ukrainian President Leonid Kuchma', press statement by the Presidential Administration of Russia, 17 May 2002
20 *War in Ukraine: Conflict, Strategy, and the Return of a Fractured World*, edited by Hal Brands, Johns Hopkins University Press, Baltimore, 2024
21 Ibid.
22 As also referred to in the article 'Why NATO must admit Ukraine', Dmytro Kuleba, *Foreign Affairs*, 25 April 2023
23 'The meaning of sovereignty: Ukrainian and European views of Russia's war on Ukraine', Ivan Krastev, Chairman, Centre for Liberal Strategies, and Mark Leonard, Director, European Council on Foreign Relations, *Policy Brief*, 3 July 2024
24 Excerpts from the closing press conference with NATO Secretary-General Jens Stoltenberg at the end of the 2024 NATO Summit in Washington, 11 July 2024
25 'How Europe Lost: Can the Continent Escape Its Trump Trap?', Matthias Matthijs and Nathalie Tocci, *Foreign Affairs*, January/February 2026
26 The Kyiv Security Compact, International Security Guarantees for Ukraine: Recommendations, by Co-Chairs of the Working Group on International Security Guarantees for Ukraine; Mr Anders Fogh Rasmussen and Mr Andrii Yermak, Kyiv, 13 September 2022
27 'Joint Declaration of Support for Ukraine', Group of Seven (G7) countries, Vilnius, 12 July 2023
28 Ukraine has signed ten-year security agreements with more than twenty countries so far, including all G7 members (Canada, France, Germany, Italy, Japan, the United Kingdom and the United States) and Belgium, Denmark, Estonia, Finland, Iceland, Latvia, Lithuania, the Netherlands, Norway, Poland, Portugal, Spain and Sweden. Ukraine also signed a separate agreement with the European Union.
29 'Victory is Ukraine's only true path to peace', Anders Fogh Rasmussen and Andriy Yermak, *Foreign Affairs*, 11 January 2024
30 Point 11, 'Statement of the NATO–Ukraine Council', Washington DC, 11 July 2024
31 'Agreement on security cooperation between France and Ukraine', signed in Paris on 16 February 2024
32 'Getting Ukraine's Security Agreements Right', Mykhailo Soldatenko, Carnegie Endowment for International Peace, 8 July 2024
33 Excerpt from 'Statements by Emmanuel Macron, President of the Republic, at his joint press conference with Volodymyr Zelenskyy, President of Ukraine', following the meeting of the Coalition of the Willing, Paris, 4 September 2025

34 'Paris Declaration: "Robust Security Guarantees for a Solid and Lasting Peace in Ukraine", issued by France', Council of the EU, 6 January 2026

35 The Treaty of Lisbon strengthens the solidarity between European Union Member States in dealing with external threats by introducing a mutual defence clause (Article 42(7) of the Treaty on European Union). This clause provides that if a Member State is the victim of armed aggression on its territory, the other Member States have an obligation to aid and assist it by all the means in their power, in accordance with Article 51 of the Charter of the United Nations. This obligation of mutual defence is binding on all Member States. However, it does not affect the neutrality of certain Member States and is consistent with the commitments of countries that are NATO members. This clause is supplemented by the solidarity clause (Article 222 of the Treaty on the Functioning of the European Union), which provides that Member States are obliged to act jointly where one of them is the victim of a terrorist attack or a natural or man-made disaster. See https://eur-lex.europa.eu/EN/legal-content/glossary/mutual-defence-clause.html

CHAPTER 11

1 'Russian attacks on Ukraine energy system caused $1 bln in damages – Minister Galushchenko', Reuters, 5 May 2024

2 'Half Ukraine's power is knocked out; winter is coming', *The Economist*, 15 July 2024

3 'Russia's glide bombs devastating Ukraine's cities on the cheap', Joe Inwood and Tania Kharchenko, BBC, 19 May 2024

4 Excerpts from the author's interview with the former Swedish NATO Ambassador, Axel Wernhoff, Stockholm, 3 August 2024

5 'Germany Will Provide Us With Another Patriot System, And We Are Working on an Additional IRIS-T System: Address of the President of Ukraine, President of Ukraine, 2024

6 'Israel has never been impressed with its version of the $1 billion Patriot air defense system. Now it could offload up to 8 to Ukraine', *Business Insider*, 2024

CHAPTER 12

1 Aggression against Ukraine, Resolution ES-11/1, adopted by the UN General Assembly on 2 March 2022, with 141 countries voting in favour, five against (Russia, Belarus, North Korea, Eritrea and Syria) and thirty-five abstaining

2 'Putin's use of military force is a crime of aggression', Philippe Sands, *Financial Times*, 28 February 2022

3 Excerpts from the author's interview with Philippe Sands, 10 February 2025

4 'Legal and human rights aspects of the Russian Federation's aggression against Ukraine', Resolution 2482 (2023), The Parliamentary Assembly of the Council of Europe, 26 January 2023

5 From the intervention of Claus Kreß, Director of the Institute for International Peace and Security Law, University of Cologne, Germany, at the Council of Europe / CAHDI seminar on the Special Tribunal for the Crime of Aggression against Ukraine, Strasbourg, 10 April 2024

6 Opening Statement before the International Military Tribunal, Robert H. Jackson, 1945

7 Excerpts from the statement by Dmytro Kuleba at the online meeting at Chatham House on 'A criminal tribunal for aggression in Ukraine', 4 March 2022

8 Ibid.

9 Ibid.

10 Statement calling for the creation of a special tribunal for the punishment of the crime of aggression against Ukraine, the office of Gordon and Sarah Brown, 6 January 2023

11 The International Court of Justice in The Hague may entertain two types of cases: legal disputes between states submitted to it by them (contentious cases) and requests for advisory opinions on legal questions referred to it by United Nations organs and specialised agencies (advisory proceedings).

12 The Russian Federation was expelled from the Council of Europe on 16 March 2022, after being a member of the most important organisation for the protection and promotion of human rights, rule of law and democracy in Europe for close to twenty-six years.
13 From the author's interview with Judge Mykola Gnatovskyy, Strasbourg, 7–8 July 2024. See also the address by Judge Gnatovskyy at the CAHDI seminar on the special tribunal and what role regional organisations, such as the Council of Europe, can play, Strasbourg, 10 April 2024
14 Statement calling for the creation of a special tribunal for the punishment of the crime of aggression against Ukraine, the office of Gordon and Sarah Brown, 6 January 2023
15 Statement by President von der Leyen on Russian accountability and the use of Russian frozen assets, 30 November 2022
16 Introductory remarks by Dapo Akande at a seminar on the special tribunal for the crime of aggression – 'What role for regional organisations such as the Council of Europe?', Strasbourg, 10 April 2024
17 Excerpts from the author's interview with Iulian Bulai, Romanian MP and leader of the Liberal group (ALDE) in the Parliamentary Assembly of the Council of Europe, 19 February 2025
18 Based on excerpts from the author's interview with Markiyan Kliuchkovskyi, Executive Director of the Register of Damage, 28 August 2025
19 Rome Statute of the International Criminal Court, Rome, 17 July 1998, and amendments to the Rome Statute of the International Criminal Court, Kampala, 11 June 2010
20 Excerpt from the author's interview with Judge Mykola Gnatovskyy, the European Court of Human Rights, Strasbourg, 8 July 2024
21 Ibid.
22 From the intervention of Claus Kreß, Director of the Institute for International Peace and Security Law, University of Cologne, Germany, at the Council of Europe / CAHDI seminar on the Special Tribunal for the Crime of Aggression against Ukraine, Strasbourg, 10 April 2024
23 Excerpt from the author's interview with Judge Mykola Gnatovskyy, the European Court of Human Rights, Strasbourg, 8 July 2024
24 Statement by Alain Berset, the Secretary-General of the Council of Europe, Brussels, 4 February 2024
25 Excerpt from the author's interview with Jörg Polakiewicz, legal adviser of the Council of Europe and Director of the Directorate of Legal Advice and Public International Law (DLAPIL), Strasbourg, 7 July 2024
26 'Ukraine and the Council of Europe sign Agreement on establishing a Special Tribunal for the Crime of Aggression against Ukraine', Strasbourg, 25 June 2025
27 Excerpts from the author's interview with Philippe Sands, 10 February 2025
28 'Ukraine and the Council of Europe sign Agreement on establishing a Special Tribunal for the Crime of Aggression against Ukraine', Strasbourg, 25 June 2025
29 From the intervention of Claus Kreß, Director of the Institute for International Peace and Security Law, University of Cologne, Germany, at the Council of Europe / CAHDI seminar on the Special Tribunal for the Crime of Aggression against Ukraine, Strasbourg, 10 April 2024
30 'Yuval Noah Harari on how to prevent a new age of imperialism', *The Economist*, 3 June 2024
31 'Merz considers extension of French, British nuclear umbrella to Germany', Nick Alipour, Théo Bourgery-Gonse, Euractiv, 2025
32 'Get Ready for the Next Nuclear Age – How Trump Might Drive Proliferation', Gideon Rose, *Foreign Affairs*, 8 March 2025
33 'Kenyan UN Ambassador compares Ukraine's plight to colonial legacy in Africa', NPR, 22 February 2022
34 'Core Group Officially Endorses the Establishment of a Special Tribunal for the Crime of Russian Aggression Against Ukraine'

CHAPTER 13

1 'The art of the peace deal', Margaret MacMillan, *Financial Times*, 1 March 2025

2 *Why War?*, Richard Overy, Penguin Random House, London, 2024
3 For the full text of the UN Charter, see https://www.un.org/en/about-us/un-charter/full-text
4 'Meeting on Zelensky's Peace Formula in Malta: Unexpected Armenia, No China', Viktoriia Stepanenko, *Kyiv Post*, 2025
5 I have amended and edited this text, mainly for ease of reading.
6 'Today Is the Day When the World Begins to Bring Just Peace Closer – by the President of Ukraine at the First Plenary Session of the Global Peace Summit', President of Ukraine, 15 June 2024
7 'Summit on Peace in Ukraine', Bürgenstock, Switzerland, 15 June 2024
8 'Russia not invited to talks to end the war', Zolan Kanno-Youngs, Anton Troianovski and Andrew E. Kramer, *The New York Times International Edition*, 15 June 2024
9 'Volodymyr Zelensky has a plan for Ukraine's victory', Joshua Yaffa, *New Yorker*, 22 September 2024
10 'Russia not invited to talks to end the war', Zolan Kanno-Youngs, Anton Troianovski and Andrew E. Kramer, *The New York Times International Edition*, 15 June 2024
11 'China's position on the political settlement of the Ukraine crisis', statement by the Ministry of Foreign Affairs, The People's Republic of China, 24 February 2023; 'Common understandings between China and Brazil on political settlement of the Ukraine crisis', Xinhua, Beijing, 23 May 2024; and 'Friends for Peace group on the Ukraine crisis set up in the United Nations', Ministry of Foreign Affairs, The People's Republic of China, 28 September 2024
12 'The talks that could have ended the war in Ukraine', Samuel Charap and Sergey Radchenko, *Foreign Affairs*, 16 April 2024
13 'Ukraine's Dmytro Kuleba: "If it continues like this, we will lose the war"', Gideon Rachman, *Financial Times*, 30 November 2024
14 'Here's what's in Zelenskyy's victory plan for beating Putin', Veronika Melkozerova, *Politico*, 16 October 2024
15 'Zelensky lays out his "Victory Plan" to defeat Russia', Alexandra Sharp, World Brief, *Foreign Policy*, 16 October 2024
16 'Victory Plan Consists of Five Points and Three Secret Annexes', President of Ukraine, 16 October 2024
17 'Pre-ministerial press conference by NATO Secretary General Mark Rutte ahead of the meeting of NATO Defence Ministers in Brussels on 17 and 18 October', 16 October 2024
18 'Victory Plan Consists of Five Points and Three Secret Annexes', President of Ukraine, 16 October 2024
19 Ibid.
20 Ibid.
21 'Zelensky lays out his "Victory Plan" to defeat Russia', Alexandra Sharp, World Brief, *Foreign Policy*, 16 October 2024
22 'Volodymyr Zelensky has a plan for Ukraine's victory', Joshua Yaffa, *New Yorker*, 22 September 2024
23 'Trump time means to do job today – Kellogg on Special Envoy Witkoff's role', RBC-Ukraine, 15 February 2025
24 Research report: 'America First, Russia, & Ukraine,' Lt. General (Ret.) Keith Kellogg and Fred Fleitz, The Center for American Security, 11 April 2024
25 Ibid.
26 'The West Needs a New Strategy in Ukraine. A Plan for Getting From the Battlefield to the Negotiating Table', Richard Haass and Charles Kupchan, *Foreign Affairs*, 13 April 2023
27 'How JD Vance emerged as the chief saboteur of the transatlantic alliance', Andrew Roth, *The Guardian*, 1 March 2025
28 Ibid.
29 'Trump's vision of a world of rival fortresses', Yuval Noah Harari, *Financial Times*, 19 April 2025

30 '"A colonial agreement" – former Ukrainian official slams US minerals deal, AP reports', Abbey Fenbert, *The Kyiv Independent*, 16 February 2025
31 'US and Ukraine sign minerals deal that solidifies investment in Kyiv's defence against Russia,' Andrew Roth, *The Guardian*, 1 May 2025
32 'US defense chief suggests Ukraine should abandon hope of winning all territory back from Russia', Lorne Cook and Tara Copp, AP News, 13 February 2025
33 'Peace Through Strength: A Plan for Ukraine', Munich Security Conference, 15 February 2025
34 https://cepa.org/comprehensive-reports/addicted-to-war-undermining-russias-economy/
35 'Conquest Is Back', Tanisha M. Fazal, *Foreign Affairs*, 21 March 2025
36 https://efe.com/en/latest-news/2024-10-11/vladimir-putin/
37 'The Russia That Putin Made', Alexander Gabuev, *Foreign Affairs*, May/June 2025
38 'Putin's endorsement of Trump's Greenland takeover reflects their vision of a new world order', Andrew Roth, *The Guardian*, 28 March 2025
39 'Putin's Point of No Return', Andrea Kendall-Taylor and Michael Kofman, *Foreign Affairs*, January/February 2025
40 'The West's Last Chance', Alexander Stubb, *Foreign Affairs*, January/February 2026
41 These points are well articulated in the op-ed in *Foreign Affairs*, 24 February 2025, 'The Right U.S. Strategy for Russia-Ukraine Negotiations,' Thomas Wright
42 'Europe's moment of truth', Wolfgang Ischinger, *Foreign Affairs*, 2 March 2025
43 'Putin's Plan for Peace Is No Peace at All', Lloyd J. Austin III and Antony J. Blinken, *The New York Times*, 14 January 2025
44 'Does Putin know why Ukraine fights on? Because we prize freedom above stability and wealth', Andrey Kurkov, *The Guardian*, 24 January 2025
45 '"Ukraine today is in the strongest position ever", ex-foreign minister Kuleba says', Natalia Yermak, *The Kyiv Independent*, 2 January 2025